FEW ARE CHOSEN

*American Women
in Political Life Today*

FEW ARE CHOSEN

American Women
in Political Life Today

BY PEGGY LAMSON

With a Foreword by
Maurine B. Neuberger

Illustrated with
Photographs

Houghton Mifflin Company · Boston

1968

1457911

TO ROY LAMSON

*who in the past months
must often have wished
that the Nineteenth Amendment
had never been passed.*

To promote a woman to bear rule, superiority, dominion or empire above any realm, nation or city is repugnant to nature, contumely to God, a thing most contrarious to His revealed will and approved ordinance. . . . For who can deny but it repugneth to nature that the blind shall be appointed to lead and conduct such as do see . . . that the foolish, mad and frenetic shall govern the discreet and give counsel to such as be sober of mind. And such be all women, compared unto men in bearing of authority.

John Knox
The First Blast of the Trumpet Against a Monstrous Regiment of Women
London, 1558

Contents

Foreword

THE ROLE OF American women in public life has had less attention than that of the pioneer mother, who endured the hardships of rearing a family and keeping house in a covered wagon during the winning of the West. Yet the women who seek office are pioneers, too. Their achievements and their contributions in politics, civil rights, education, diplomacy and the law have enriched all of society.

Women have been lauded in song and story as mothers and homemakers. In many cases, their traditional role has fostered an awareness of the relationship between their private lives and the legislation that governs them. Some have entered public life to strive for improved education for children, for traffic safety, or fluoridation of the water supply; their concern for the family budget, depleted by unfair consumer practices and the cut made by the annual tax payment, has involved them directly in affairs of state.

The women of the sixties are not the militant feminists of the past who blazed the trail. In a sense, they do not need to be. The women of today have had opportunities for better education and they have used them. Modern women owe much to President Kennedy, who established the Commission on the Status of Women, which set in motion a two-year study on the needs of women for protection from discrimination because of sex, for equal pay and for correction of the social security laws which did not treat women with the same consideration as men.

Many women going about their tasks at home, at school, or on the job accept their way of life with no knowledge or little thought

of the women who have gone to the city council, the state legislature or the national Congress to make their lot a better one.

In this book Mrs. Lamson has concentrated on ten women who
have made such contributions. Having been active in political life
for twenty-five years, I know that much of the story of the inter-
minable meetings, the campaigns and frustrations endured by these
women had to be left unwritten. But I can share with them the
excitement of their success. Eight of these women have sought and
won elective office and two have had their talents recognized as they
have been appointed to high posts in government.

After two terms in the Oregon Legislature I was elected to the
United States Senate. The question I was asked most often was:
"What is the hardest thing about being a woman Senator?" I an-
swered, "The hardest thing is being elected." Once I had attained
office I considered myself a United States Senator — not a woman
Senator — and I was on my own to rise or fall.

There is a second question that comes up frequently: "When
women comprise more than half of the population, why are there
so few of them in public office?" I have thought about this a great
deal. I believe traditional education has not offered incentives for
women to participate in public life. As the child of the day laborer
has much less opportunity to become a doctor or an engineer than
the offspring of a family in the professions where educational advantages are taken for granted, so the girl-child has been denied encouragement and the guidance which would give her the confidence
that she, too, might become a Senator, a doctor or a judge.

From my own experience I have found that women perpetuate
the prejudices against themselves. They denigrate their own abilities
and are uncertain that they can deal with the problems of the cities,
of taxation and international diplomacy. Is there something in our
national mores that makes us think that women are unable to help
direct the ship of state? We trust them to manage a home, rear
children and live within a budget, but not to make the laws that
vitally affect the family.

Then there is the hardship of the campaign itself. Women tend not to like the rough-and-tumble life that an active candidate must lead. As young girls they are indoctrinated with the quality of modesty, but a politician has to go before the Chamber of Commerce or the Farm Bureau and say, "Look at me. I can do it better."

They need to be told that participating in a campaign is like having a baby. There are months of planning, of discomfort, of wonderment that are a test of physical endurance, but all of that dims with the pleasure of accomplishment. A woman who dares to expose herself to the electorate will have more days of frustration and heartache than any other combatant. Her family will be criticized, the length of her skirts will be cause for comment, and her every remark will be weighed for its veracity.

But the goal is worth the race. To be a participant in governing the country is ample reward. If it is an elective office she has sought and won, she will find a self-fulfillment each time she responds to a roll call, whether it is an aye or nay.

Perhaps the single biggest handicap for a woman seeking public office is her lack of money. Where does she go for campaign funds? The P-TA or the League of Women Voters does not give that kind of support. Inevitably, it is her husband who through his business, his union, or his profession has made the contacts that are the lifeblood of a successful politician.

These are the stories of ten women who are unique in that they have overcome the prejudices and the handicaps that I know most women face. The accounts of their service and success are written with humor and objectivity, and should provide encouragement for other women who have felt the call to public service.

Maurine B. Neuberger
Former United States Senator from Oregon

Illustrations

SENATOR MARGARET CHASE SMITH RECEIVES CONGRATULATIONS FROM MAJORITY LEADER SENATOR MIKE MANSFIELD AND MINORITY LEADER SENATOR EVERETT M. DIRKSEN.

REPRESENTATIVE FRANCES P. BOLTON, STANDING WITH SECRETARY OF THE INTERIOR STEWART L. UDALL AND MR. TURKEY TAYAC, A MEMBER OF THE PISCATAWAY TRIBE.

ESTHER PETERSON KEEPS A SHARP EYE ON CHAIN STORE PRICES IN HER CAPACITY AS SPECIAL PRESIDENTIAL ASSISTANT FOR CONSUMER AFFAIRS.

REPRESENTATIVE MARTHA W. GRIFFITHS MEETS WITH THREE YOUNG CONSTITUENTS FROM MICHIGAN STATE UNIVERSITY IN THE RAYBURN RECEPTION ROOM AT THE CAPITOL.

REPRESENTATIVE PATSY T. MINK ADDRESSES THE LADIES' AUXILIARY OF THE VETERANS OF FOREIGN WARS.

AT A LUNCHEON SEMINAR FOR NEW REPUBLICAN MEMBERS OF CONGRESS, REPRESENTATIVE MARGARET M. HECKLER IS WELCOMED BY AN EXPERIENCED COLLEAGUE, REPRESENTATIVE FRANCES P. BOLTON, AND MRS. GERALD R. FORD.

REPRESENTATIVE MARGARET M. HECKLER TALKS WITH A CONSTITUENT ON THE "HOT LINE" FROM HER WASHINGTON OFFICE.

CONSTANCE BAKER MOTLEY AND JAMES MEREDITH ATTEND A CONVOCATION OF THE NAACP LEGAL DEFENSE AND EDUCATIONAL FUND, INC.

AMBASSADOR EUGENIE ANDERSON VISITS A COLLECTIVE FARM IN BULGARIA.

ANN UCCELLO, HARTFORD'S FIRST WOMAN MAYOR, TAKES HER OATH OF OFFICE.

MAYOR ANN UCCELLO AND SECRETARY OF THE STATE ELLA T. GRASSO APPEAR AT A SYMPOSIUM SPONSORED BY HARTFORD COLLEGE.

ELLA T. GRASSO, DEMOCRATIC FLOOR LEADER, CONFERS WITH MEADE ALCORN AND JOHN M. BAILEY.

SENATOR MARGARET CHASE SMITH, WEARING HER TRADEMARK, HOSTESSES AT A SENATE LUNCHEON.

ESTHER PETERSON PRESIDES WITH ELEANOR ROOSEVELT AT THE THIRD MEETING OF THE PRESIDENT'S COMMISSION ON THE STATUS OF WOMEN.

Introduction: Not Many Are Called

THE YEAR 1918 saw the beginning of the end of women's long struggle to win the vote. In a sense then this book may be regarded as a fiftieth anniversary salute, one of many that will be written to commemorate the final victory in a battle which began in Seneca Falls in 1848 with the Declaration of Women's Rights and ended in Washington in 1920 with the passage of the Nineteenth Amendment.

When the House of Representatives finally surrendered on January 10, 1918, and passed the Federal Suffrage Amendment, the women who jammed the galleries and corridors burst into spontaneous song; "Praise God from Whom All Blessings Flow" rang from the rafters of the Capitol. Seventeen months later the Senate, which had always been the more obdurate legislative body on the woman suffrage question, also gave in and voted for the amendment. "The ayes were the ayes of Congress," wrote the *Woman's Citizen*, official publication of the National American Woman Suffrage Association, "but the voice was the voice of the people."

The suffragists under the leadership of the brilliant and tireless Carrie Chapman Catt at once began their campaign to secure the ratification by thirty-six states which would make the Nineteenth Amendment a fact and permit them to vote for the first time in the 1920 Presidential election. Two states, Illinois and Wisconsin, vying with each other for the honor of ratifying first, voted favorably on June 10, 1919. In Wisconsin, however, a nay vote was recorded by one Senator Herman Bilgrien. When questioned by reporters the Senator declined to explain his reasons; he had too often been misquoted, he said. Instead he agreed to write out a statement which the press could use. In her book, *Woman Suffrage and Politics,* Mrs. Catt records Senator Bilgrien's manifesto as it appeared in the *Wisconsin State Journal* under the heading "Why I voted against Woman Suff."

I. I and my wife agree on point I, a hous Wife belongs to home near her children and to keep hous, and not in open public Politic.

2ond. it is only for the city Women in larger Cities that want to vote and to get the controll of the Country vote. to Elect State officers and President of the U.S. because a Country Women wont not go to vote they have all they wont to do to take care of their children and House Work garden etc.

3th a Danger that the men will not go to the poles if the Women get Elected to any state Legislature. the big Danger will be that some hair pulling will going on if there will be Women Elected in the State Legislature they will be worse as the Attorneys at present.

For Carrie Chapman Catt there was no surprise but only a "grim humor" in the evidence that such a man should sit in a high place and "pass judgement on women of brains and culture in their appeal for justice." All too often the suffragists had had to present their case "before a tribunal of just such a grade of intelligence and literacy."

When they presented their case for the final time, it was before a tribunal in which many members may have been ignorant, but most members were drunk to boot.

By June of 1920 thirty-five states had ratified the amendment. As they studied the roster of the states that were still stubbornly holding out, Mrs. Catt and her lieutenants decided to confer upon reluctant Tennessee the "honor" of becoming the thirty-sixth state.

On Saturday, August 7, two nights before the special Assembly was due to convene, a bizarre scene was enacted in Nashville. Senators and representatives were seen reeling through the lobby and corridors of the Hermitage Hotel in what Mrs. Catt referred to as "an advanced state of intoxication." The legislature was drunk, the dismayed suffragists were told, because "in Tennessee whiskey and legislation go hand in hand, especially when controversial questions are urged." Anti-suffragists who had converged on Nashville to make a last-ditch stand against votes for women saw to it that this particular local tradition prevailed throughout the special session.

The senate sobered up enough to pass ratification first, but when the vote was finally taken in the lower chamber the count, with 96 members present, stood at 48 to 48. Then on the third roll call a young man who might otherwise have gone to his grave unheralded assured himself a place in history by voting "aye." His name was Harry Burn, he was twenty-four years old, he came from the town of Niota in McMinn County and his mother had made him promise to vote for ratification if a stalemate developed. "Be a good boy and help Mrs. Catt," she exorted him. And Harry Burn was the good boy whose single vote finally enfranchised the women of America.

"The vote is the emblem of your equality, the guaranty of your liberty," said Carrie Chapman Catt at one of the many victory celebrations that followed the Tennessee ratification. "Women have suffered agony of soul that you and your daughters might inherit political freedom. . . . Their motive has been the hope that women would aim higher than their own selfish ambitions, that they would serve the common good. . . . The vote is won. . . . Progress is calling to you to make no pause. Act!"

On another occasion, and in a more practical vein, Mrs. Catt told the women, "The only way to get things done is to get them done inside of a political party. You will have a long hard fight before you get inside, but you must move right up to the center."

Unfortunately the great suffrage leader did not follow her own advice. No sooner were the ceremonies marking the passage of the Nineteenth Amendment finished than Mrs. Catt announced she would retire to her farm in Westchester County and spend a year canning fruits and making jellies. Her withdrawal was the more puzzling since Carrie Chapman Catt, twice widowed and childless, had never been a domestic person. She had spent her life battling for a great cause; she was more at home behind a speaker's lectern than in front of a kitchen stove. Yet at the critical moment when her own actions would signal a new era in women's emancipation, she chose with almost mid-Victorian propriety to retreat to woman's traditional role in the home.

Many men politicians who had been eyeing her next move anxiously in 1920 must have sighed with relief that this Titan of a woman with her vast legislative skill and experience had decided to renounce public office. And her enormous following, the more than two million women who had fought with her to win the vote, docilely followed her lead back into domesticity.

Mrs. Catt herself never joined a political party. Furthermore by creating the League of Women Voters as a successor to the Woman's Suffrage Party and by committing the League to operate within a totally non-partisan framework, she in fact turned her back on the entire party system.

Today neither the worst fears of Senator Bilgrien of Wisconsin nor the fondest hopes of Carrie Chapman Catt have been realized. Today women are in the majority in America, yet only a tiny fraction have managed to "move right up to the center of a political party." This book concerns a fraction of that tiny fraction.

The ten women who are the subjects of these chapters are all members of a political party. I have selected them partly for their personal attributes but more because they hold positions which cover the spectrum of high public office in this country. They are not women who generally make the headlines, nor do they shape the larger course of the nation's destiny. However, they are all deeply concerned with today's issues. They are, in sum, the very stuff of which our government is made.

One common theme unifies them. As women they are all very much in the minority in the fields in which they work. Although this generality would hold true for *any* group of ten women in public life, I should explain — or perhaps justify — my selection of *this* group.

I began with the office, not the office holder. In the legislative branch there is only one woman Senator and thus there was no problem of choice in the upper house. There are eleven women Representatives, I picked four of these ranging from the oldest in service and years to the youngest in service and years. From the executive branch I selected one woman from those holding Presidential appointments which include Secretaries, Under Secretaries, Assistant Secretaries and Special Presidential Assistants. There are three women in this category. From among four women presently holding the rank of Ambassador or Minister I chose one. In the judiciary I included one of four women federal judges. At the state level I picked one woman from among the elected constitutional officers — Governor, Lieutenant Governor, Secretary of State, Treasurer and Attorney General. Fifteen women hold such offices throughout the fifty states. To represent municipal government, I wanted to include the mayor of one of America's hundred largest cities. Only one woman holds this office within the continental United States.

In these top categories of our federal, state and municipal governments are a total of approximately 1,400 elective and appointive officers. Only forty of them are women. A quarter of that number seems a fair sampling for this book. Still, I am aware that any choice is bound to appear somewhat arbitrary. Many will object to my selection and no doubt object even more strongly that there are some I have left out. Yet others will reprove me for not going further afield to cover women members of various commissions, women Bureau Chiefs and Deputy Assistant Secretaries or women members of state legislatures and city councils. I might of course have done so, but even if I had broadened the base to encompass these and other categories, the number of women who have achieved public office would still have emerged as dismally small.

I should mention that I deliberately did not include women holding traditional "women's jobs," and, to forestall one further criticism, I must emphasize that the scope of this book is only women who are presently in office. I feel obliged to labor this point because of the number of people whose first question, on learning that I was writing a book about women in public life *today*, has been, "Have you got Clare Boothe Luce in it?"

I began my researches with a number of preconceptions, most of which turned out to be wrong. Seeking an explanation for the very small proportion of women in public office (the percentage remains constant at about 2.5 per cent), I conveniently placed the blame on the male electorate. In our present matriarchal society, I reasoned, American men, who feel themselves challenged on all sides by women, are clinging obstinately to their right, within the privacy of the polling booth, not to vote for women candidates.

On the evidence now before me I am convinced that this is not so. Eight of the ten women discussed in these pages have held elective office. Six of the eight have never been defeated. Two of the six have consistently topped their entire state ticket; all but one was elected in her first try for public office. Between them these eight women have stood for an aggregate of fifty-eight elections. They have suffered a total of *three* defeats.

I doubt if any random choice of eight men elected officers would produce a better record; few, I think, would equal it.

My further belief that there was also a widespread resistance among women themselves to voting for women candidates appears equally shot full of holes by this and other statistics. I do not, of course, have figures covering women who have run for office, been defeated and who have not been heard from again. I strongly doubt, however, that many able, qualified candidates have been lost to public service because of the electorate's unwillingness to vote for a woman. Certainly for the vast majority of women now in public office at all levels, winning the election has been far easier than capturing the nomination.

If blame is to be attached to any group of men it must not be to those who pull the voting machine lever inside the polling booth but to those who pull the strings inside the political parties. Two parallel statements by party leaders who should know attest to the continuing frustration suffered by women seeking party endorsement. The first from India Edwards, for many years the Vice Chairman of the Democratic National Committee, who says, "If the party backs a woman you can be pretty sure they do it because they think it's a lost cause but they know they have to have *some* candidate." The other from John Bailey, Chairman of the Democratic National Party and for years the leading power broker in the state of Connecticut. "The only time to run a woman," he says cheerfully, "is when things look so bad that your only chance is to do something dramatic."

It is of course quite possible to run for office without party endorsement. Three of the eight women in this book have done so with repeated success, although with prodigious effort. In sum, then, political parties while often a considerable deterrent do not constitute the major roadblock in women's path to public office. A far greater obstacle looms for them before they ever start up — or down — the path in the attitudes of family and friends. (I do not refer here to women who have small children, many of whom are too young themselves to seek public office.)

Certainly the misgivings of a husband are readily understandable. It is the rare and unusually flexible man who can accept having his wife move to Washington, D.C. with or without him. There are some such men, as this book shows; it also shows that while five wives have managed an accommodation between Washington and home, one has not seen her way clear to causing such an upheaval in her family.

All political roads do not lead to the nation's capital, however. Only a small percentage of the opportunities for women in public life need take them away from home for an extended period, if at all. Millions of women live in or near capital cities, and even for those who do not, state assemblies sit for only a few months a year — in many states they convene only every other year. Yet women's participation in state legislatures remains proportionately as small as in the federal Congress.

Mayors by definition are always near home. Yet here the statistics on women in office are far below the already very low norm.

Quite apart from the purely practical difficulties, a woman in the public arena can create other problems for her husband. He may feel that his position as head of the family is compromised, or even that his manhood is challenged. As might be expected, husbands whose wives are already in office scoff at such a notion; there is no way to judge the feelings of those whose wives are not in office, but would like to be. Undoubtedly there are some, though not an abundant number of, reasons why a husband might feel more threatened by a wife who is a politician than by a wife who is a lawyer or a doctor or an artist or a college professor or a businesswoman. On the other hand, a man's pride in his wife's achievement and in her personal satisfaction is a plus factor which should be weighed in the balance.

All too often, I suspect, women who say they would like to enter public life hover on the brink and then turn back because they tell themselves it would not be fair to their husbands to go forward. They then regard their retreat as a sacrifice when it is, in fact, an excuse. The likelihood is that they were not really drawn to public life as activists but only as interested observers. Widowed or unmarried, childless and without family responsibilities, these women would probably always remain on the sidelines because — and here it seems to me is the crux of the matter — most women do not really want to get involved in what James Reston has called the "noisy brutalities of partisan politics."

I believe without question that if women, who are a majority of 51 per cent in America today, really wanted a wider participation in public life they could certainly have it; if they worked through the many powerful women's organizations to demand a greater representation as law- and policy-makers they would not be denied.

There is no organized resistance in today's society which keeps women out of the mainstream of public affairs. Perhaps it would be better if there were. The suffragettes of fifty years ago had solid doors to batter down; they joined together and became the militants. Today such barriers as exist are invisible and illusive, and almost the only group of militants who still flourish are those who have joined Betty Friedan, the author of *The Feminine Mystique,* in her organization called NOW (the National Organization of Women). But to most observers NOW's 1,200 members seem to be merely shadow-boxing. What exactly do they want that they don't already have?

What they want is an equality of opportunity, a full partnership with men. The vast majority of thoughtful American women want that too, but most do not want it enough to fight for it and to risk being called a feminist — a word which has come to have decidedly pejorative overtones — to get it. Today feminist and feminine are regarded as contradictory terms; one cannot, it seems, be both, as the suffragettes once were.

By the same token political and feminine are mutually exclusive. Politicians by definition are aggressive. A woman seeking political office must therefore behave like a woman and not like a politician since aggressive women are of course not feminine. A woman who fights for her beliefs is shrill; a man is forceful.

I have been puzzled in my researches by the attitude of certain women, themselves partisan politicians working behind the scenes in the party, toward the women who are on stage as candidates. Secure in their know-how and in their obscurity, these gray eminences regard the women office seekers not as dauntless standard bearers, but as tough, determined exhibitionists, driven not by idealism but by some inner frustration.

I was also struck by the response, which I trust is an isolated example, of a man with whom I talked about one of the women in this book. He had taught her in college and he spoke warmly of her fine capabilities as a student. He seemed surprised, however, that I should include her in a book about women, because as he said, "she thinks and works just like a man."

There seems no way to get around this dichotomy between men and women. To do her job successfully in public office a woman must occasionally appear unfeminine. But to do the same job successfully a man may under no circumstances appear unmasculine.

Given these prejudices, so deeply rooted in American society, it must be very difficult indeed for a young woman to visualize herself in the role of a politician. Little girls do not dream of growing up to be Governor; women's fantasies do not carry them into the realm of public office. Neither, it seems, do the realities.

Yet there are many exceptions, and they of course are the reason for this book. There are also those who have gone before and to whom I here pay brief tribute, beginning with at least a few of the notable firsts among American women in public life.

The first two American women to hold "appointive office" in the federal government were Sarah Waldrake and Rachel Summers who were employed in 1795 by the United States Mint as adjusters to weigh gold at a salary of $.50 a day.

The first woman to run for President of the United States was Victoria Claflin Woodhull. Although she was highly aggressive, self-seeking and a wild exhibitionist, no one ever accused Mrs. Woodhull of being unfeminine. She was an advocate of free love, and she practiced what she preached so successfully — or rather with such successful partners — that she managed not only to become the first Presidential candidate but also the first lady stockbroker in America. She was the first woman ever to appear before the House Judiciary Committee where she presented a "memorial" arguing that women already were enfranchised by the Fourteenth Amendment. When she was rejected by the National Woman Suffrage Association, she created her own Equal Rights Party and made herself its Presidential standard bearer. Her further claim to fame was that she broke the famous Beecher-Tilton case in the scandal sheet, *Woodhull and Claflin's Weekly*, which she owned and published with her equally notorious sister, Tennie C. As a result she spent election night of 1872, the year of her "candidacy," in jail. As far as is known no one voted for her. Victoria Woodhull cannot be considered to have established a precedent for women in public office.

The first bona fide candidate for public federal office was Jeanette Rankin who was successfully elected from Montana to the House of Representatives in 1916 — four years before the passage of the Federal Suffrage Amendment. Miss Rankin, serving at two widely separated periods in Congress, cast her vote against America's entrance into both World War I and World War II. In the spring of 1968 at a sprightly eighty-two, she returned to Washington to lead women of the Jeanette Rankin Brigade in a march on the Capitol to protest her country's involvement in the war in Vietnam.

In the Senate the first woman, Mrs. Rebecca Latimer Felton, was appointed by the Governor of Georgia to serve *one day*, November 21, 1922. It was not until ten years later that the next woman Senator, Hattie W. Caraway, was appointed to fill the unexpired term of her husband. Mrs. Caraway was subsequently re-elected to become the first woman Senator to serve a full six-year term. Since then only two other women have been elected to the Senate.

Nellie Tayloe Ross of Wyoming replaced her husband on his death in 1925 to become the first woman Governor. Later in the same year Ma Ferguson stepped into Pa Ferguson's shoes when he was impeached and took office as the nominal Governor of Texas. During her campaign, buttons and stickers proclaimed, "Me for Ma. And I Ain't Got a Dern Thing Against Pa." The striking similarities between the Wallaces of Alabama and the Fergusons of Texas have often been noted.

When Frances Perkins was named Secretary of Labor and became the first woman Cabinet member, many hoped that her appointment would be a breakthrough for women in top appointive offices. But although Miss Perkins served with distinction for twelve years, only one woman has since been in the Cabinet. Oveta Culp Hobby was named by President Eisenhower as the first Secretary of Health, Education and Welfare and served for two years.

Undoubtedly the most outstanding woman of the past four decades has been Eleanor Roosevelt, who never held an elective or a full-time appointive office. Vigorous, uncompromising and committed always to the cause of human rights, Mrs. Roosevelt set the highest possible standard for women in public service. Whether she would have made as effective a contribution had she had a constituency to satisfy is open to question. Certainly she enjoyed the luxury, rare among public figures, of being able to express her beliefs openly, undistilled by consideration of any special interest groups. But with her bold, imaginative and always humane outlook it is probable that Eleanor Roosevelt would have achieved distinction in any capacity in which she served her country. She cared greatly about the status of women. The women in office today, both Democrats and Republicans, owe much to her. Without Mrs. Roosevelt their legacy would be all too slight.

I move now from the past to the present, and from the general to the specific to introduce the subjects of this book: Senator Margaret Chase Smith, Representative Frances P. Bolton, Assistant Secretary of Labor Esther Peterson, Congresswomen Martha W. Griffiths, Patsy Takemoto Mink and Margaret M. Heckler, Judge Constance Baker Motley, Ambassador Eugenie Anderson, Mayor Antonina P. Uccello and the Honorable Ella T. Grasso, Secretary of the State of Connecticut.

These ten women are of course just as different as any comparable group of ten men would be, yet they have more in common. Although they all strongly proclaim their desire to be regarded not as women but as ordinary public officers they remain acutely conscious of being women and of being thus set apart. How could it be otherwise? Margaret Chase Smith, to take the most obvious example, is one lone woman, sitting with ninety-nine men in the Senate chamber.

Each of the women occupies a place in a similarly male-dominated world. Each feels that she has had to fight twice as hard to win her position and that she must work twice as hard to gain recognition. Each is painfully aware that a failure on her part could have an adverse effect on the aspirations of other women in public life.

As a group the women are both self-protective and protective of each other. They are proud of their own accomplishments, which is normal in politics; they are also proud of each other's successes, which is not. One after another has boasted to me that women in public office are far more attentive to details than their male counterparts, more conscientious and more genuinely concerned with people.

I believe in the main that this is true. I am further impressed by the fact that each of these women has carved a place for herself in some special area of legislation or policy and has committed herself to the issues involved. They take themselves and their work very seriously. In my dealings with them I have seen few if any traces of cynicism. They are all realists, fully aware of the limitations placed upon them because they are women, and of the compromises they must sometimes make because they are politicians. In some instances they seem more cautious than men would be, and they are often more defensive. They are ambitious, and none is without at least some small degree of the ruthlessness that invariably accompanies ambition. They have all displayed a dauntless determination to stay the course.

These ten women are very much of the people. With one exception they come from families of modest means. Their fathers' occupations are a testament to the American dream; they include a minister, a superintendent of schools, an engineer, a barber, a letter carrier, a baker, a chef and a shoemaker.

Nine of the ten are married, two are widowed and these two both entered public life by replacing their husbands in office. The other six who have held elective offices won them entirely on their own merits. Six are Democrats, four are Republicans. All but two are college graduates; five hold higher degrees. The women range in age from eighty-two to thirty-nine, they came from nine different states, and between them they have sixteen children. For what it is worth, not one of the ten was ever elected to a school committee.

These then are the trail-blazers; they are still, after fifty years of votes for women, in the vanguard of *representation* by women. But when one considers that it took seventy-two years to win the vote, perhaps fifty years is not quite long enough to win full acceptance.

It is my pleasure to acknowledge here the kindness and coopera-tion of the many persons who helped me in the preparation of this book.

My first thanks are of course to those ten who *are* the book for their courtesy, their generosity and for their brave spirit. Each woman but one took time from her incredibly busy schedule to talk with me, in most instances at considerable length. (The exception was Constance Baker Motley who felt that because of her position as a federal judge it would not be suitable for her to be interviewed.) Giving interviews is a part of every public official's life, but no matter how often one goes through it it cannot be easy to talk to a perfect stranger who is not only judging you by every word you utter but who intends to make her assessment known to the public. Complete frankness is obviously impossible in these circumstances, but I am grateful to my subjects for at least seeming to talk openly with me, for never misleading me, for submitting patiently to my questions and for giving thoughtful answers. I thank them for the good grace with which they accepted me and the book I proposed to write about them.

The secretaries and administrative assistants of all the women treated my many requests with unfailing courtesy. I thank them all most warmly with a special mention for Vivien Meisen, Irene Lewis and Patricia Kelly.

In addition to talking with the women themselves, I of course had to talk with others about them. Many persons were generous in sharing their insights with me. Within the government I gratefully acknowledge the kindness of Senators George D. Aiken, Karl E. Mundt, Edmund S. Muskie and Stuart Symington; of Secretary of Agriculture Orville L. Freeman, of the late Joseph W. Martin, of David Swankin, Alex Bloomfield, Richard Johnson, John Leslie and in particular of Mary N. Hilton of the Women's Bureau and Derrick A. Bell of the Department of Health, Education and Welfare.

Others outside of the government who gave freely of their time were Norman C. Amaker, Robert Carter, Paul Christopher, Leroy D. Clark, Jesse DeVore, George Ducharme, Donald Jacobs, James Meredith and James M. Nabrit, III. Agatha Fullam and Oliver Bolton merit my special gratitude.

Within the political parties Howard Haussman, John M. Bailey, C. Perrie Phillips, Meade Alcorn and India Edwards all contributed enlightening, lucid and pungent comment.

Members of the press shared their keen perceptions with characteristic generosity. Among them were James Doyle, Doris Fleeson, Donald Larabee, Edward L. Penley, Jack Zaiman, James O'Hara, Charlayne Hunter, Irving Kravsow and James Loeb, Jr.

All these people and many others, some of whose names I have deliberately left out to preserve their anonymity, responded unhesitatingly and graciously to the request of a stranger who was writing a book.

Many old friends were also commandeered by me to try — usually without notable success — to educate me in the areas of their own expertise and to put me in touch with others who might do so. I

offer my warm thanks to John D. and Martha B. Briscoe, to James
MacGregor Burns, Dorothy Kenyon, Joseph E. Johnson, Margot
Lindsay, Katie Louchheim, Mary McGrory, Joseph L. Rauh, and
Polly Shackleton. Jane Murray and Ann Stone contributed valuable
editorial assistance.

Felicia Lamport Kaplan, herself a writer of distinction, undertook
to read my manuscript fresh off the typewriter and with her quick
wit and eagle eye forestalled many blunders which might otherwise
have been compounded. Catherine Abbot Johnson put her fine
mind to the task of helping me to prepare the index, and turned
what must normally be a dull chore into a delightful and spirited
battle of wits.

Members of my family were not spared. I am grateful to my
daughter, Pat Fischer, for research assistance, to my daughter-in-law,
Gay Lamson, for her help in preparing the manuscript and especially to my husband, Roy Lamson, for his wise and experienced
editorial guidance and for his help in countless other areas.

I have been particularly fortunate in the two young women who
have been most closely associated with this project. DeAnn Burrows
has not only typed and retyped the manuscript but has cheerfully
and efficiently performed a wide variety of other tasks, not the least
of which has been to keep up my morale by her own good spirits.
My affectionate thanks go finally to my editor, Daphne Ehrlich,
who has guided this book from conception to completion without
ever losing her sense of humor, her critical judgment or my complete respect.

If, despite the best efforts of all these gifted, conscientious, helpful people, any errors of commission or omission appear on these
pages, they are entirely my own.

PEGGY LAMSON

Cambridge, Mass.
April, 1968

ONE IN A HUNDRED

Margaret Chase Smith

O<small>N</small> S<small>EPTEMBER</small> 24, 1963, the United States Senate voted on the Nuclear Test Ban Treaty. At the time the vote was scheduled to take place, President John F. Kennedy was meeting at the White House with a German delegation headed by the German Ambassador. Protocol demanded that he take no phone calls, but since he was understandably eager to know the results of the vote which could mark the beginnings of a *détente* between Russia and the United States, he asked his secretary, Mrs. Evelyn Lincoln, to bring him a note the moment she heard from the Capitol.

The slip of paper she handed him, now a part of the memorabilia of the Kennedy Library, said:

"Vote 80 to 19. Mrs. Smith went wrong."

This note, apart from its historical import, dramatizes in four terse words the imposing position occupied by Senator Margaret Chase Smith, Republican from Maine.

Obviously her defection was of particular significance to the President, not because she represented a politically sensitive area, which Maine is not, nor because she spoke for the Republican Party, which she does not, nor even because she and the President were particularly close friends, which they were not. Her negative vote must have been a disappointment to the President because he knew that she had voted out of conviction and because he, like most high officials in the capital, recognized the value of having Margaret Chase Smith on his side.

She was then and is today one of the most important and highly regarded people in Washington. The reason for her pre-eminence is something of a riddle, however, for she has almost none of the attributes generally ascribed to the power politician.

She is no image maker. Not for her the florid oratory of an Everett Dirksen, the crusty irascibility of a Wayne Morse, the charismatic flair of a Robert Kennedy, the voluble good nature of a Hubert Humphrey, or the slick charm of a Mark Hatfield. By contrast Margaret Chase Smith seems colorless and ordinary to the point of banality. A sweet-looking woman, she is notable to many people only for the single rose she always wears pinned to her unadorned, straight-cut, round-necked dresses.

Passing her on the street one might easily have only a vague feeling of having seen that rather pretty white-haired lady before. But the rose would place her. Wearing her trademark, she is unmistakably Margaret Chase Smith.

Whether deliberately or not, Senator Smith herself seems more than willing to perpetuate her bland, unexceptional image. A masterpiece of unremarkableness is her account to her constituents of "A Senator's Day." It is quoted here in full.

In reporting to you on my work in the Senate, I should like to emphasize the fact that the life of a Senator is not an easy one and that it is predominately work with little time for social activities. Contrary to some reports, their official duties give little time and opportunity for participation in the Washington Social Merry-Go-Round.

I have a long working day. I arise at 6:45 in the morning — even earlier in the Spring and Summer for I have a tendency to arise with the sun. This gives me a chance to walk around the yard and tend to plants, shrubs, and trees that I have planted. It is difficult to describe what this means to me in the contrast that it brings to the eight a.m. to eight p.m. daily pressure.

I prepare my breakfast and read the morning paper. One of the things I enjoy the most in my day is sitting in my living room with a breakfast tray in my lap, drinking my coffee, eating toast and honey, and watching through the picture windows the wonderful little inhabitants in my yard — the cocky squirrel, the nervous little chipmunk, a cautious rabbit or two and the many varieties of birds scurrying around and vying with each other at the feeding box in the mimosa tree.

After breakfast I drive from my house in the country twelve miles from the office, arriving at my office desk about eight a.m. From eight to ten I attend to my mail and matters on my desk, talk to the departments and agencies, confer with my staff and see constituents calling at the office. From ten to twelve I am in committee sessions—as I go to the Appropriations Committee or the Armed Services Committee or the Aeronautical and Space Sciences Committee.

My afternoon starts when I go to the opening of the Senate session at noon. Fifteen minutes later I have my lunch which is usually fresh fruit salad with cottage cheese — occasionally a cheese sandwich. Lunch by myself usually takes no more than thirty minutes. After that I return either to the Senate Floor or to my office. If there are committee meetings in the afternoon, I go back to them around two p.m. or two-thirty p.m. and remain there until called back to the Senate Chamber for a quorum call or a roll call vote.

Usually at four-thirty or five I return to my office to sign my mail and study other matters on my desk. More often than not, I don't leave my desk and my office until around eight in the evening. I drive home, prepare my dinner and finish between nine and nine-thirty. Perhaps then I watch television for half-an-hour, followed by a look at some files I have brought home with me and I go to bed about eleven and go to sleep on the newscast.

While this recital throws little light on the substance of Senator Smith's day, it reveals a good deal about the Senator herself. She is a loner, a lover of nature, out of place in the social life of the nation's capital. She is hard-working, methodical, and orderly; she is simple, thrifty, sensible, and conscientious. In sum she is the product of her environment, the perfect representative of her constituency — she is Maine.

Two other qualities not reflected in "A Senator's Day" but possessed in full measure by Margaret Chase Smith — her spunk and her independence — further endear her to the majority of voters in the state of Maine.

But a Senator's home-state popularity, while it assures re-election, by no means assures a place of prominence on the national scene, and in Senator Smith's case the reasons why she might *not* be important nationally far outweigh the reasons why she might be. In the first place she represents a small, rural state with only five electoral votes, which, despite its famed "as Maine goes" slogan does not carry much political weight in Washington. She is a woman of no substantial means and of only limited education.

In the second place, like most elected officials, Mrs. Smith has a public and private personality. But her public posture, though pleasant and steadfast, can hardly be called dynamic, and since she tends to be suspicious and wary of the press, only a few reporters get close enough to penetrate into her private aspect and to portray her with the warmth and charm she is said to possess. Furthermore the Republican Party has never accorded her a very great personal recognition, while she for her part has always stayed quite clear of the party organization and has, in fact, established herself as an independent force. And finally, she is one lone woman among ninety-nine men in the Senate, and not inclined by temperament or conviction to play along and be one of the boys.

Yet despite these formidable drawbacks, according to Senator Stuart Symington of Missouri, her long-time Democratic colleague on the Armed Services Committee, she is one of the most powerful and respected people in the Senate and, as Symington points out, if the Republicans should gain control of the Senate in 1968, Mrs. Smith would be among the five or six most potent legislators on Capitol Hill.

Her name has been mentioned repeatedly for Vice President, a suggestion which she scorns, and she is the only woman ever to have been placed in nomination at a major political party convention for President of the United States. She received twenty-seven votes on the first and only ballot. Senator George D. Aiken, who nominated her in 1964, says wryly, "If she had been the candidate she would have done better in the election than the fellow we chose."

Senator Smith has received no less than fifty honorary degrees from colleges and universities throughout the country, and she is justifiably proud of this widespread recognition. In addition she has always won a high place in the Gallup poll to determine the most admired women in the world, advancing from one of the ten most admired women in 1954 to one of the four most admired in 1963.

Other awards, all duly listed in her official biography, include the Honest Politician Award from *Liberty Magazine*, the Most Charming Woman in Government Award by the Charm Institute, and the Economy Champion in the Senate by the Council of State Chambers of Commerce.*

Doris Fleeson, the distinguished columnist, and a close friend of Margaret Smith, once wondered whether the people of Maine were aware of their Republican Senator's great national distinction. Traveling through the state with Mrs. Smith on one occasion Miss Fleeson found an opportunity to ask a down-easter if he knew just how important Margaret Chase Smith really was in the Senate.

"Aiya," he said. "We know. And she did it without kissing anybody's backside either."

She did it, in fact, in the only way she knew how, by earnest, dedicated, hard work. She is by no means the first person in high office to come from a simple background; she is one of the few to have risen to prominence without catering to anyone.

Margaret Chase Smith was born in Skowhegan, Maine, on December 14, 1897, the eldest of six children. Her father, a man of not very robust health, was the local barber. Legend has it that when Mr. Chase was stricken with one of his severe headaches, little Margaret would take over the shop and give the customers a shave and a haircut. Romantic perhaps, but, according to Mrs. Smith,

---

* On October 19, 1949, according to the *Portland Press Herald*, Mrs. Smith added an accolade of her own to the list. "I am one of the five least talkative members of the Senate," she stated. Her administrative assistant, William C. Lewis, added that since the "study" had been made, of the other four taciturn ones, Senator Bert H. Miller had died, Senator Robert F. Wagner had retired and Senators Milton Young and Virgil Chapman had "talked extensively," so that in point of fact Mrs. Smith deserved first place in the nontalkative contest but was too modest to say so.

not quite accurate. "I was always ambitious in wanting to try new things," she has said, "and at the time there was a good deal of talk about women barbers and about beauty parlors and so on, so I thought my father should teach me the business. He did. He taught me how to give a shave and I got so I could do a fairly good job when I could find anybody who would let me try."

Apparently there were not enough such brave souls around Skowhegan to keep the twelve-year-old girl thus occupied, so she applied for a job at the local five-and-ten-cent store. Here the problem was that she was too small to reach the stock shelves, so she had to wait a year or so to acquire the necessary inches before beginning her first gainful employment. She worked nights and holidays at the five-and-ten. Seventy-five cents was her take-home pay from noon until ten at night, a dollar for a full day. At Christmas she worked practically around the clock for a few days and earned a total of $3.50. "But it was great, great experience," Mrs. Smith says.

The year after her graduation from high school she taught in a primary school, but, although she often refers to herself as a "former schoolteacher," her classroom experience was rather limited. After one year's teaching she moved on to become a telephone operator. This too was good training she says, for handling a switchboard taught her how to do several things at once — an invaluable preparation for public office.

She was to derive even greater benefit from her job at the switchboard. It was over the telephone that she first "met" Clyde Smith, the man who fourteen years later became her husband. "He had a beautiful voice," says the Senator.

Perhaps the work that best fitted her for her present role was her next job as circulation manager for the *Skowhegan Independent Reporter*, a weekly paper. Here Margaret Chase came into constant contact with the public, and she soon found herself running a quasi-employment-information service; she also helped the merchants to write their advertisements and thus came to know the business community in her small world. Subsequently she was instrumental in starting a local Business and Professional Women's Club, and, at the age of twenty-eight, she became president of that organization's state federation.

After a few years she advanced from the newspaper job to a much better paying position as office manager of the Cummington Woolen Mills. Among her other duties there she made up payrolls for men and women who worked "anywhere from 75 to 105 hours a week at less than thirty cents an hour," an inequity which later resulted in her strong stand in favor of wage and hour legislation.

Miss Chase was thirty-three years old when, in 1930, she married the fifty-four-year-old Clyde H. Smith, who was then a member of the Governor's Council. The couple spent most of their time at the state capital in Augusta until 1936, when Clyde Smith was elected to the Congress.

Mrs. Smith, who had been very active in her husband's campaign, and who was used to putting in a full working day, did not relish the idea of sitting around, when they moved to Washington, playing the part of the decorous congressional wife. She wanted to go to work for her husband. For his part, Mr. Smith did not relish the idea of having his wife on the payroll. What turned the tide in her favor was a petition from some constituents saying that they *wanted* Margaret to play a part in his political life and would Representative Smith please put her on the payroll. He did.

"I think I got $3000 a year," says Mrs. Smith. "So I'm the living example of the results of nepotism."

Working full time in her husband's office, Mrs. Smith had little time for outside activities. She did, however, join the Congressional Club, which is made up of the wives of Congressmen, and as an experienced businesswoman she soon became treasurer of the club, a job which helped to keep her in tune with the social side of life in the capital. Thus, when a women's club in Waterville, Maine, asked her to speak about social activities in Washington, Mrs. Smith felt qualified to accept. Her speech, which was to have a far-reaching effect on her career, happened to fall on Navy Day.

"Thinking as I always have that social activities are delightful and a necessary part of life," the Senator said recently, "it still seemed to me that there were many other things that women should do — especially women of club age, after they'd gotten their families going. Clubs were wonderful, and cards were wonderful, but I just felt there ought to be some contribution made. So, it being Navy Day, I decided to talk first about social activities in Washington but then to throw in a few paragraphs about the inadequacy of our Navy."

Those few paragraphs, "thrown in" thirty years ago, marked the beginning of Margaret Chase Smith's long commitment to military preparedness.

Clyde Smith was re-elected easily in 1938, but in April, 1940, just a few days before he was due to file again for the primaries, he suffered a heart attack. He seemed much concerned about the imminent filing date, and his doctor, to quiet him, suggested that his wife file instead. Then when he recovered Margaret could withdraw her name and he could replace her.

Mrs. Smith, who had never given a moment's thought to elective office for herself, went along with the idea simply to set her husband's mind at rest. He seemed greatly relieved and his health apparently improved, but shortly afterwards he suffered another attack and died.

Ironically, the doctor who, for medical reasons, made the decision which started Margaret Chase Smith on her political way was a Georgia Democrat.

As a freshman Representative she had hoped to carry on her husband's work on the Labor Committee, but was assigned instead to the usual minor committees such as Invalid Pensions, War Claims, Post Office and Post Roads. With her growing interest in military preparedness, the assignment she really wanted was the Naval Affairs Committee, but each year she shrewdly requested Appropriations as her first choice and Naval Affairs as her second, knowing that she had little chance for an appointment to Appropriations, which required considerable seniority, but that if she made enough fuss about it she would eventually get her second choice as a consolation prize. Still it was five years before she finally achieved her goal and gained her first major committee assignment to the Naval Affairs Committee. Joseph W. Martin, Republican of Massachusetts, was Speaker of the House at the time. Interviewed shortly before his death Mr. Martin recalled, "I put Margaret Chase Smith on Naval Affairs and at the same time I put Clare Boothe Luce on Military Affairs so I made two women happy in one day which is more than most men can say."

Serving with Mrs. Smith on Naval Affairs was Lyndon B. Johnson, and her friendship with the President dates from this period. In 1947, when the House considered the bill for unification of the armed services, Congresswoman Smith was the only member of the Naval Affairs Committee to vote for it. Thereafter she served on the first Armed Services Committee in the House.

Looking back on the early days of her public service, Senator Smith says, "I had two objectives when I first started out. One was to stay on the job and two was to stay close to the people. How well I've stayed on the job is indicated by the fact that I have not missed a vote since June 1, 1955. [Her consecutive roll call count as of April, 1967, was 2,443.] And for the other, I have for years gotten into Maine at least once a month."

Besides going into the state every month, Mrs. Smith during her term of office as a Representative developed numerous other constituency-endearing habits which she has continued to observe faithfully. She answered every letter on the day it arrived, she was always in her office at nine in the morning to receive phone calls from constituents, she never broke appointments, she paid conscientious attention to the smallest details. In all of her dealings she was friendly, homespun, down to earth, and helpful.

The voters of the Second District of Maine were solidly behind her. The word was that "Margaret Chase Smith can stay in Congress as long as she wants. She's set for life."

But Margaret Chase Smith had other ideas.

Almost all Representatives, whether they admit it or not, and most of them do not, really want to move to the Senate chamber. Mrs. Smith was no exception.

One of Senator Aiken's earliest recollections of her was during the 80th Congress when she and Sherman Adams met with him to try to devise ways of bringing feed from Canada for northern New England livestock. In the course of the meeting Aiken offered the Representative from Maine the seat behind his senatorial desk. "Sit in my chair," he told her. "You may want one for yourself some day." The very next election she had one, Senator Aiken adds.

When Maine's senior Senator, Wallace White, announced his intention of retiring at the end of his term, Margaret Smith decided to run for his seat. It was a bold move. No woman had ever been initially elected to the United States Senate on her own merits.

Maine in 1948 was still solidly Republican, so that the problem was to win the nomination in the primary race. Here Mrs. Smith faced extremely tough competition. Running against her were three powerful men; one opponent, the Reverend Albion Beverage, was a spellbinding pacifist and isolationist who, though not likely to win, was a threat since it was believed he would have great appeal to the women voters. The other two, a former Governor, Sumner Sewall, and the incumbent Governor, Horace Hildreth, were seasoned, successful, able politicians, backed by well-oiled and well-heeled machines. All in all it was a formidable challenge.

"This little lady," pronounced a Maine politician, "has simply stepped out of her class."

Others, besides the candidate herself, were more optimistic. Representative Frances Bolton, who might have relished such a race herself had it been possible — which it was not in Ohio — went all out to help her fellow Representative and friend.

"Listen," Mrs. Bolton was quoted as saying, "you know the support Margaret has developed in her own district. If she just has the
time and strength to campaign through the rest of the state so people there can get to know her as the home folks do, she can make
it."

In an article published in the September 11, 1948, *Saturday Evening Post*, Beverly Smith, the magazine's Washington editor, describes Mrs. Smith's hardships on the icy Maine campaign trail in a
way that makes Peary's expedition to the North Pole seem like a
lawn party.

First there was the problem of getting to the state each week
from Washington. At best the flight to Portland required a change
in Boston or New York (sometimes both), and during the winter
months flights were more often grounded than not, which meant
day coaches, usually sitting up most of the night. Once in Portland
Mrs. Smith still had to make the hundred-mile trip to her home in
Skowhegan. Here she picked up her car and took to the icy roads,
the snowdrifts, the sub-zero temperatures as she covered the state
of Maine, reaching even the remotest spots where occasionally
she had to put up for the night at a farmhouse.

She managed it through the ice and sleet and snow into mid-
February unscathed, but then in what has been referred to as a
"politically lucky break," she slipped on the ice and fractured her
arm. She was rushed to the hospital in Bangor by ambulance, and
two hours later was keeping a speaking engagement in Rockland,
sixty miles away. No doubt the sight of a lone woman, arm in sling,
carrying on undaunted against three healthy male opponents won
many hearts and votes.

Margaret Chase Smith was her own campaign manager. She
had no paid staff, and depended entirely on volunteers, many of
whom she had known through her activities as president of the
Business and Professional Women's clubs. Even the telephone oper-
ators, ever loyal to one of their own, conspired to get long distance
calls through faster for her.

She campaigned on her record in the House, using such slogans as the Can Do Candidate with the Can Did Record. It was all very folksy and amateurish and enthusiastic, and the political big-wigs in and out of the state saw no reason to take it very seriously.

As for the pro-Smith forces, they hoped at most that, with four candidates in the race, their candidate would squeak by with a plurality based on perhaps as little as 30 per cent of the vote. No one, including Margaret Chase Smith, was prepared for what happened.

When the votes were counted on June 21, 1948, primary day in Maine, which also happened to be the day the Republican National Convention opened in Philadelphia, Margaret Chase Smith had come up with more votes than all three of her opponents put together.

It was a stunning victory. Not only had Mrs. Smith won the Senate seat (the Democrats ran only a pro-forma candidate in the actual election), but she had won complete independence from the Republican Party organization.

Her astonishing feat was almost totally eclipsed, however, by the day's bigger political news of a coalition between Senator Robert A. Taft and Governor Harold E. Stassen, formed in an attempt to stop the nomination of Governor Thomas E. Dewey. Ironically today, twenty years later, it is the two surviving members of that Republican triumvirate, Dewey at sixty-eight and Stassen at sixty-one, who are almost totally eclipsed while Margaret Chase Smith at seventy-two is still on her way up.

As a freshman Senator she once again had to begin with minor committee assignments — District of Columbia, Expenditures in the Executive Department, Rules and Administration. It was not until toward the end of her first term in 1953 that she won major appointments to the Appropriations and the Armed Services committees. She continued on Expenditures in the Executive Department, by now renamed Government Operations, but here she became a controversial figure, for reasons which were much to her credit.

When Margaret Chase Smith took her seat in the Senate in 1949 another seat on the Republican side of the aisle was occupied by a man who had been elected two years earlier and who so far seemed to most of his colleagues an inconsequential vulgarian. He was the junior Senator from Wisconsin, Joseph P. McCarthy.

All through 1949 Senator McCarthy acted the part of rabble-rouser without a cause. Then he discovered Communism. He had done little in his first term in the Senate to strengthen his position with his constituency, and he hit on Communists in government as an issue that might give him some mileage in his home state and help his 1952 campaign for re-election.

On February 9, 1950, he launched his trial balloon in Wheeling, West Virginia, in his now famous speech: "I have here in my hand a list of 205* [men in the State Department] who were known to be members of the Communist Party." It was the beginning of Joseph McCarthy's mercifully short but successful career as a demagogue.

Repercussions from the Wheeling speech were swift. On February 20th he was summoned to defend his charges on the floor of the Senate, and for six hours he threw up a smoke screen of confusion, contradictions, evasions, and total disregard for the truth which was to become his stock in trade. An *ad hoc* committee, constituted a few days later to investigate McCarthy's wild, unsubstantiated charges and headed by Senator Millard Tydings, began hearings that dragged on all spring. They proved nothing, but gave the Senator a forum in which to continue his smear tactics under the protective cover of congressional immunity.

Although most Republicans had been repelled by Joe McCarthy's February performance in the Senate chamber, many soon began to see in the man and in the movement which bore his name a campaign issue which would repudiate the Democrats and finally bring the Republicans back to power. Even Senator Taft, "Mr. Repub-

* Richard Rovere in his book *Senator Joe McCarthy* points out that the figure 205 was to change in the next months to 57, to 80, to 10, to 116, and at a certain juncture to 1 when he said he would stand or fall on the single case of Owen Lattimore.

lican," whose political purity was a byword, was willing to exploit
McCarthyism and to encourage the Senator to persist in his reckless
attacks. "If one case doesn't work, try another," he is said to have
told McCarthy.

Not so Margaret Chase Smith. On June 1, 1950, she spoke out —
the first Republican to do so — on the floor of the Senate. "I speak
as briefly as possible because too much harm has already been done
with irresponsible words of bitterness and selfish political oppor-
tunism," she said in her speech. "As a woman, I wonder how the
mothers, wives, sisters, and daughters feel about the way in which
members of their families have been politically mangled in Senate
debate — and I use the word 'debate' advisedly. As a United States
Senator I am not proud of the way in which the Senate has been
made a publicity platform for irresponsible sensationalism. I am not
proud of the reckless abandon in which unproved charges have
been hurled from this side of the aisle. . . . I don't like the way the
Senate has been made a rendezvous for vilification. . . . I am not
proud of the way we smear outsiders from the floor of the Senate
and hide behind the cloak of congressional immunity. . . . As an
American I want to see our nation recapture the strength and unity
it once had when we fought the enemy instead of ourselves."

Senator Smith concluded her speech by offering a statement — a
resolution which she called a "Declaration of Conscience," in
which she "expressed concern over the growing confusion that
threatens the security and stability of our country." Without actually naming McCarthy, she denounced "certain elements of the
Republican Party [who have] materially added to this confusion in
the hopes of riding the Republican Party to victory through
the selfish political exploitation of fear, bigotry, ignorance, and in-
tolerance."

When she first drafted the "Declaration of Conscience," Mrs.
Smith had showed it to Senator Aiken, who said he would like to
co-sponsor it. Subsequently they were joined in sponsorship by
Republican Senators Charles W. Tobey of New Hampshire, Wayne

L. Morse of Oregon (he had not yet gone across the aisle to the Democratic side), Irving M. Ives of New York, Edward J. Thye of Minnesota, and Robert C. Henrickson of New Jersey. But it was Margaret Chase Smith who took the initiative.

She was not rewarded by the Republican Party, however, for her brave and timely action, and if she had hoped it might start a ground swell which would stem the tide of McCarthyism, she was disappointed. Most Republicans, while perhaps applauding her privately, publicly continued to tiptoe around the junior Senator from Wisconsin, afraid to incur his wrath, hoping to capitalize on his growing popular following.

By 1953, when the Republicans did come to power, even President Eisenhower declined to declare against McCarthy. Instead, the Wisconsin Senator was rewarded with a committee chairmanship, an unprecedented position for one with so little seniority.

The committee was Government Operations, of which Margaret Chase Smith was a member. And the sub-committee, which was soon to overshadow the parent committee altogether, was the Permanent Investigating Committee, on which Mrs. Smith also served. But not for long. One of McCarthy's first acts — as unprecedented as his chairmanship — was to drop Senator Smith from the Permanent Investigating Committee. Senator Taft, still the most powerful Republican in the Senate, who could have interceded to prevent her demotion to a lesser sub-committee, did not. Although he had once referred to her as the Joan of Arc of the Republican Party, he did nothing now to help her continue in the role of savior. It is interesting to speculate on how the subsequent and notorious Army-McCarthy hearings would have differed had a Republican of Margaret Chase Smith's conviction still been a member of the Permanent Investigating Committee.

Joe McCarthy not only wanted her off the committee, he wanted her out of the Senate altogether, and to this end he selected, launched, and financially backed a candidate to run against her in the 1954 Maine primaries for her Senate seat. Robert L. Jones of

Biddeford, Maine, had been the executive assistant to Senator Charles E. Potter, Republican from Michigan, on the Permanent Investigating Committee. Jones was a McCarthy man, and, following in the footsteps of the master, he was alleged to have started a whispering campaign that Mrs. Smith had cancer and would probably be unable to run. Mrs. Smith promptly filed her nomination petition, announced that she was in the best of health, and pointed, as she was so fond of doing, to her unbroken roll-call attendance as evidence of her robustness. "I think the records will show," she said in a later interview, "that I have missed only one vote in my years of service on anything that could be called illness, and that was one Saturday afternoon when I thought I had a headache."

Furthermore, she declined to campaign vigorously against the thirty-four-year-old Jones, saying, "My record is so outstanding and so effective that there isn't any use running around the state defending it against someone who has been assigned to do the job."

She was entirely correct — at least about the futility of running around the state — for the people of Maine gave Jones a very cold shoulder. He carried exactly four out of 621 precincts on June 22, 1954, and succeeded only in making Senator Smith look more deserving than ever in the eyes of the electorate.

The actual election in September was quite a different matter, however. For the first time in years, Maine was about to become a two-party state. The renaissance of the Democratic Party, begun a few years earlier, now resulted in a strong candidate for every spot on the ticket. Edmund S. Muskie, today the junior Senator from Maine, led the slate as candidate for Governor. Running against Margaret Chase Smith was a popular history professor from Colby College named Paul Fullam. Though he had never before sought public office, Fullam was cast in the Adlai Stevenson image — attractive, articulate, intelligent, and a master of understatement. Senator Smith started off by publicly commending her worthy opponent as a man of principle and intelligence whose only drawback was his lack of experience. After that she completely ignored him until the final days of the campaign.

Fullam for his part made the usual announcement about campaigning only on the issues, but instead of mouthing it as a tired old political cliché, he actually meant it — and furthermore he stuck to it. He had no illusions about defeating Margaret Chase Smith. He ran partly because he truly believed in a two-party system, but largely because he was deeply concerned about the grave problems which confronted the government. In announcing his candidacy he said, "We are all of us living our daily lives under three terrible realities: the ruthless forces of Communist aggression, the presence of appalling instruments of physical destruction, and a growing national disunity. . . ."

Privately he believed that Mrs. Smith was beyond her depth in dealing with these vast questions but that she managed to conceal her basic inadequacy by clever wiles and dodges. "Operation Margaret," he wrote to a friend, "is a favor-dispensing service which has managed to build over the years a solid corps of blind followers who identify with her personal integrity and womanly honor . . . I say this not in malice but in charity; I shall take my stand on the issues and rise or fall on that ground. Perhaps to the stock-jobbing in ships, to lobsters and potatoes, I shall be able to add consideration for the future in which our children must live."

Though Paul Fullam did indeed take his stand on what he considered to be the important issues — federal aid to education, unemployment compensation, foreign policy, taxation, defense, and the development of Maine as an independent economic unit in the total New England economy — he was unable to persuade his opponent to do likewise.

"My outstanding and effective personal record is too well known to need repeating," she claimed. As before, she continued to campaign on a person-to-person basis and to invoke as often as possible the magic name of Eisenhower. This was, of course, the first time she had ever faced Democratic opposition. Her previous fights had all been in primaries against Republicans. Her problem in this campaign was further complicated by the fact that the Democrats were making appreciable capital of the widespread unpopularity of the incumbent Republican Governor, Burton M. Cross, and Mrs. Smith, a loner at best in campaigns, had no desire to be associated with a possible loser.

In the last days of the campaign Fullam got more and more down to cases on the specifics of his opponent's voting record. "In order to make clear to the voter the sharp alternatives offered between my views and Senator Smith's," he said in a speech on September 6th, "it was incumbent upon her to make clear her position on these issues too. She has not done so." Citing chapter and verse then, he went on to examine parts of her voting record and to say where and why he was in disagreement with it.

Margaret Chase Smith's response was to charge that he was "becoming more and more personal."

Fullam answered that he had consistently made a careful distinction between *Mrs.* Smith and *Senator* Smith, but that in the latter capacity she must realize that "her public acts and words and record are not her private property, but the property of the people of this state and of all the states. As such they are subject to legitimate criticism and disagreement." He added that he would be glad to provide her with manuscripts of all his speeches.

She would have been well advised to accept this offer. She did not, however. She said nothing further about or to Fullam until 11:05 P.M. on the night before the election. Then, with no advance notice whatsoever, she made an "impromptu," live, television appearance and delivered what can only be described as a diatribe against Paul Fullam.

She began by stating that although she had wanted to wage the campaign on issues, not on personalities, her opponent to her "surprise and disappointment" had become increasingly "personal and erroneous" in his attacks on her. "When I said so the other day, he accused me of trying to keep my public record private and secret," she added.

During a political campaign it is considered quite normal to twist your opponent's words. But, though a certain degree of distortion is permissible, a one-hundred-and-eighty-degree wrench is beyond acceptable limits. Over and over again during her televised speech Mrs. Smith claimed that Paul Fullam had said one thing about her when in fact he had said exactly the opposite. Even in his citing of her clear and indisputable voting record Mrs. Smith contended that her opponent had lied. Mr. Fullam, she said, had accused her of voting *against* an amendment of the Taft-Hartley Act. Mr. Fullam had done nothing of the sort. He had accused her of voting *in favor of* the amendment and said that *he* would have voted against it.

There were other such direct reversals of "for" and "against" which made her case sound extremely strong to those who did not know what Paul Fullam had actually said.

It is probable that Senator Smith herself did not know exactly what he had said since she did not at any time ask for copies of his speeches and apparently relied on newspaper accounts and on the reports of people who had heard him speak. Still, although her failure to check facts was not consistent with her reputation for careful preparation, there is no reason to think that her misstatements were deliberate.

But if carelessness is not a characteristic of Margaret Chase Smith, a need to justify herself by citing her honors is.

My opponent has accused me in effect of being an enemy of air power. [He had not, even in effect, done so.] For your information, Professor Fullam, I am not an enemy of air power. Instead, I have been acknowledged by such organizations as the Air Reserve Association and the Air Force Association to be a champion for air power. For your information, sir, I am a lieutenant colonel in the Air Force Reserve.

The speech was filled with variations on this theme.

I note that on your campaign poster you brag of your membership in the American Political Science Association. Now you may be ashamed of me, Professor Fullam, but the members of that group of which you are so proud of your association — the members of that group disagree with your shame of me — because they once took a poll in rating senators and they rated me sixth best of all 96 members of the United States Senate. . . . And your own former newspaper, the *New York Times,* of which you are so proud of your association with, has commended my record repeatedly — even the Massachusetts Senator you had on your telecast [John F. Kennedy*] publicly commended my record. . . . And Bowdoin College — the great institution once headed by a great man who appeared on your telecast [Kenneth M. Sills] was proud enough to award an honorary degree of Doctor of Laws, Honoris Causa to me in 1952. . . . The University of Maine also disagrees with your shame of me, Professor Fullam, for it has expressed its pride in my record by awarding me an honorary Doctor of Laws degree . . . and your own great Colby College gave me an honorary degree of Master of Arts.

Considering Senator Smith's usually cool, well-reasoned public performance, one can only assume that this erroneous and exaggeratedly defensive speech was hastily prepared and motivated by alarm. For by election eve Muskie appeared to be a shoo-in for Governor (as indeed he turned out to be) and this, plus Fullam's vigorous and substantive campaign, so unlike any she had encountered before, may have thrown Mrs. Smith momentarily off balance.

But if the speech can be excused on these grounds, its timing cannot be. Coming as it did just before Station WCSH went off the air for the night, literally and figuratively at the eleventh hour, it allowed Paul Fullam no opportunity to respond before the polls opened the next morning. Recognizing the injustice of this tactic,

---

* Kennedy was vacationing near Bar Harbor during the heat of the campaign. Fullam went to see him to seek his support and as a result of this meeting Kennedy agreed to come to Portland at his own expense and at a time when he was suffering severe discomfort with his back, to speak for Fullam. Mrs. Smith was said to have been very piqued because Kennedy came to Maine to speak for her opponent but did not go into Massachusetts to speak for the Democratic senatorial candidate, Foster Furcolo.

WCSH allowed Fullam equal time — albeit four days after the election — to answer Mrs. Smith's charges.

He was somewhat handicapped in preparing his response since he had not heard Senator Smith's broadcast. He was appearing on a program from Bangor at the time; his wife and his close associates, who were of course listening to him, had not heard Mrs. Smith either. Fullam requested a copy of the text from Senator Smith's office. It arrived just before he was scheduled to go on the air, typed, rather incongruously, on the back of stationery from a New York hotel. With it came a covering letter from Mrs. Smith's secretary, said to have been slightly apologetic in tone, suggesting that perhaps the Senator had been misinformed about some of Professor Fullam's charges.*

Paul Fullam died in June, 1955, of a heart attack. Had he lived he would probably have continued his auspicious start in politics. Those who were close to him say that he would have run next for the House, waited until 1960 when Margaret Chase Smith came up for re-election, and then challenged her again.

As it was, he had the satisfaction of knowing that he had played a vital role in the resurgence of the Democratic Party in Maine and that Margaret Chase Smith's plurality of only 40,000 votes made his the best showing against her of any candidate before — and, as it has turned out, since.

Back in Washington for her second term, Senator Smith continued in her capacity of watchdog on all matters pertaining to national defense. As time went on she gained a reputation as a tenacious, determined prober, particularly in committee hearings where her ability to ask the questions behind the questions often confounded the witnesses. A general, for instance, who had been carefully

---

* No film of Mrs. Smith's TV appearance nor any copy of her text is available from Station WCSH in Portland. Nor was there any mention of the speech in either the morning or afternoon editions of the *Portland Press Herald* on the following day. The quotations above are taken from the text which Senator Smith's office sent to Professor Fullam, and from copies of his own speeches.

briefed by his staff on the point at issue, but who was perhaps a bit hazy on some of the details, was fair game for Mrs. Smith. Thanks to her habit of scrupulously careful preparation, she knew all the details — down to the last triviality — and knew how to use them to great effect.

Never was her penchant for meticulousness, coupled with her sense of righteous indignation, more devastating than in the summer of 1957 when the now famous skirmish took place over the promotion of actor James Stewart to brigadier general in the Air Force Reserve.

Shortly after Senator Smith learned that President Eisenhower had nominated Stewart for promotion, she began asking Air Force personnel for a detailed report on his participation in reserve activities. Stewart, who had risen from private to colonel and combat wing commander, had a brilliant combat record both in World War II and in the Korean War. According to Senator Symington, formerly Secretary of the Air Force, he had done as much for air power as any man in the country. To the public at large, who loved him anyway, his service seemed quite exemplary, especially for a movie star. But as Margaret Smith dug into the records she found that his postwar attendance at reserve meetings and drills had been very spotty. He had, in fact, had only nine days of active training in the past eleven years, and only when the possibility of promotion loomed had he started going to meetings regularly.

Senator Smith was outraged. "Suggesting Stewart for promotion places success in big business and in the movies above military training," she said. In addition to her disapproval of giving Stewart unfair preference over less famous reservists who had dutifully completed their requisite training, her greater concern was that Stewart's mobilization assignment, in the event of hostilities, was to be as chief of staff of the Strategic Air Command's 15th Air Force, a post for which she, with considerable justification, did not consider him qualified.

General Emmett (Rosie) O'Donnell was sent to Washington to

appear before the Armed Services Committee in defense of Stewart's nomination. The General may have been a good combat man, but in this case he failed to take the measure of his adversary. Senator Smith shot his testimony full of holes and effectively demolished his arguments. Stewart's promotion was denied.*

Just as she had routed General O'Donnell, Mrs. Smith could pulverize fellow legislators who opposed her without constructing a watertight case. The wiser of her colleagues soon found it easier to stay on her side of the argument than to risk taking the floor against her in a debate. And herein lies at least part of the secret of her importance in Congress. Because she is so tenacious and well prepared and because she is fearless in defense of her convictions, Senators on both sides of the aisle go out of their way to gain Margaret Chase Smith's support, knowing the value of having her with them and the hazards of having her oppose them. She resists blandishments, however, and she does not often tip her hand in advance.

"I do not commit myself to legislation until I am ready to vote," she once said in a television interview. "Legislation is a matter of compromise and you just don't know what is coming. So I work very hard on my votes, and once I cast one I forget it."

It is doubtful if she, or any of the other Senators who were present at the time, will ever forget one of her most celebrated votes on the confirmation of Admiral Lewis L. Strauss for Secretary of Commerce.

Few appointments have ever stirred a more bitter controversy on Capitol Hill. Eisenhower had named Strauss for an interim appointment in October, 1959, while the Congress was recessed, pending confirmation when the Senate, which was heavily Democratic, reconvened. Strauss had long had a personal conflict with Democratic members of the congressional Atomic Energy Committee,

---

* Three years later Stewart had completed the requisite reserve training, and was again nominated for promotion to brigadier general. Mrs. Smith voted in favor of his promotion after assuring herself that his mobilization assignment in the event of hostilities would be in public relations.

notably Senator Clinton Anderson of New Mexico, who considered
him dictatorial and who had questioned his integrity in the matter
of the Dixon-Yates power contract.* In addition, many other
Democrats objected to Lewis Strauss for his part in terminating
the government service of Dr. J. Robert Oppenheimer on the
grounds that Oppenheimer's past association with known Communists made him a security risk. Some Democrats, however, considered Strauss well qualified for the post of Secretary of Commerce
because of his broad experience in business, finance, and in the administrative machinery of government.

For the Republican minority in the Senate the confirmation was
a point of political honor. Not since 1925 had a President's appointment of a cabinet member been rejected by Congress. Failure to
deliver this nomination to their Republican President now would
result in a severe blow to the party's prestige.

For seven months the confirmation dispute simmered in an atmosphere of extraordinary bitterness on both sides. Then on June
19 Senate Majority Leader Lyndon B. Johnson announced that
the Senate would stay in session "today, tonight, and tomorrow"
until the nomination was disposed of. The Republicans fought to
delay the vote by long speeches (Goldwater even threatened to
filibuster) until they could round up any absent members who could
tip the balance in favor of Strauss. Only two Republicans and three
Democrats were not present that night when, in an atmosphere of
high tension, with the galleries packed, the final tally began.

Senator Smith had not announced her intention in advance. When
her turn came, she voted no. There was an audible gasp. She was
one of two Republicans to vote against Lewis Strauss (the other

---

* In 1954 the Atomic Energy Commission made a contract with the Dixon-
Yates power company to furnish power in the Memphis area to AEC installa-
tions, thereby replacing the Tennessee Valley Authority power which had
been previously used. The contract was canceled when it was found that
Adolphe Wenzell, vice president of the First Boston Corporation (who was
to have supplied the monies for the transaction), had acted as an unpaid con-
sultant to the Bureau of the Budget on this contract. Strauss denied knowing
that Wenzell had acted in this dual capacity and said he would approve the
contract again if circumstances were the same.

was Senator William Langer of North Dakota). The nomination was not confirmed. The final vote was 49 against and 46 in favor.

By thus defying her party and her President and voting according to her own conviction, Margaret Chase Smith reaffirmed her independence and served notice once and for all that she could not be taken for granted by the Republicans. She would call the shots as she saw them even if it meant standing alone.

She is never quite alone, however. Always with her, though often remaining in the background, is William C. Lewis, her fifty-five-year-old administrative assistant, whose association with the Senator dates from the days when she was on the House Naval Affairs Committee and he was on the committee staff.

Wherever Margaret Chase Smith goes, William C. Lewis goes. They own adjacent property in Chevy Chase, Maryland, and in Maine, and Lewis's presence is taken for granted both in the capital and in the state. He is a lawyer, the son of two lawyers, and is said to be a man of great intelligence and is of invaluable help to Senator Smith in shaping her legislative and political positions.

Many people, among them both friends and opponents, feel, however, that Lewis has come more and more to exercise a Svengali-like influence over Mrs. Smith, that he has made her increasingly suspicious and petty and has planted the idea in her mind that people are out to get her.

Whether or not Lewis is responsible, there seems to be ample evidence that Mrs. Smith is considerably more contentious than she used to be. There is even an unofficial society of those who were once quite close to her but who have, for one reason or another, fallen from grace. It is called the Order of the Wilted Rose.

But if she is querulous and defensive with some people, she is also capable of being charming, down to earth, and warm with others, and it is difficult to determine what motivates her reactions. Certainly she does not pander. She can be unforgiving and vindictive to a political figure who has crossed her, loyal and attentive to an obscure friend who has faithfully done her bidding. It is puzzling that she should be so thin-skinned, so quick to take umbrage at words and deeds that most politicians of her long experience have learned to shrug off as part of the game. And unquestionably she is a good and shrewd politician. Not only has she never lost an election, she has won them all by large majorities, nearly always topping the ticket; in 1960 she set a new all-time record for Maine, with more votes than Eisenhower had won in the state in 1956.

Her legislative record, fond as she is of citing it, would hardly justify her extreme popularity, for she has introduced very little new legislation affecting the state, although she has staunchly protected what others have created. Nationally her name is connected with even less legislative action, but as Senator Aiken suggested recently, she will go down in history not for the good legislation she passed but for the bad legislation she kept from passing. Future historians will look on her as one who stood firmly in favor of a strong military, and an adequate, economically sound space program. They will remember her also as a woman. In her reluctance to be so considered, however, she can also be her own worst enemy. When asked if she could explain why more women do not go into public life she answered tartly, "I wouldn't have any idea. I'm in. I know why I'm in. I don't know why other people aren't."

Her answer, implying that she has never given this matter a thought, does not do her justice. She has on several occasions delivered a clear and forceful speech on "The Challenge to Women" in which she discussed the question of women's limited activity in public life and suggested that the reason for it is that women lack incentive and determination, that they have failed to stand together to exercise their majority voting power. "If women are to claim and win their rightful place in the sun on an equal basis with men then they must not insist upon those privileges and prerogatives identified in the past as exclusively feminine."

It is Senator Smith's contention that as a woman in public office she has never insisted on a woman's prerogatives. "I've never asked for privileges as a woman, I never accept privileges as a woman, and I've never been given privileges as a woman. I accept my responsibilities, do my homework and carry myself as a member of the Senate — never as a woman member of the Senate. I'm always happy to be recognized as a woman — and as a lady, but I do not let it enter into my official affairs."

Her opponents do not agree. "She plays her womanhood to the hilt if anyone attacks her," said one. Perhaps privately, but she does not do so publicly. She even insisted that in her bid for the Presidency in 1964 the fact that she is a woman was only secondary, that her real reason for entering the New Hampshire primary against Rockefeller and Goldwater was to demonstrate that one did not need to be a millionaire to run for the office. In addition she wanted to show what could be done by a moderate, without money, who also happened to be a woman. She does admit that it was a breakthrough for women, but she was determined that her sex not be stressed as the key issue. Thus when Senator Aiken made the nomination speech for her in San Francisco, on July 16, 1964, he had to do it without once referring to her as a woman.

Senator Aiken handled his assignment adroitly. He first explained that since his candidate had returned to her well-wishers every penny of money she had received for her campaign, he could not even offer the delegates a cigar or some chewing gum or a cup of coffee. Then he set forth the qualifications a President should have.

"A President should have integrity. . . . My candidate stands ace-high in this respect. A President should have ability. . . . If my candidate does not have ability then the forty-four universities and colleges that have awarded her degrees based solely on merit have been wrong. A President should have had wide experience in government. . . . A President should have courage . . . common sense."

It was a skillful job of highlighting the good qualities of his candidate and, as nominating speeches go, without undue exaggeration.

But do these qualities alone make a President? Probably not in today's complex world. They do, however, make a Senator who is the pride of the state of Maine.

LADY OF THE HOUSE

Frances P. Bolton

SHE INSISTS on being called Congress*man* Bolton. But occasionally, even after her twenty-eight years in the House of Representatives, some hapless soul mistakenly refers to her as "Congresswoman." It makes Frances Bolton very cross.

"Try to find 'Congresswoman' in the dictionary," she says. "It doesn't exist." In point of fact it does, but Mrs. Bolton is so emphatic about it that one feels the dictionary must be wrong.

"We've had Congressmen here for a good many generations," she contends. "But we've *never* had Congresswomen. You're a woman Congressman. It's just like a chairman. Some people say chairwoman. But that's just silly."

The fact that most of the other ten women in the House use "Congresswoman" — some even making a point of it — only adds to Mrs. Bolton's scorn. "They think they're building up women that way. I say I do more for women than they do by being a woman Congressman."

If being called Congressswoman irks her, being referred to on the floor of the House in paraliamentese as "gentlelady" (Will the gentlelady from Ohio yield?) causes her to be neither gentle nor quite a lady. "Ignorance. Just ignorance," she fumes. "It's more than I can take. And whenever anybody does it that I can really talk to I tell them exactly what I think. Carl Albert, for instance, was in the chair one day and called me a gentlelady. And I went right up to him and banged on the desk. 'Carl,' I said, 'never again let me hear you say that! You're the gentleman from Oklahoma and I'm the gentlewoman from Ohio! Do you understand?'"

Reflecting on it, Mrs. Bolton suddenly chuckles, the fierce expression fades, and her face lights up with a mischievous grin. "Poor

Carl. I scared the living daylights out of him. He slipped once after that, but believe me he went right back to 'gentlewoman' just as fast as he could get there."

The quick switch from testiness to drollery is very characteristic of Frances Payne Bolton. She is eighty-two years old. She is keen witted and strong willed, sprightly, emphatic, humorous, and astonishingly vigorous. As the ranking woman in the House, the second ranking member of the Ohio delegation, and the ranking minority member of the Committee on Foreign Affairs, she keeps up a dizzying day-in, day-out schedule that would wear down many a thirty-year-old Marine. Mrs. Bolton thrives on it.

A typical day, taken from her engagement calendar, began at "the ungodly hour of eight" with a breakfast for the House Republican Conference. At nine she attended a State Department briefing in the House Office Building. At ten there was an executive session for the full Committee on Foreign Affairs which lasted until the House convened at noon. At twelve-thirty she had lunch in the Capitol Dining Room with the Ohio Republican delegation, after which she was scheduled to be in two places at once; as ranking minority member of the Committee on Foreign Affairs, Mrs. Bolton is an ex-officio member of all ten of its sub-committees, and at two o'clock that afternoon the Near East Committee was meeting in open session with Dr. Charles Malik of Beirut, while the Asian and Pacific Affairs Committee met with two AID representatives from Saigon. Mrs. Bolton looked in on both meetings before going on at three-thirty to a Foreign Aid "Coffee" in the Speaker's Dining Room. From four to six she was honorary hostess at a reception at the International Club honoring women members of Congress, followed at six-thirty by cocktails at which she was actual — not honorary — hostess. At seven o'clock she went to the Madison Hotel for a dinner in honor of Dr. Malik.

At all times Mrs. Bolton, like the other Representatives, must keep an ear cocked for the bells and an eye on the lights over the clock in her office which call her to the floor of the House.

One bell and a red light signify that the House is in session, four bells and four lights mean the House is adjourned. But three bells is a quorum call and two bells a "yeas and nays" call, and when these ring the Congressmen start scurrying out of their offices, out of the committee rooms, down the endless corridors of the Rayburn, the Longworth, or the Cannon Office Buildings, into the subway across to the Capitol and into the House chamber. 1457911

As the legislators pour in answering quorum or yea-nay calls, Mrs. Bolton's progress to her seat is slow, not because she walks slowly — she doesn't, she trots — but because she is greeted by so many people on both sides of the aisle. A squat little figure with her perfectly coiffed red hair, her remarkably unwrinkled skin, her piercing blue eyes, dressed usually in bright colors, she is hugged by some, patted on the back by others, shaken hands with, waved to, whispered to, nodded to by still others, ignored by none.

Everybody knows Frances Bolton. Ask an officer at the entrance of the Rayburn House Office Building for Mrs. Bolton, he will give her room number without consulting his directory. Ask another officer which way to Room 2373, he will answer "Yes, Mrs. Bolton's office, three right turns then a U turn, then a left. . . ." Ask the attendant at the Capitol subway if Mrs. Bolton has gone over yet. He will remember that she went a few moments ago.

She is, in fact, an institution in the House, as, after twenty-eight years, she deserves to be. Only eight members, including Speaker John McCormack, have been there longer.

Mrs. Bolton doesn't relish being known for her longevity, however. Nor does she like to be known for standing on her head (she has practiced yoga for years) or to be pointed out as the only mother whose son served with her in the Congress of the United States. Although all these distinctions are notable, the Congressman considers that she has worthier claims to fame.

Outstanding in her legislative career are her associations with nursing, with foreign affairs — in particular with Africa, in which areas she has made significant contributions. Senator Karl E. Mundt,

Republican from South Dakota, who has known her since they were both first elected to the 76th Congress, calls her a "sort of modern up-to-date Florence Nightingale," an estimate Mrs. Bolton would probably find a bit too saccharine.

She has, however, introduced countless bills designed to improve the status of nurses, increase their pay, and expand their training facilities, thereby providing better care for the sick. And it was the bill which bears her name that created the Cadet Nurse Corps during World War II and supplied 125,000 nurses for the war effort.

Less well known in nursing legislation than the Bolton Bill but occupying a special place in its author's affections is Public Law 89-609, which Mrs. Bolton first sponsored in 1966 at a time when talk of equal rights for women was particularly rampant.

"Mr. Speaker," said Frances Bolton on the floor of the House, "I am today introducing an Equal Rights for Men bill."

It was just that — a bill to authorize the commissioning of male nurses in the regular Army and regular Navy Nurse Corps, and its text, which should be dear to the hearts of all who had fought to include the word "sex" in Title VII of the Civil Rights Act, specified over and over again that the word "she" or "her" be struck and that for the word "women" the word "persons" be substituted. The bill became law on September 30, 1966, since which time the Army has complied cheerfully but the Navy, Mrs. Bolton feels, has been slow to mend its ways, and still tends to discriminate against male nurses.

Mrs. Bolton has had a lifelong interest in nurses, regardless of their sex, race, or nationality. Her active concern with nursing began when she was eighteen years old and a debutante in Cleveland, Ohio.

Frances Payne Bingham came of excellent stock. Her forbears were early settlers; the Binghams arrived in this country in 1659, the Paines (which was the original spelling) came to Plymouth Colony in 1650. Among her distinguished ancestors are Robert Treat Paine, signer of the Declaration of Independence, Thomas

Paine, and also John Howard Payne, author of "Home, Sweet Home." Her maternal grandmother was a Perry — kin to Commodore Perry. Her Bingham grandfather migrated from the East to Cleveland in 1816 and amassed a considerable fortune in the metal business. Her other grandfather, Henry Payne, was a United States Senator — a Democrat.

Though Frances Bingham grew up in a privileged environment, her education was, to say the least, sketchy. She says, "I had a brother who was ill and the climate down in Florida seemed to agree with him. So every winter I'd go to school in Cleveland from September to November and then we'd move down to Florida. My brother had a tutor, a Yale man with a scroll and key and all that business, but nobody cared what the little girl learned. So I studied the sea and the sky and the birds and the beasts and loved it. I never studied American history, for instance. In fact I had no proper schooling at all."

At fourteen, after her mother died, Frances was sent abroad to a school outside of Paris, where she learned French and Spanish ("I still have a beautiful French pronunciation") and after two years there she came home to be "finished" in New York at Miss Spence's School for Girls — not for young ladies, she emphasizes. Even in 1901 it was just plain "for girls."

"It was a wonderful school," she says. "It still is. But I didn't do very well." In her senior year she was told she could not graduate with her class; instead of a diploma she would get only a certificate. "So," Mrs. Bolton recalls, "they gave me a piece of paper that said, 'she hasn't done very much, but the little she did wasn't too bad.'"

There her formal education ended. Back in Cleveland, keeping house for her father, Miss Bingham prepared to make her debut along with the girls she had known since childhood. As little girls they had all been members of the Brownie Club and had, among other activities, each year given a "lawn fete" at which long-suffering parents had been obliged to "buy" their homemade products, the proceeds going to charity. As debutantes in 1903 they reconstituted the club in order that they might continue to conform with the *noblesse oblige* of the day, which demanded that each year's group of debutantes adopt a charity of their very own.

The Brownies, however, faced a dilemma. All the good causes had been pre-empted, it seemed, by their predecessors, the Rainbows, the Sunbeams, and the Baker's Dozen. There just wasn't a single charity left for the Brownies to adopt.

What to do? Frances Bingham was president, and she had an idea. The Baker's Dozen had claimed the Visiting Nurses Association, so why not latch onto that cause and become the Visiting Nurse Supply Corps? Accordingly, a delegation of Brownies waited upon the head of the Visiting Nurses Association, who said, by all means, she would be only too happy to have vigorous young debutantes go around with her hard-working nurses and carry their heavy supply bags for them.

Some of the Brownies, who had in mind an activity more in the bandage-rolling line, demurred. They were certain their parents would not let them go into the sordid homes where the visiting nurses' duties took them. Mrs. Bolton says, "I was certain my father wouldn't let me go either, so I didn't ask him. I just went.

"I'd dance all night, then get up to have breakfast with Father at seven and then off I'd go to the clinic around eight." All day long she made rounds with the nurses to the Greek district, to "Little Italy," changing sheets, ministering to the most miserably squalid poor, to dope addicts, to fourteen-year-old pregnant girls.

When Charles Bingham eventually caught up with his young daughter's activities, he was stern but wise. "I wouldn't have allowed you to go if I'd known about it," Mrs. Bolton recalls his saying, "but now that you are doing it, my dear, don't stop. It's the only way you'll learn how most of the world has to live."

Sixty-five years later his daughter still remembers, "his tone of voice and the expression in his very bright blue eyes."

"I had a good many shocks," she says, "but it was an important revelation for me to learn what life really is." "Mercy," she adds,

"I was born into this terribly conservative family. Fine people, but very, very conservative. I had to try to haul myself out of it. All those experiences stood me in such good stead. It was wonderful for me."

The protected, favored young woman was not the only one to benefit, however, for, thanks to her early experiences, the nursing profession gained a great champion.

If Frances Payne Bingham was born into a conservative milieu, she did not greatly broaden her horizons by marrying Chester Castle Bolton, whose family tradition was, if anything, more strait-laced than her own. She had known Chester Bolton all of her life. He was a neighbor, the son of family friends; he had gone to Harvard before settling down to work in the family steel business. He was in every way considered a most suitable match for Miss Bingham.

They were married in 1907, and their sons Charles and Kenyon were born in 1909 and 1912. Their son Oliver, who was later to serve with his mother in the 83rd and 84th Congresses, was born in 1917. In that year Frances Bolton also inherited a considerable sum of money from her bachelor uncle, Oliver Hazard Payne, an inheritance which she shared, incidentally, with her second cousin, Payne Whitney. The Boltons bought property in Lyndhurst, a Cleveland suburb, and started to build their house, which they called after the fashion of the day, "Franchester."

They might well have stayed right there in Cleveland, respectable, solid pillars of their community, never penetrating the national scene, had not the First World War interrupted their complacent existence.

Against his will, for he had been trained at Plattsburg and wanted to get into the action, Chester Bolton was called to Washington to work for the Munitions Standards Board. He remained chained to a desk job until near the end of the war, when he was commissioned as a lieutenant colonel in the Army, but, although he trained for overseas duty, the armistice came before he was shipped off.

He returned to Cleveland and Franchester, feeling restless and with no enthusiasm for picking up the threads of his business life. His postwar dissatisfaction was further exacerbated by President Warren G. Harding, whose sorry performance in Washington was, he felt, bringing discredit to both the Republican Party and the state of Ohio. He was a young, clean-cut, solid businessman, of sound Republican ideas. One day in 1922, according to the story handed down to his son Oliver, Chester Bolton picked up the phone in his office to hear the quiet voice of Cleveland's Republican boss, Maurice Maschke, say to him, "Chester, I have two seats in the Ohio Senate." (Not, there are two seats, but, *I have two*.) "You are going to take one of them and you're going to get another high-class fellow you can work with to take the other."

Such was the power of ward leaders in those days. Chester Bolton himself attended exactly one political meeting, and was easily elected. On the first of January he closed his desk in Cleveland and went to Columbus, Ohio. For six years he served as an Ohio state senator before being elected in 1928 to represent the Twenty-second District in the Congress of the United States.

Frances Bolton remained rather aloof from her husband's political life in Columbus, Ohio. She had interests of her own, and at the time politics was not among them. She was more stimulated by music, for example, and had for years studied voice, even harboring dreams of becoming an opera singer. Furthermore, Chester Bolton was a somewhat austere man who was not inclined to bring his office troubles home.

But if her husband's political activities in the state did not create much of a ripple in her day-to-day life, the move to Washington caused quite a big splash. So much so that Frances Bolton says, "I felt as if I'd jumped into the Indian Ocean — over my head."

There is something about this description that seems hard to credit. Mrs. Bolton, who has a lively spirit of adventure, gives the impression that if she were to jump into the Indian Ocean, it would be because she *wanted* to jump in to find out what it was like.

Equally unconvincing is her recollection of herself eleven years later, in 1940 when, after Chester Bolton's sudden death, she was persuaded to run for the Congress to complete his unexpired term. "I was just as green as grass," she says.

In fact she was not. She was a fifty-five-year-old widow with three grown sons who was very much at home in official Washington. In her years in the capital she had been increasingly involved both with her husband's career in Congress and with organizational party politics. In 1938, the year before Chester Bolton's death, she had served as a member of the Ohio State Republican Campaign Committee. Furthermore, public service was a tradition in her family. Both her grandfathers had served in the Ohio state legislature and one of them, Henry B. Payne, had gone on to Washington, first as a Representative and then as a Senator.

The only area in which Mrs. Bolton might have been called green was at the local party level in her own Twenty-second Congressional District. There she had still to learn such niceties as who the leader of Ward 15 was, what his wife's name was, how many children they had, and what church they attended. Fortunately Mrs. Bolton was not only instinctively adept in her relations with people, but she was blessed with the politician's indispensable tool — a remarkable memory.

On Capitol Hill Frances Bolton did not at first appear to have a great deal in common with the majority of her fellow legislators, most of whom were of more modest means, and lacked her first-family D.A.R. background, and nearly all of whom were men. There were only six other women in the 76th Congress and all but one had been elected, as Mrs. Bolton had, to fill vacancies caused by the deaths of their husbands. Margaret Chase Smith entered the House shortly after Mrs. Bolton. Edith Nourse Rogers of Massachusetts, the other Republican woman, had been a Representative for fifteen years and was to remain one for another twenty. Senior among the women was Mary T. Norton of New Jersey, the first woman Democrat to have been elected to the House strictly on her own merits.

Other notables in the 76th Congress included Martin Dies of the Dies Committee and J. Parnell Thomas of the House Un-American Activities Committee. Everett Dirksen and Charles Halleck (who had not yet become Ev and Charlie) were serving their third terms in the House. Estes Kefauver and Albert Gore were in the middle of their first terms. Sam Rayburn was the Speaker, and the Representative from the Tenth Texas District was Lyndon Baines Johnson.

In the Senate was the first woman Senator, Hattie W. Caraway of Arkansas, who had been appointed to replace her husband. (Senators can be appointed to fill vacancies caused by death. Representatives cannot. They must stand for special election.) There was also Robert M. La Follette, Jr., Arthur H. Vandenberg, Styles Bridges, Carter Glass, Millard Tydings, Robert F. Wagner, Pat McCarran and Robert Taft. The two Senators from Missouri were Champ Clark and Harry S Truman, the former being rather better known at that time than the latter.

Mrs. Bolton looks back with some nostalgia to the early Congresses in which she served. The atmosphere she thinks was more relaxed, somehow the legislators had more good times together. She remembers particularly that at the end of a session when the Representatives were waiting for the Senate to finish up so they could adjourn, they would all gather in the "well" of the House and everyone would be singing and whooping it up.

Today there is less friendly feeling because there are more people who "insist on making everything so terribly partisan," which she says is not *her* idea of serving the country.

Be that as it may, Frances Bolton is not above partisanship of her own. "They," said in a particular tone of voice automatically means the Democrats. "They" of course control all the committees, and the legislative agenda is set according to the "lilt of their chairman." She has tried to sit with some of "them" in the members' dining room in the hope of "getting better acquainted," but nothing much ever comes of it.

It is not surprising that there should be an invisible line between

Mrs. Bolton and the Democrats, many of whom look on her as a reactionary. She is, in fact, a straight-down-the-line Republican, particularly in domestic matters. An advocate of sound fiscal policy and private enterprise, she opposes such government spending as federal rent subsidies, for example, believing that they would undermine "moral strength and spiritual fiber" and "take away from part of our people the consuming need to be responsible."

In November of 1967, however, her vote on a poverty program bill appropriating funds for the Office of Economic Opportunity was so surprising that it received special notice in the press. After voting for the bill, which called for 2.06 billion dollars, she said on the floor of the House, "I am not here in this well to say we must give so huge a sum — certainly not before every effort has been made to cut down and do a better job. We should be able to do much more and do better with less. I am here to say that I cannot live with myself if we stop the doing."

Still, the word "liberal" is a pejorative one to Frances Bolton, and it could therefore only be a source of satisfaction to her that on the A.D.A. (Americans for Democratic Action) legislative scoreboard her voting record for 1965 was zero. It was fifteen in 1964 when she voted with the A.D.A.'s preferred position for final passage of the Civil Rights Act and also against reduction of the foreign aid authorization.

Although she may not agree with their ideology, Mrs. Bolton nonetheless has had some very warm Democratic friends. Helen Gahagan Douglas was one. Mrs. Bolton remembers a day in the House when, after Mrs. Douglas had finished speaking, another Democrat got up and "tongue-lashed" her. Mrs. Bolton happened to be sitting in the front row of the Republican side. Seeing Mrs. Douglas's distress, she crossed over to the Democratic side and sat down beside her — an action which created quite a stir. People on both sides of the aisle told Mrs. Bolton they'd never before seen anything like it.

"What else could I do," Mrs. Bolton snorts. "I was so angry."

She reacts with equal indignation to the treatment Helen Gahagan Douglas received in the 1950 senatorial campaign from her Republican opponent, Richard M. Nixon. "Shocking. Perfectly shocking."

Mary T. Norton, the Democrat from New Jersey, was another great favorite. In a more partisan vein, Mrs. Bolton remembers a day in the House when she crossed over to the "other side" to talk to Mrs. Norton about something. It was early in the first session of the 77th Congress before she or Mrs. Norton had got to know the new members. "Suddenly I looked up," Mrs. Bolton recalls, "and there coming into the chamber on their side was this woman. She had on a white shirtwaist, and one of those very wide belts, and she was chewing gum, and she had some of her hair up in curlers."

Gleefully Mrs. Bolton nudged Mrs. Norton. "I said, 'Mary, do you see what I see, dear?'" Mrs. Norton looked up and, according to Mrs. Bolton, "turned as white as a sheet." "Well, she's yours," Mrs. Bolton crowed. "She's not mine."

Mrs. Norton, it should be recorded, saved "their" honor by going over to the new Congresswoman and suggesting that chewing gum and hair-curlers were hardly the proper accoutrements for a member of the House of Representatives. It might also be added that the woman was not re-elected.

Mrs. Bolton says she is very jealous of the records of "women Congressmen," and if any of them behave unsuitably she resents it bitterly, albeit slightly less so if the offenders happen to be Democrats. But during her twenty-eight years there have been few such miscreants. Almost all the women she thinks have been fine, serious, dedicated, and hard-working public servants. And here with a partisanship of another sort she adds, "We women are much more conscientious than the men. And also we do so much better with the little things."

In the present 90th Congress, she is very proud of the fact that Martha Griffiths, a Democrat from Michigan, is the first woman ever to serve on the powerful Ways and Means Committee. She thinks Lenore Sullivan, another Democrat, from Missouri, is fine, "one of the best," and she is extremely fond of Charlotte Reed, a Republican from Illinois. The mother of four children, Mrs. Reed, who used to be a singer on radio, is probably the prettiest of the Congresswomen and a great favorite among her male colleagues. "She has a charming smile and uses it well," says Mrs. Bolton, who sees no reason for women to play down their femininity.

"The fact that we're women sometimes goes a long way," she says, and again that mischievous little grin, as she is reminded of the time Senator Mundt had a bill coming up on the floor of the Senate. It was a foreign affairs bill, one that she had been instrumental in getting through the House. "So I asked Karl if there was anything I could do to help with it in the Senate. 'Oh, no,' he said very airily. 'We'll be all right. No problem at all.' Two hours later he was calling me back frantically. 'Francie,' he said, 'put on all your war paint and go over there and get it for us.' " So Frances Bolton went over and charmed the bill into law.

Getting that bill through was only one of her accomplishments in the field of foreign affairs, which has been her principal committee assignment since her first re-election to the 77th Congress. (During the 76th as a freshman, she served on the Indian Affairs and Government Operations committees.)

Mrs. Bolton has never been inclined to sit back and gather information at second hand. Thus her participation on the Committee on Foreign Affairs led her to go on fact-finding trips long before such "junkets" were as common as they are today. When, in 1945, she approached Secretary of State Dean Acheson to ask if he could arrange for her to go to Russia, it must have been a little difficult for the highly professional Secretary of State to take Congressman Bolton's reasons very seriously. She wanted to go to Russia, she told him, because her father had been there in 1868 just after his graduation from Yale, and had talked so much about what a beautiful country it was that she thought now she would like to see it for herself. If the Secretary was skeptical he was also certain that Mrs. Bolton could not get a visa. She was certain that she could. Acheson told her that in any case it would be a month before the Russian Ambassador, Andrei Gromyko, would even see her. Mrs. Bolton called and got an appointment for the next day.

In reminiscing, as she likes to do, about moments in her past, Congressman Bolton is inclined to act out the key scenes, taking all the parts herself. Since she is particularly fond of recounting her interview with the Russian Ambassador, her performance as Gromyko is one of her best. The *mise-en-scène* is the Russian Embassy in Washington. Extras include a female receptionist wearing a checked skirt and black top and smoking Russian cigarettes in a long Roosevelt cigarette holder, and the soldiers who line the stairway as Mrs. Bolton is escorted past them into a very long room; at the far end of it, behind a huge desk, sits Ambassador Gromyko.

MRS. BOLTON (*aside*): This room certainly must be awfully well wired for sound. I'd better give them something to think about. (*To Gromyko*) Mr. Ambassador, I've come here to request a visa for Russia.

GROMYKO: And vot do you vant to go to my country for?

MRS. BOLTON: Well, you've got a great country, Mr. Ambassador, and I've got a great country, and we have to live on the same earth with each other, so I think we might as well get to know each other. And I think there's no better way for countries to know each other than to have the women get acquainted.

GROMYKO: And vy?

MRS. BOLTON: Well, you know we women really have so much more in common than you men do.

GROMYKO: Zo? Vy is zat?

MRS. BOLTON: Because, Mr. Ambassador, all babies come the same way.

Gromyko (*Throws head back, laughs and laughs and laughs.*)

MRS. BOLTON (*aside*): Well, at least we're making a good recording.

It is hardly necessary to report that the visa was immediately forthcoming. Subsequent visas were then granted to three other members of the Near East sub-committee and an official junket to Russia resulted, the first time, Mrs. Bolton claims, that any member of the Committee on Foreign Affairs had been permitted to travel.

The four members flew into Russia in an Air Force plane, clearly marked with an American flag, rather than in a Russian plane. In 1945, when the Iron Curtain was more impenetrable than it has since become, this irked Stalin so much that he refused to see the Representatives during their two weeks in Moscow. They settled, however, for Vishinsky, whom Mrs. Bolton describes as "great fun."

Always with an eye on nursing and hospital problems, Frances Bolton began almost as soon as she arrived in Moscow to nag their interpreter-guide, Serge, to take her to see a hospital. He kept making excuses until the day before they were to leave when Mrs. Bolton fixed him with an eye and said, "Now see here, Serge . . ."

Serge knuckled under and took her right off to the hospital where she was very cordially received. When asked what in particular she wanted to see, she said she understood that the Russians had been doing some extraordinary plastic surgery and opted for that ward. Plastic cases are punishing to look at even for those with strong stomachs and it soon proved more than Serge, who was doing the translating, could take. "The first thing I knew," Mrs. Bolton says, "There was six feet at least of Serge on the floor in front of us, out cold." This left Mrs. Bolton with no interpreter, but undaunted she "stepped over Serge" and went on to visit the rest of the ward. She was both impressed by the Russian medical achievement and depressed by the terrible poverty and deprivation she found in the hospital.

On its return the sub-committee made a report * to the House. "They weren't much interested in it," Mrs. Bolton says, "but they should have been. It was very good."

---

* Later expanded into a lengthy treatise and published in 1949 by the Committee on Foreign Affairs under the title *The Strategy and Tactics of World Communism.*

Congressman Bolton's next official trip came in 1947, when she took members of the Near East sub-committee, of which she was then chairman, to Palestine. Their November visit coincided with the dramatic and, to her, unhappy moment when the partition of Palestine into the sovereign Jewish and Arab states became a fact.

On their way to the Near East the Bolton party stopped first in London, where the big four foreign ministers, Marshall, Bevin, Bidault and Molotov, were meeting. Feeling in London was running very strongly against the division of Palestine, and Mrs. Bolton cabled home her unequivocal opinion that the worst thing our country could do would be to have any part in it. She implies that General Marshall's sentiments about partition agreed with her own. It is true that there was great conflict at the time between the State Department and the Zionists, but officially Marshall was certainly in accord with President Truman and in favor of the creation of the Jewish state.

The committee members went on to Palestine from London and were staying in a little hostel in Jerusalem, their every action being viewed suspiciously, when, early on the morning of November 28, a cable from General Marshall was handed to Mrs. Bolton telling her that partition had that day been voted by the United Nations.

In view of the extremely tense situation the British in charge felt it wise for the American Congressmen to leave Palestine as soon as possible. Accordingly, it was arranged for them to fly out the next day. Five minutes before they left a bomb was thrown into the American consulate, fortunately harming no one. One woman had hysterics, Mrs. Bolton remembers, but adds that she probably would have had them anyway.

Few people are able to be objective about the Palestine decision. Mrs. Bolton is no exception. To her it was and is a tragedy. Her sympathy was entirely with the Arabs. She maintains that the famous Balfour letter of 1917 offered the Jews only a home, not a country of their own. She objects to the fact that Israel has been built and is largely supported today by the millions of tax-free dollars contributed annually by American Jewry. It should be pointed out that although her objection was valid in the past, American money is now being used in Israel only to support such organizations as hospitals and schools, which would be tax-exempt in this country as well.

Frances Bolton went back to Palestine several times after 1947 to see what had happened to "those poor, poor Arabs." However, following the Arab-Israeli war in the spring of 1967, she at once issued a statement which was generally sympathetic to the Israeli position:

> If one nation is permitted to claim as its own a vitally needed waterway in order to harass a neighboring state, what assurance is there that any nation will be safe? Indeed, to permit this would set a most dangerous precedent. . . . Let us support our President who has voiced strong protest, and urge him to act with understanding, patient diplomacy and calm cooperation to ease this crisis and promote lasting peace in the Near East.

Of all of her travels Mrs. Bolton looks on her three-month trip to Africa in 1955 as her "great adventure." Here again her timing was opportune, for this was a period of great hope in Africa, foreshadowing momentous changes to come, yet still a time of relative calm before the various countries' struggles for independence erupted with such violence.

While many of her colleagues in the House either were not thinking of the "Dark Continent" at all or were thinking of it only vaguely in "Whither Africa" terms, Frances Bolton was more beguiled. Perhaps, as one cynical detractor suggests, "she had a mental picture of herself surrounded by a group of adorable little half-naked black children all singing 'Welcome Frances Bolton!' " In any case, with her let's-us-women-get-together-and-straighten-things-out approach, she decided she wanted to see for herself what was going on in the African countries' evolution toward independence.

When the chairman of the Committee on Foreign Affairs agreed to sanction an official trip for Mrs. Bolton, he assumed that other members of the African sub-committee would accompany her. But none of the Congressmen on the committee felt they could be out of the country for such a long period, so Mrs. Bolton traveled instead with a doctor from the Mayo Clinic, an African expert from the State Department, and a photographer from the Signal Corps. The fact that her three male escorts were the identical ages of her three sons gave the twenty-thousand-mile trip a little extra fillip for Mrs. Bolton. "We had a perfectly marvelous experience together." Starting from Dakar and Senegal they worked their way right down the west coast of Africa to Capetown.

On her return Frances Bolton assumed the benevolent Mother Africa role which she has maintained ever since, although her critics, particularly those who are themselves thoughtful students of Africa, claim that her knowledge is highly superficial. "She has never," says one observer, "really done anything legislatively to advance Africa and she has no real understanding of the continent. She supported independence in an enchanted period but she seems now to be leaning more toward the conservative side."

The same critic acknowledges, however, that Mrs. Bolton genuinely likes Africans as individuals. She loves to entertain for them, and to encourage others to do so she started the Women's Committee of the African-American Institute in New York. She has performed many generous acts on a personal basis — recently, for example, she put a young girl from Kenya through medical school in this country.

In 1957 she returned to Africa as one of four official United States delegates to the independence ceremonies of the new state of Ghana.

Just before she left on her African trip, Mrs. Bolton became involved in a problem which was as far removed physically as it was ideologically from Africa but which was to become a "great adventure" of its own.

She had long been interested in Mount Vernon, and when she learned unexpectedly that the land across the Potomac from it was

about to be sold to a Texas oil company she acted with characteristic generosity and equally characteristic impatience. In order that
the peaceful rolling view of the Maryland shore which George
Washington had known and cherished and which had for two hundred years been carefully preserved would not be ruined by oil
storage tanks, Frances Bolton bought the land herself — 450 acres
of it — for something over $750,000.

Subsequently she formed the Accokeek Foundation, named for a
river on the property. A neighboring parcel of a hundred or so
acres was owned by the similarly conservation-minded Alice Ferguson Foundation, so that approximately half of the 1152-acre tract
along seven miles of the Potomac was protected. Then in 1960 dis-
aster threatened again when the Washington Suburban Sanitation
Commission proposed to take the land by eminent domain to construct a sewage plant on it.

Mrs. Bolton's fury at this indignity, which must have been awe-
some, still did not leave her speechless or actionless. Within two
months, thanks to her leadership, the Congress had enacted legislation, and President Kennedy had signed into law an act authorizing
the acquisition of the 1152 acres by the Department of the Interior
to establish Piscataway Park.

The Accokeek and Ferguson Foundations agreed to turn over
their acreage to the Interior Department, and, to further protect
the Mount Vernon overview, more than a hundred and fifty landowners donated scenic easement covering 2500 surrounding acres.
In signing scenic easements the landowners voluntarily agreed to
keep their land in five-acre lots, to preserve all trees, and to build
nothing unsightly in the way of the view. Mrs. Bolton calls it
"the greatest joining together of private, foundation and government effort in any preservation-conservation project." There
was one vital condition, however. All easements and the land gifts
were contingent on the federal government's acquisition of the 600
additional acres by August of 1967.

Although $1 million was authorized by the Congress in 1960, six
years later only a few parcels had been acquired, the August dead-

line was approaching and the purchase price of the land had quadru-
pled. Once again the Congress acted and increased the authorization accordingly.

Unfortunately to negotiate from authorization to actual appropriation, it was necessary to contend with Representative Michael
J. Kirwan, a Democrat from Ohio, who, as second-ranking member
of the Appropriations Committee, is chairman of the Democratic
Campaign Fund. The two positions give him a neat interlocking
directorate.

Rolling her eyes upward at the thought of her fellow Ohioan,
Mrs. Bolton says of Kirwan, "He's the one who dispenses all the funds
to the Democrats, and then he's also the one who says, 'If you want
that new Post Office . . .' "

For some reason Representative Kirwan was opposed to Piscataway
Park.* He did not care *what* George Washington looked at from
his front piazza two hundred years ago; he stated flatly that he was
not going to "give" a penny for a public park for Washington, D.C.
(voteless Washington, D.C.), not while "a single member of my
district is unemployed." Accordingly, when the Interior budget
came before the House Appropriations Committee in February,
1967, all of the funds allocated for Piscataway Park were cut.

Mrs. Bolton expected as much. Forestalling all well-intentioned
attempts to protest the cut when the Interior bill came up for vote
in the House, she got the bill over to the Senate "clean, with no
nasty business attached to it." She knew, having carefully paved
the way for it, that the Senate Appropriations Committee would
restore the cuts. They did, and in May the Senate appropriations
bill passed with $1.5 million included for Piscataway Park.

---

* One explanation for Kirwan's intransigence sounds like a monumental fish
story, and is. For many years Michael Kirwan had a devoted administrative
assistant who was very fond of fish. Some years ago, as the legend goes, the
assistant took sick, and as he lay dying he told his boss that his fondest dream
had always been to see a magnificent aquarium in the District of Columbia.
Determined to gratify the deathbed wish of his employee, Kirwan set the
wheels in motion to construct a ten-million-dollar aquarium on Haines Point
in Washington. The theory is that Kirwan, a strong scratch-my-back-and-I'll-
scratch-yours man, would not okay any funds for Piscataway Park unless he
got the money for his aquarium.

With the House and Senate appropriations bills differing so substantially, a conference committee made up of key members of
both chambers was called to work out a compromise. As a result
the appropriation, while not sufficient to complete the project, did
save the land gifts and the scenic easements.

On Washington's Birthday, 1968, Secretary of the Interior Stewart L. Udall presided at the inauguration ceremony formally establishing Piscataway Park. Mrs. Bolton and representatives of
the other participating foundations presented their land deeds to
the government of the United States. In the Senate, Margaret
Chase Smith paid a glowing tribute to the decade of time and effort and to the generosity of her "beloved colleague from Ohio."
From the White House came a warm letter of appreciation signed
by the First Lady.

Though millions of citizens will soon benefit from Piscataway
Park, few of them will be in a position to express their gratitude to
the progenitor of the project by voting for her, a circumstance
which will doubtless be pointed out to the citizens of the Twenty-
second Ohio District who *are* in a position to vote for her. Why,
Frances Bolton's opponents may ask, should an Ohio Congressman
be spending all her time in Washington getting parks for the residents of Maryland, Virginia, and the District of Columbia? As an
old pro, Mrs. Bolton is well aware of this particular pitfall. In an
inverse ratio, it often seems that the more effective the legislator
is in the larger national and international issues, the less satisfactory
he is to his constituents.*

* Richard Rovere, in his book *Senator Joe McCarthy*, writes, in this case
about Senators, "They come to it [the Senate] as ambassadors from rather
meager sovereignties, and before long they are likely to find themselves dealing with the affairs of the entire nation and of the great world beyond its
shores and borders. If their interests and aptitudes are engaged by their opportunities, they are very likely to alienate—and become alienated from—the
provincial politicians upon whose favor they are dependent. The more time
they devote to seeking just solutions to national and international problems,
the less time they have for dipping into the pork barrel for the people back
home, for chatting with constituents who have just come to Capitol Hill from
the Washington Monument, or for touring the county seats and market towns
at home."

But Mrs. Bolton's twelve re-elections to office attest to her success in bridging the gap between her divergent responsibilities. Although she has devoted much of her legislative energy to nursing, to foreign affairs, and to the Mount Vernon overview, she has remained close to the grass roots of Ohio and through the years has paid scrupulous attention to her constituents' needs.

Commenting on this attainment, her son Oliver says, "One of the reasons Mother has been able to do the job that she has is that in the first place she's an exceptional woman with a very large breadth of understanding. And in addition to that, quite frankly, she has been able to afford a structure which permits a servicing of her district that has been just fantastic."

Congressmen are allowed a staff of eleven people to divide between their Washington and their district offices. Mrs. Bolton, whose constituency before the 1950 redistricting used to be the second largest in the country, encompassing all the suburbs of Cleveland and some 970,000 people, maintains two Ohio offices, one in the Federal Building in downtown Cleveland, which is connected to the Washington office by teletype, and the other in suburban Mayfield, which is in the district proper. She has been able to afford additional and better-paid staff members, many of whom have been with her for years and have evolved an extremely smooth procedure in dealing with constituency matters.

But while her large and expert staff frees Congressman Bolton from routine duties to some extent, she is still obliged to return to her district at least once in every three or four weeks; she encourages her constituents to bring their problems directly to her, whether they deal with an urban renewal project involving millions of government dollars, or with getting a passport in a hurry, or even finding motel reservations for Easter week in Washington.

"I don't even remember a Christmas or a Thanksgiving or any sort of family dinner at all," says Oliver Bolton, "when the phone hasn't rung with somebody calling Mother to say something like,

'Mrs. Bolton, my husband's dying and my boy's in Japan or Persia or wherever and how do I get him home?'

"Of course," Bolton adds, "The job of a Congressman has changed radically since the 1930's when Dad was in. In those days a citizen wouldn't have thought of going directly to his Congressman. He went first to his ward leader, and the ward leader would go to the county chairman, and then the county chairman would go to the Congressman."

Today, Bolton feels, party structure in the old sense has disintegrated; in many states there is only a loose organization and as a result little party discipline. Oliver Bolton, who is fifty years old, speaks from his unique experience as the son of two Congressmen and as a former Congressman himself.

In 1950, after an arduous campaign in which he was determined to prove to the voters of the Eleventh Ohio District (which is east of his mother's) that he would go to Washington as himself, not as his mother's or his father's son, Oliver Bolton was elected to the 83rd Congress.

In the capitol his effort to establish his own identity in the eyes of the other Congressmen was enhanced by the first record vote of the session. As the clerk read the roll call it went: Frances Bolton — Nay, Oliver Bolton — Yea. A roar of laughter followed. It was so pat that one might almost have accused the Boltons, who are nothing if not hams, of planning it. But actually it was a simple matter of their voting in the best interests of their constituency. The question concerned a fertilizer subsidy bill; Oliver Bolton's district was agricultural, Frances Bolton's suburban. Hence yea — nay.

Though the first of their differing votes, this was by no means the last. "We're a funny family," Oliver Bolton says, "Mother's brought us up to run our own lives until somebody else starts picking on one of us. Then we all go to his defense. We've been a close family, but a very independent one. During the campaign I wouldn't even let Mother come into my district. And that's the way it was in Washington. It was great fun serving with her — in fact it was wonderful — because we let each other alone."

Bolton did not even discuss his intention of running for Congress with his mother, though she was delighted when he told her he was going to try it. For his part, he was anything but delighted when his mother told him in 1940 that she was going to run for his father's seat. "I kind of thought of politics as a man's job," he says and adds with, all things considered, a commendable courage, "I still think so."

His own political career was cut short when at the end of his second term in Congress he had a heart attack and decided not to seek re-election. He does not, however, rule out further political activity in the future.

An obvious possibility would be for him to run for Frances Bolton's seat when she vacates it, thus becoming the third Bolton to represent the Twenty-second District. But he declines to consider such a course for three reasons: first, he would have to move his residence, which he does not want to do; second, if he ran in the Twenty-second District he might, with some justification, be accused of running on his mother's apron strings; third, and most important, he does not think he could be elected from the Twenty-second which, since the 1950 redistricting, has radically changed character and is more and more Democratic.

"I don't believe a normal Republican could win," Oliver Bolton says. And indeed in the 1968 election Frances Bolton, who has never been a "normal" Republican in that so many Democrats have always voted for her, will face perhaps the stiffest test of her political career. In the spring of 1968 the Twenty-second District was again substantially redistricted to include a large number of working class and Jewish voters, all strongly inclined toward the Democratic side.

The changed make-up of the Twenty-second District has led incumbent Ohio Democratic Congressman Charles A. Vanik to shift from his own Twenty-first District and to run instead in opposition to Frances Bolton in the Twenty-second. Both districts are in Cuyahoga County.

If he wins the primary, Vanik will be a formidable opponent. The fifty-five-year-old Congressman, who has served for seven terms in the House, has proved himself very strong indeed at the polls. In the last election he won 90.1 per cent of the vote.

Frances Bolton, running at eighty-two years old for her fourteenth term in the House has also scored decisive victories in the past, though she concedes that her margins have been going down as the number of Democrats in her district have gone up. "It's *almost* a question of whether I'll be elected," she has said.

Much hangs on the word "almost," for the stakes in the 1968 election are very high. If Mrs. Bolton is re-elected and if the Republicans should gain control of the House, she would become chairman of the Committee on Foreign Affairs. Frances Bolton is not known for her diffidence; in her view the chance to achieve this much-coveted position far outweighs the chance of being defeated at the polls.

She knows that her age will be a major issue and that to combat it she will have to campaign vigorously, showing her sprightly self to voters all over the Twenty-second District. She will have to convince her constituents, as she has obviously convinced herself, that she still has much to accomplish for them and for the country in the Congress of the United States.

In an interview at her Palm Beach home on the occasion of her eightieth birthday, Congressman Bolton was asked if she had any plans to retire before the next election.

"Retire!" One can imagine her recoiling. "Heavens no. I expect to be here until I die."

PRESIDENTIAL APPOINTMENT

Esther Peterson

SHORTLY AFTER President Johnson appointed Assistant Secretary of Labor Esther Peterson to a second post as his Special Assistant for Consumer Affairs, she was asked by a colleague just how she planned to divide her time between the Labor Department and the White House.

"Two-thirds here, two-thirds there," she answered imperturbably.

Her response was entirely characteristic, for Esther Peterson is a realist, accustomed to walking into situations with her eyes open and her sense of humor intact.

Nor are two jobs at once any particular novelty for this energetic, candid, sixty-one-year-old woman. She has, in fact, known little else but double demands in her comparatively short career in the federal government.

When President Kennedy appointed her, just after his election in 1960, to her first position as director of the Women's Bureau of the Department of Labor, he lost little time in also making her the executive vice chairman (the chairman was Mrs. Roosevelt) of the President's Commission on the Status of Women. While serving in this dual capacity, she was promoted from director of the Women's Bureau to Assistant Secretary of Labor for Labor Standards and continued to hold two jobs until late 1963, when the Commission on the Status of Women published its report and the Commission was dissolved.

Then, early in 1964, before she had really had time to catch her breath, she became Special Presidential Assistant for Consumer Affairs, and the pattern of double-job-juggling persisted until February of 1967, when President Johnson finally relieved her of her

White House position and replaced her with Betty Furness. She then returned full time, that is four-thirds time, to the job to which she had been appointed by Kennedy and the then Secretary of Labor, Arthur Goldberg, the job for which she had been confirmed by the Senate and for which she was eminently qualified by years of experience in the labor movement.

As an Assistant Secretary of Labor, Esther Peterson is either the highest ranking woman or the second highest — depending on how one interprets the protocol — in the executive branch of the government. The only other woman Assistant Secretary, Dorothy H. Jacobson in the Department of Agriculture, was appointed much later to her office, which, according to some stylists, gives Mrs. Peterson the rank. On the other hand, Agriculture ranks Labor because it was founded first, which, in the view of another school of thought, gives Mrs. Jacobson the edge. As a matter of fact, when Mrs. Peterson was a Special Presidential Assistant, she outranked herself as Assistant Secretary of Labor.

"Frankly, I don't pay any attention to this sort of thing," she says, and there is reason to believe she means it or that she at least pays it less attention than most. In status-conscious Washington, where the pecking order is usually paramount, she stands out as a woman completely without side. She exhibits no trace of self-importance, only a strong sense of the importance of her work.

What is significant to her about her position is that as an Assistant Secretary she is occupying a post which has traditionally been held by a man. To her the whole concept of women in specifically women's jobs is archaic. Although her interest in women's affairs has been an abiding one, she firmly believes that classification by sex is not a valid basis for employment at any level.

Her belief that women can no longer be regarded as a special group is central to all of her thinking, yet she is not a feminist. Feminists, she feels, tend to wave the flag over an issue which is not related to today's reality. She is convinced that the principle of equal rights for men and women is clearly embodied in the Fifth and Fourteenth Amendments to the Constitution, that it is the *practice* of full partnership which is not yet an accepted fact because of the many discriminatory policies, often justified sincerely as protective measures, which continue to set women apart.

"It isn't a matter of coming down to sameness," she insists. "We *are* women. We're different, of course. And an interplay is good. But that doesn't mean we need to have walls built around us."

Feminist she is not. Feminine she most certainly is. She is, in fact, a woman of many paradoxes. The complete antithesis of the hard, chic, cool, well-turned-out, successful career woman, her look is the look of a fresh country girl grown up. She wears her hair braided around her head; her skin is pink and white, her eyes a very clear blue; her voice is soft, her manner gentle and direct. She is wholesome. She loves her family — her husband and her four grown children — and her home life with an unaffected exuberance. "Beautiful" is one of her favorite words, and when she applies it to people, which she frequently does, she is not thinking of the Acapulco jet set.

Today's youth, while perhaps regarding her as square, would still be forced to admire her thinking. "Our time is a time for crossing barriers, for erasing old categories — for probing around." The words are Marshall McLuhan's, but they might well be Esther Peterson's.

Her probing around, her attempts to change old categories cause the Assistant Secretary of Labor some uncomfortable moments of conflict, however. For her constant drive toward the practice of full equality is not always popular with the trade unions leaders who constitute her power base. To an appointive officer, a power base is the equivalent of a constituency for an elective officer, and for all her directness, her apparent lack of guile, Mrs. Peterson is still a politician. But, even apart from the practical necessity of not offending those who have put her in office, the labor movement is her commitment. For almost forty years it has been her cause.

Nothing in Esther Peterson's background or upbringing preordained her for the course she chose. Everything, in fact, pointed her in an opposite direction.

Born and educated in Provo, Utah, and reared in the strict atmosphere of the Mormon Church, Esther Eggertsen was one of four daughters in a family of Danish descent. She graduated from Brigham Young University with honors (in the same class with Ezra Taft Benson, with whom she used to "double-date" occasionally) and, after teaching for two years in Cedar City, Utah, came East to take her master's degree in physical education at Columbia.

Shortly after her arrival in New York, she met a young student named Oliver Peterson, who was working for his doctorate in sociology and who soon began opening the eyes of this unsophisticated girl to a world she knew nothing about. It was a world of ferment, of hunger and suffering — this was during the great 1930 depression — from which she had been largely insulated by an upbringing that had led her to believe simply that "he prospers who deserves to prosper."

After she received her master's degree from Columbia, she went to Boston to teach gym at the exclusive Winsor School for Girls — a "beautiful school." In Boston, as a matter of course, since she had been brought up to be active in church work, she volunteered to help out at the YWCA. The Y in those days ran evening classes, part recreation, part current events, for various categories of workers — Thursday nights, maid's day off, for the domestic workers, another night for secretaries and business women, another for industrial workers. Esther Eggertsen chose to teach the last group and there had her first experience with the working women and with the problems of this as yet unorganized segment of our society.

One memorable evening during her first year in Boston she went to the Y and found no class. Not one of the girls in her particular section of the industrial division had turned up. Puzzled, she consulted Oliver Peterson — they were not yet married but would be soon — who advised her to find the girls and see what had happened. Knowing only that they were mostly garment workers who lived in the Italian section of town, Esther set out to locate her missing class.

"It was my first experience of going into real low-income homes in the slums. Utah is rural, and you didn't know the cold-water flats and the kind of things that existed in the 'thirties during the depression. So climbing up those rickety stairs to find those kids was one of the dramatic experiences of my life."

Going into their homes she discovered why her girls hadn't come to class that week. They were on strike.

"I can remember how my old Republican feelings came over me when I heard that word 'strike,' " Mrs. Peterson says. "Look, I was raised to think they all had bombs in their pockets. I had a completely different idea about these things, even though Oliver had been teaching me a lot."

What she learned that night in those cold-water flats she thinks probably changed the course of her life. The girls were all doing piece work, cutting and sewing wrap-around housedresses at the rate of $1.32 per dozen dresses. (Their weekly pay checks came to between five and seven dollars.) Suddenly they had been given orders to change the pockets on these dresses from a square, which was quickly sewed, to a heart shape, which took much longer, and for which they were to receive no increase in pay. They struck. They were not organized; they just got together and struck. And they called it the "heartbreak strike."

The next morning, with the last vestige of her conservative background stripped away, the twenty-five-year-old gym teacher went to see Miss Katharine Lord, the revered headmistress of Winsor School for Girls. "I was obviously concerned and moved," Mrs. Peterson says, "and I knew I wanted to help those girls, and Miss Lord — oh she was a beautiful woman — can you imagine her tolerance? She told me to go ahead and follow what I believed, as long as it didn't interfere with the efficiency of my work for which I was paid. And that was in 1930!"

One has to pause for a moment to consider 1930, to remember the breadlines and the apples sold on street corners, to recall "the worker" and how he was exploited and how the "radical," whose conscience was stirred by the worker's plight, inevitably came to be looked on as a "pink" or a "fellow traveler." In the 'thirties, the struggle of labor to organize played a role in our national life which was the equivalent of the Negro's struggle for equality today.

The "heartbreak strike" was one of the incidents which led to the big garment workers' uprising of this period. The International Ladies' Garment Workers' Union came to Boston to organize the strikers; soon there was a bona fide picket line. Early each morning Esther Eggertsen joined this picket line for an hour or so before trotting off to teach gym to the Winsor School girls. And if any of them or their parents ever heard that their Miss Eggie of the Department of Peristalsis and Perspiration, as they called it, was engaged in that unique form of moonlighting, none of them ever objected.

"At least I never heard of it if they did," Mrs. Peterson says, and adds with the characteristic optimism which her more cynical colleagues sometimes feel borders on the Pollyanna, "To me, it was just one more example of the integrity of people who can separate these things in their minds and really have a basic respect for the individual."

To cement her first highly subjective experience with working women, she got a job that summer as recreation director at the newly formed Bryn Mawr Summer School for Women Workers in Industry.

The school, one of the first to use a college campus in summer for the benefit of less privileged special students, was the brain child of Bryn Mawr's president, Dr. M. Carey Thomas, who remains one of Mrs. Peterson's idols. (Today on the wall of her office she has a panel of twelve such pioneer women whom she looks on as her heroines. They include Susan B. Anthony, Carrie Chapman Catt, Jane Addams, Florence Kelley. Eleanor Roosevelt as the most revered occupies a special place of honor. Curiously, Frances Perkins, the only woman Secetary of Labor, who founded the Bureau of Labor Standards which Esther Peterson administers, is missing.)

There were no educational requirements for entrance into the Bryn Mawr Summer School for Women Workers; the only condition was that the girls must have supported themselves for three years. The curriculum was built, as Mrs. Peterson puts it, "out of the warp and woof of their daily lives." Years later Esther Peterson was to be instrumental in starting another such school for working women at La Brevière, near Paris.

For six years she continued working at Winsor in winter and Bryn Mawr in summer. When she and Oliver Peterson were married, he moved to Boston to complete his doctorate at Harvard. Both Petersons worked actively with the trade unions. In addition to her work with the International Ladies' Garment Workers' Union, Esther Peterson was a moving factor in organizing the progressive Teachers' Union which brought her into contact with many of Harvard's liberal intellectuals.

Together the Petersons also formed a Citizens' Committee, designed to interpret strikes and labor problems to the public. Thus began a pattern which has run all through Esther's life — a pattern of keeping people informed.

"Perhaps I'm naïve," she says, "but I just feel so sure that if people have the right facts they make the right decisions." She adds that perhaps we'd have less of a "credibility gap" in respect to Vietnam if this pattern were more widely followed.

During these early years and later, when the Petersons moved to New York, Esther had her first contact with the Communists, the agitators of the 'thirties and 'forties, whose seductive, proselytizing attempts were familiar to many liberals of that period. She was working for the Amalgamated Clothing Workers, and her boss, J. B. S. Hardman, a Russian who was anti-Communist, was a particularly important influence during a difficult time in her life. He helped her to see the blandishments of the party members for what they were and to resist the many overtures made to her. "And of course," she adds, "there was always my very strong Oliver to make me test my own reactions."

Because of the total communion of ideas between her and her

husband and because they have from the beginning engaged in such complementary activities, few of the usual conflicts of home versus career have dogged Esther Peterson's life.

Furthermore, she has been fortunate in her timing. Unlike many young married women who grope, trying to get their bearings, Mrs. Peterson found her way very quickly. By the time her first child, Karen, was born in 1938, she not only had her feet firmly on the ground, but she had had a valuable internship, a first-hand experience with the early activities of the emerging labor movement and, in particular, with women workers and their problems. She was dedicated, tireless, and enthusiastic. She had many friends in the trade unions who were grateful for any work she could manage to do for them, whether volunteer or part time. So, until the last of her four children was grown, she never had to face a nine-to-five job, yet she could continue to be useful and to learn on her own terms.

In 1947 Oliver Peterson, who had joined the Foreign Service after the war, was assigned as labor attaché, first to Sweden and later to Belgium. During the following ten years, while they lived abroad, Mrs. Peterson devoted her prodigious energies mainly to being the wife of her husband and the mother of Karen, Eric, Iver, and Lars (all family names, incidentally, which did not hurt the popularity of the Peterson family in Sweden). Her success is amply demonstrated today by her four handsome children. Karen, now Mrs. Gene Cady Wilken, is a Wellesley graduate, who got her doctorate at Berkeley while her husband got his. Eric, who was in the Peace Corps, is an architect in New York and married to a journalist. Iver is in the Washington Bureau of the *New York Times*, and Lars, like his two brothers a Harvard man, is in the class of 1968.

When the family returned to Washington in 1957 after their years abroad, Mrs. Peterson went to work on the Hill as a lobbyist — "legislative representative" is the euphemism — for the Industrial Union Department of the AFL-CIO. One day shortly after her return she was walking down a corridor in the Senate Office Building when she heard a familiar voice with a New England accent calling to her, "Hey, Esther, where've you been? I've missed you." She had known John F. Kennedy back in the days when he was first serving on the House Labor Committee and she was lobbying for the Amalgamated Clothing Workers.

Mrs. Peterson tends to speak in terms of "one of the most dramatic moments of my life — the most exciting — the most significant." This encounter with Kennedy was "one of the nicest moments." It also proved one of the most important, since it led to her entrance into public life.

Highly placed though she was in the Kennedy administration as Director of the Women's Bureau, as Assistant Secretary of Labor, and as Vice Chairman of the President's Commission on the Status of Women, Mrs. Peterson did not really burst into the public eye until she became Special Presidential Assistant for Consumer Affairs under Johnson. Then all at once she seemed to be everywhere, and, for the first time in her life, she became a highly controversial figure.

To fulfill a campaign promise to establish consumer representation in the government, President Kennedy had made a gesture by setting up a loosely organized Consumer Advisory Council, and then he had more or less forgotten about it. His inaction won him unprecedented praise from *Printers' Ink*, trade journal for advertising and marketing interests. To *Printers' Ink* readers, any government activity in the field of consumer affairs is looked on as Big Brotherism.

President Johnson went much further than President Kennedy had. He wanted the consumers to know he cared; he also wanted them to know it in an election year. So, in 1964, he hired Esther Peterson to demonstrate his concern to the housewives of America. *Printers' Ink* regarded *this* action as "ominous," and indeed, its worst fears were realized as soon as Mrs. Peterson really swung into her job.

From the consumers' point of view, however, she proved a brilliantly apt choice for the newly created post of Special Assistant to the President for Consumer Affairs. Her directive from Johnson

was vague, and with no established procedure to follow, Esther
Peterson simply attacked the job in the only way she knew how —
directly. She told the consumers to write to her and tell her their
problems.

The results were overwhelming. Letters poured in from ag-
grieved consumers, mostly women, who had never before had anyone willing to listen to their troubles, let alone someone who was in
a position to do something tangible about them.

Shopping constantly to check facts, traveling around the country
to set up consumer conferences, appearing on television and in the
press, Esther Peterson soon became a familiar and refreshing champion of the housewives, someone with whom they could identify.

"I was fascinated by her," said a young woman who had followed
Mrs. Peterson's activities closely during this period. "She looked so
normal. I know she has to be brilliant and high-powered to have the
kind of job she does, but she just looked like an ordinary person that
you'd see pushing a shopping cart into the check-out line at the
supermarket. Probably it was an act, but even so, it convinced me."

It was not an act, of course. Esther Peterson not only looks like a
normal housewife, she is one. She is other things as well, but with her
remarkable ability to empathize, when she talks to housewives, the
housewife side of her predominates.

From the start Mrs. Peterson took the view that the consumers
were an unorganized segment of our society that defied effective
organization. She sought, therefore, to create interest in them by
working through existing organizations — trade unions, women's
groups, professional associations. As a result of her actions, a great
stirring of interest in the consumer began. The sleeping giant
awakened. Once politicians started to think of their constituents as
consumers, consumer problems became politically sexy. With the
legislators thus aroused, Mrs. Peterson's implied threat to business
was that unless it took care of the consumers' interests, the Congress
would. She became known in some circles as "Pass-a-Law Peterson."
Businessmen quaked when she started talking about their particular

industry, knowing that if they resisted her, she could, and probably would, introduce a bill which, like motherhood bills, would certainly pass. Many wise industry leaders complied voluntarily, some even enthusiastically.

But though she carried a big stick, she used it very sparingly. According to her able young assistant, David Swankin, she spent the bulk of her time during her three years as Special Assistant meeting and working out problems with industry. Mrs. Peterson is a great believer in getting everyone around a table to thrash out a question at issue. When she organized a consumer conference on food marketing, for example, she was careful to arrange parallel meetings with the retail grocers to keep them informed.

When she set up a "The Most For Your Money" conference, she brought together variety store interests from Woolworth's and Penney's down to the very small chains to try to find solutions to the age-old problem of why the poor always pay more. One result of this particular conference was a joint recommendation that the war on poverty had an obligation to inform the disadvantaged consumer, which resulted in an effective consumer-education program within the Office of Economic Opportunity.

When the dry cleaning industry came to her to complain that because of the proliferation of new synthetic fabrics they were ruining many garments, not through carelessness but through ignorance of the fabric's properties and characteristics, Mrs. Peterson promptly called representatives of the textile industry together. Manufacturers of clothing, rugs, drapes — all articles that could be sent to a cleaner — met and pledged not merely to append a cardboard tag, but to *sew* into each garment permanent care instructions.

Not all problems were so simply and harmoniously solved, however. The more Esther Peterson probed the consumer question, the more marketing practices she found to denounce. She cited deceptive labeling, misleading come-ons, and tie-in sales. "Giant" pints, king- and jumbo-sized boxes, "cents off" sales (cents off what?) were aberrations, she said, of "manufacturers who found it profitable to confuse." She spoke out against built-in obsolescence and shoddy, "slickly put together" products, warning the consumer to be more concerned about quality and performance than about whether the product would "increase his prestige or excite envy on the part of his neighbors." She called for "full disclosure," meaning simple, accurate, visible information about the nature and quantity of a product, to be embodied in a truth-in-packaging bill.

The advertising industry, which was the most directly in her line of fire, began to fight back. Ten months after she took office in the White House, they fired their first volley at point-blank range in the form of an editorial in *Printers' Ink* titled, "Is She Ignorant?" Accusing her of "deliberately pitting consumers against advertisers for her own purposes," they referred to her, rather aptly it must be said, as an "articulate, ingratiating woman with the well-scrubbed exuberance of a scoutmistress leading the first hike of spring" and called her office "the most pernicious threat of advertising today." In paragraph after paragraph they heaped abuse upon her:

> Mrs. Peterson is an enigma wrapped up in an anachronism. . . . The consumer conferences that Mrs. Peterson has initiated give her the means of indoctrinating consumers so that they will be what Mrs. Peterson thinks they should be. . . . [She] is a woman with a cause; even if her position is irrational, she presses on . . . she abhors persuasion, embraces the impossible idea of "full disclosure" in advertising and would destroy advertising as it exists today. Does she comprehend what she is doing? Does President Johnson know about it?

Leaping to get an anti-Peterson bandwagon rolling, Mark Cooper, the president of the Advertising Federation of America, promptly sent a copy of the editorial and a memo endorsing its stand to all members of the Advertising Federation of America. His action boomeranged somewhat, however, because the AFA, prior to the

Printers' Ink blast, had invited Esther Peterson to be the main speaker at their next regional meeting. Mrs. Peterson canceled the speech. "Apparently," she said publicly, "the AFA believes that advertising should be completely immune from criticism. Well, the AFA is wrong."

At once another group, the American Association of Advertising Agencies, stepped into the breach and gallantly invited Mrs. Peterson to speak at their next meeting. But many business leaders interpreted this as an endorsement of Mrs. Peterson's sweeping public charges against advertising, and accused the 4 A's, in hurt tones, of letting down the side. In point of fact, it is very doubtful that their invitation implied an all-out approval of Mrs. Peterson. Rather it was said to be a slight rap on the knuckles of the younger, less powerful, slightly upstart AFA.

Amid all the ensuing hubbub Mrs. Peterson stood firm and remained outwardly calm and good-humored. Her picture, laughingly holding a large banner proclaiming, "Printers' Ink Loves Esther Peterson," which some undercover admirer on the *Printers' Ink* staff had given her, appeared in the national weekly magazines. In fact, though, Mrs. Peterson says she became a little uncomfortable about the possible effect on her family of so much sudden and partly adverse publicity. But when she phoned her youngest son, Lars, to ask him solicitously if anyone around Harvard had said anything about her that made him feel uncomfortable, he replied with suitable Harvard insouciance, "Oh, come on, Mother. Who the hell do you think you are?"

"These kids," Mrs. Peterson reflects, "can really put you in your place."

The furor quieted down eventually, but there is little doubt that a considerable degree of residual dissatisfaction remained. Privately, industry men continued to mutter that "the whole business of consumer protections is hogwash" and that Mrs. Peterson's office was "unnecessary and undesirable."

Early in October of 1967 a group of Colorado women organized themselves as the Housewives for Lower Food Prices and began a boycott of Denver's five leading chain foodstores. On October 17, with ten thousand militant women picketing their stores, the first of the five chains capitulated and closed the doors of its markets to begin marking down prices. The other chains, left with more employees than customers in their stores, were shortly forced to follow suit.

At once the boycott idea spread to other cities. In Dallas it was called a Ladycott; in Florida it became MILC—Mothers Interested in Lower Costs. Chain foodstores from Michigan to Texas, from New Mexico to New York, faced determined hordes of women pickets demanding reduction in food costs.

Esther Peterson's name was not mentioned in any of the news stories, but on October 26 Senator Barry Goldwater attacked her directly. He would "lay odds," he said, that the women who were boycotting the stores to protest food prices were being led by "left-wing groups that had been organized by Esther Peterson."

Although Mrs. Peterson had been in various of the cities just before the boycotts began, she denied that she had anything to do with fomenting them or that they were being led by left-wing groups. The boycotts, she said were "a spontaneous reaction" to matters of genuine concern by housewives "who are not a left-wing group." She also took the opportunity to add that Goldwater's statement "again demonstrated the insensitivity of the Republican Party to the needs and problems of American citizens."

It was, of course, perfectly clear to everyone who followed the boycotts that if Esther Peterson was not actually out leading the troops, she had, in spirit, sounded the call to arms. Eventually she suffered from the repercussions of having done her job too well. In the opinion of many in-the-know Washington observers, disgruntled industry finally prevailed with the President, who a few months later agreed to have Mrs. Peterson leave the White House and return to the Department of Labor.

Esther Peterson's accomplishment as a trail blazer in the field of consumer affairs was undeniably great. The report of the President's Committee on Consumer Affairs, summarizing activities between 1964 and 1967, lists a hundred and seventeen public appearances which she made during this period. It details multitudinous actions by the business community, by private organizations, and by the government at state and federal levels, to assure consumer protection and education. And finally the report cites achievements during the three-year period which range from the passage by the 89th Congress of the Fair Packaging and Labelling Act to the establishment of a Denim Council which has issued a one-page *Consumer's Guide to Buying Blue Jeans* and a fact sheet on *Blue Jeans Terminology*.

In addition to dividing her time between labor and the consumer during those three years, Mrs. Peterson had occasionally to divide her allegiance, and here it was more difficult to apply the two-thirds, two-thirds formula. While serving the special interests of consumers, she was sometimes obliged to take action contrary to the special interests of labor. As a result she had some fence-mending to do on her return to full-time activity in the Department of Labor.

On the other hand, she had picked up a whole new following among the women of America, which gave her a certain measure of political independence. This was useful, for Esther Peterson soon found herself facing an ideological conflict between her own convictions and those of her labor constituency. It was, furthermore, a conflict of old versus new concepts.

When Frances Perkins first created the Bureau of Labor Standards in 1934, her objective had been to assure the physical well-being of all workers by protecting them from industrial hazards, undue overtime, and overtaxing occupations for which they were unfit. In particular, Miss Perkins sought to correct the working conditions of women who during the depression had been severely exploited by low pay and long hours. Spurred by the Department of Labor, the states began to adopt special laws to safeguard the rights of women against such abuses. Legislation, varying from state to state, put "floors under wages and ceilings on hours."

It is ironic that thirty years later what had been regarded as enlightened protection of women workers came to be branded as unfair discrimination against them. The Civil Rights Act of 1964 provides in Title VII that employers shall not discriminate on the basis of race, national origins, or sex.

Many working women today emphatically *do not want* protection. As Assistant Secretary of Labor for Labor Standards, Mrs. Peterson must try to put herself in the shoes of a woman who is a member of a well-organized union, working in a plant which has a defense contract requiring frequent overtime. While a man, often doing an identical job, may work overtime and fatten his take-home pay envelope with time-and-a-half, the woman may not — not because she, as a person, is physically unable to handle the extra hours, but because she is a woman and because the *state law* says that women may work only eight hours and no more. Naturally she wants the premium overtime pay, and naturally she protests, the more vigorously now that Title VII backs her up and says she is being discriminated against.

But Mrs. Peterson must also consider another kind of woman, one in a less well-paid trade union. Say she is the mother of three children. She works a seven-to-three shift because she must be home when the children get home from school. She also needs time to do the washing and ironing, the shopping and cooking. If she is forced to work overtime, even her time-and-a-half probably will not bring in enough money to pay for these necessary household services. Besides, she *wants* to be home; she wants to combine her job at the factory with her job as a wife and mother. But if she were to refuse to work overtime, and if there were no law to prevent her from *having* to work overtime, she would undoubtedly lose her job. So this woman — also emphatically — wants the state's protective legislation to continue.

Labor is on the side of this woman. Labor is pledged to protect her rights, to safeguard her from abuse, to see that she is not exposed to physical risks, to the operation of hazardous machinery, to heavy lifting, or, at the lowest level, to the performance of the most onerous and unpleasant industrial tasks. In the view of the trade unions, women *are* a special category and should be treated as such. Nor do the unions feel that Title VII applies to labor laws in which the intent is clearly protective and therefore non-discriminatory. In sum, labor strongly believes that *state* laws must prevail in the area of labor standards.

Opposing them and backing the woman worker who is asking no quarter and is prepared to do a man's job at a man's hours and a man's pay are the militant feminists, whose chairman and most verbal spokesman is Betty Friedan, and whose organization, NOW (National Organization of Women), is strongly committed to the conviction that women are not a special category and that they should not and *will not* be treated as such.

In the main, Esther Peterson shares this belief, while not applauding the combative, flag-waving, aggressive tactics of NOW or of its chairman. Mrs. Peterson is in favor of legislation for people. She feels that much of the protective legislation is in fact outmoded today and that, whether male or female, an individual's fitness to perform a job or to work overtime should be established by a physical examination. She wants "specific bills for specific ills." She believes that we should meet the problems of workers by recognizing the special needs of special groups, whether they be the handicapped, or the aged, or widows, or even persons whose transportation to and from work presents particular difficulties. In the matter of pay, her creed is the "rate for the job." She points with satisfaction to the federal Fair Labor Standards Act which, as amended in 1963, established equal pay for men and women doing the same job.

At the same time she is against hard confrontations with the trade unions, and she is very much against any premature lifting of protective legislation until other safeguards are established. She favors a step forward, then a pause to consolidate gains, then another step forward. Above all, she favors knowing clearly in which direction the forward steps are taking us.

In her official capacity, Mrs. Peterson is constantly under pressure to take definitive action, to throw the full weight of her office behind one faction or another. Representatives from the Consumers' League — an organization founded by one of the heroines on her wall, Florence Kelley — wait upon her to demand that she urge the Secretary of Labor to do everything in his not inconsiderable power to compel state legislatures to hold fast to their protective labor laws.

Just as vociferous on the opposite side, though perhaps for the wrong reasons, are the members of that hardy perennial, the Woman's Party for Equal Rights Amendment (chairman, Mrs. Emma Guffey Miller, Bryn Mawr, 1899). The last vestige of the militant suffragists, the Woman's Party broke off from the powerful Woman's Suffrage Party in 1915 to fight not only for the vote but for the passage of an amendment to the Constitution which clearly states that women are the equal of men. They are fighting for it still.

Each year this gallant little band of diehards, irreverently referred to as the "Tennis Shoe Ladies," appears on Capitol Hill to present the "old amendment." Each year President Pro Tempore Carl Hayden phones Mrs. Peterson to announce, "Esther, the ladies are here again." Each year when the bill reaches the floor of the House the President Pro Tempore has attached onto it the Hayden rider which says in effect that the equal rights amendment cannot invalidate any legislation, thus assuring that all of the states' protective (i.e. discriminatory) laws remain, and vitiating the intent of the amendment.

Through the years the advocates of the equal rights amendment have tended to be conservatives. It is not surprising, therefore, that Margaret Heckler, the freshman Republican Representative from Massachusetts, should have been asked, almost as soon as she took office in the House, to sponsor the amendment. Frances Bolton, ranking woman Republican in the House, has always declined to do so.

In her capacity as executive vice chairman of the Status of Women Commission, Esther Peterson managed to bring many of these divergent viewpoints together and to get their advocates to agree to a single broad statement. The Commission's published report, *American Women* (a Government Printing Office best seller, by the way), opens the section on "Women Under the Law" with the words: "Equality of rights under the law for all persons, male or female, is so basic to democracy and its commitment to the ultimate value of the individual that it must be reflected in the fundamental law of the land." Mild as that may sound, it was considered by Mary Hilton, now deputy director of the Women's Bureau, who worked closely with the Commission, to be a landmark of harmonious agreement.

More specifically, the report continues that since equality of rights is already embodied in the Fifth and Fourteenth Amendments of the Constitution, a further amendment is no longer needed to establish this principle. But judicial clarification, the Commission believes, is "imperative in order that remaining ambiguities with respect to the constitutional protection of women's rights be eliminated." And finally the Commission calls for an "early and definitive" Supreme Court case which will challenge state discriminatory laws and conclusively prove women's rights under the Fifth and Fourteenth Amendments.

The chairmanship of the Status of Women Commission was one of the last official duties performed by Eleanor Roosevelt. As always, Mrs. Peterson says, Mrs. Roosevelt was ahead of her time. She was the first to say that women really didn't need a lot of those old protections any more and to call for the elimination of "outmoded barriers to women's aspirations."

Many people think that Esther Peterson looks like Mrs. Roosevelt. Mrs. Peterson is delighted to have even a physical resemblance to the woman she admires above all others.

"In so many situations," she says, "I keep thinking, 'How would Mrs. Roosevelt handle this one?' She was a wonderful balance in a lot of delicate situations, but somehow she always came out just so straight!"

While Mrs. Roosevelt remained completely unself-conscious, Esther Peterson finds that, particularly since the Status of Women report, she has become more self-conscious, that is more conscious of being a woman and more uncomfortable about acting like one. "We're still so afraid that if we're a little bit aggressive, we'll be un-feminine," she says ruefully.

It is a ticklish problem. The wife of a former Assistant Secretary of Labor who has herself worked within the Democratic Party to get women elected thinks that all women in public office are and must be aggressive and that Esther Peterson is no exception, but that she covers up better than most with a lot of Scandinavian folk-siness.

On the other hand, John W. Leslie, director of information in the Department of Labor, who takes a rather dim view of most women he deals with in his work, believing that they either go "all emotional" to get their way or else "chew up everything in sight to show they're equal," says that Esther Peterson does neither. "She thinks straight and behaves honestly, which is of course not like a woman *at all*, yet she remains completely feminine."

Mrs. Peterson herself admits to a certain amount of maneuvering — a little of *What Every Woman Knows* — in the performance of her duties. "Often when I have an idea I think is pretty good," she says, "I find myself trying to get it through by making some key man think it was his idea in the first place. I can think of a lot of cases where if I'd been a man I would just have put the idea through without any of this working around. But then if I hadn't done some maneuvering I probably wouldn't have been able to accomplish as much as I have."

The fact that she is pliable does not mean that she can be either pushed around or flattered into doing anything she does not believe in. Working over a draft of a report with her not long ago, a young man in her department pointed to a line he disagreed with. "You're a sweet, lovely, charming Assistant Secretary," he said, "but this sentence is irrelevant. I've crossed it out."

Mrs. Peterson studied the paper for a moment, then gazed thoughtfully at the young man over her glasses. Smiling she picked up an eraser. "I'm glad you've crossed it out lightly," she said.

She is not always so sure of herself. But if she is sometimes indecisive, her admirers say it is because she is not convinced of the infallibility of her own ideas. Her detractors say it is because she does not really know enough.

One such "detractor" prefaced his appraisal of Mrs. Peterson by saying, "You know the thing about Esther is that she's for real. She's just as nice as she seems to be and believe me in Washington that's refreshing."

"But," he added, "I don't suppose three things in the world have ever happened because of Esther Peterson. She speaks and thinks entirely in terms of vague, hopeful, beautiful generalities for a better world. She can never get down to the real specifics."

Others, notably her own staff, disagree. Mrs. Peterson is of course a relative newcomer to public office. From her early Winsor School days until 1961 when she entered government service, she operated in an area where her ebullient optimism, her hard work, her sincere concern for the less fortunate, her unwavering courage, and her essential good sense paid the greatest possible dividends.

She has brought these same qualities into public office. Perhaps they are not enough. Perhaps her warm, sometimes unsophisticated and oversimplified belief in the essential goodness of people does not sufficiently take into account the baser realities of their greed, corruption, and venality. Perhaps the more experienced officials in Washington, who appear cynical beside her, do in fact dig deeper in dealing with the massive complexities of their jobs.

Yet Esther Peterson's effectiveness is undeniable.

Her private life is fully achieved. Her four children are all outstanding; her husband remains the strong, useful, cheerful human being he has always been. The Petersons live in a large, comfortable, red brick house near the Walter Reed Hospital in Washington and get away whenever they can to their farm in Townshend, Vermont. Their social life is simple. Both love to play poker, both love to drink beer, so they do much of their entertaining by giving poker parties with kegs of Danish beer tapped in the cellar. Once or twice a year, however, they give a larger, more chic, more typically Washington cocktail party. When she is feeling particularly troubled or in need of diversion, Esther Peterson likes to make bread. This is a hangover from her girlhood days when she didn't like it so much but had to do it anyway. For the rule in the Eggertsen house was that whichever of the four daughters came home last at night had to mix the bread dough for the next day. Mrs. Peterson became extremely sharp, she says, at detecting signs that her sisters were getting ready to say good night. Then she would whisk out quickly ahead of them and get home in time to avoid the bread detail.

In her public life Esther Peterson is an innovator. She continues to be dynamic, to move and to try to move others forward with her. In some instances, however, she is not able to articulate her ideas very precisely. When, for example, she talks of a "time when labor standards will be more subjective and more concerned with the satisfaction workers get out of their jobs," tough-minded, realistic labor experts tend to smile. They regard this as a high-flown utterance, typical of someone long associated, as Esther Peterson has been, with the "needle trades" whose workers are traditionally among the poorest paid of any union. Whereas a heavy industry like the building trade gets good wages for their workers, but is little concerned with the atmosphere in which they work, the needle trades rely on liberal-sounding generalities about better working conditions as a substitute for the higher pay scale they are not powerful enough to win for their workers. Still, not even the cynics can deny that pride of workmanship, while it may not pay for the groceries, is an intangible asset to the worker and one which may, as Mrs. Peterson believes, give added meaning and dignity to his job.

Mrs. Peterson is more specific about her hopes for the future of women. She looks forward to "full partnership" between men and women, but she believes it will never be a reality until the mass media stop portraying women exclusively as "sweet fragile little wives on a pedestal" and until women themselves stop clinging to this false picture of themselves and accept their rightful places as doers and contributors.

Esther Peterson's hopes for her own future are quite clear. "I want to wind up lobbying again," she says. Then, always the romantic, she qualifies it. "I mean I want to wind up lobbying for *lost causes.*"

The phrase has a nostalgic ring of the 'thirties. But the lost causes, when Esther Peterson finds them, will be strictly of the 'seventies.

THREE CONGRESSWOMEN: WHAT MAKES THEM RUN

Martha W. Griffiths, Patsy T. Mink, Margaret M. Heckler

In the fifty-one years since Jeannette Rankin took her seat as the first woman to be elected to the House of Representatives, sixty-seven women have served in Congress, the vast majority of them having been elected to fill unexpired terms of husbands who had died while in office.

By the 1950's this pattern began to change. In 1954 four new women were elected to the House, none to fill a husband's seat, bringing the total number of women in the 84th Congress to its all-time high of seventeen.

Among the four freshmen that year was a Democrat from Michigan named Martha Griffiths. On the day Mrs. Griffiths took her seat after the swearing in, a fellow Congressman sitting next to her shot her a dispirited look and said glumly, "At this rate it won't be any time at all before you ladies have the majority here."

One of Congresswoman Griffiths' first official acts was to ask the Legislative Reference Service of the Library of Congress to figure out just how long it would actually take at the then present rate for women to gain the majority in the House. The answer came back, 432 years.

Today the computers would probably put the millennium even further into the future, because there are now only eleven women in the House and one in the Senate.

But though their numbers have decreased, the qualifications of the women serving in the legislature today have markedly improved. The law is widely considered the best preparation for public service as evidenced by the fact that 61 per cent of the men Representatives are lawyers. Today, for the first time in the history of the Congress, three of the eleven women are also lawyers.

They are Martha W. Griffiths, Patsy Takemoto Mink, Democrat from Hawaii, who was elected in 1964, and Margaret M. Heckler, Republican from Massachusetts, now serving her first term in the House.

These three Congresswomen, who may be said to typify a new wave among women legislators, have more in common than just their law degrees. Each has worked as a practicing lawyer, each had held state elective office before coming to Washington, each won her seat in the House entirely on her own merits.

But perhaps their most important bond is that each of their husbands has been the moving factor in shaping the course of their public service. Hicks Griffiths, John Mink, and John Heckler have all served as their wives' campaign managers; they remain actively involved as advisers, strategists, and sounding boards.

Much hope for women's greater participation in public life lies in the solidarity of purpose between husband and wife which marks the careers of these three Congresswomen.

Martha Griffiths, the most senior in rank and in years, is a slim, youthful-looking woman with a pronounced Midwestern accent and a friendly, direct manner. In talking with her one senses little discrepancy between her private and her public personality. She is brisk and to the point, and where her strong convictions are concerned, she speaks her mind without equivocation. From the beginning a forthright independence of thought and deed has marked her public career.

She comes of sturdy pioneer stock. Martha Wright was born in Pierce City, Missouri, as were her great-great-grandparents on both sides, on January 29th, 1912. Her father was a rural letter carrier and her mother, who served as a substitute mail carrier, could, and often did, drive a double team of horses in the performance of her duties. Her father's father had been the county sheriff; he was killed by outlaws when Martha Wright's father was eight years old. Her grandmother took what little money she had, went to St. Louis, learned to be an expert tailor, and returned to Pierce City to support her three little boys by her newly acquired trade, thus establishing the precedent of a woman in a man's job which her granddaughter would someday follow.

On her mother's side, one of Martha Wright's uncles married a granddaughter of Daniel Boone; the daughter of this union became the first woman attorney in the state of Missouri. Given this heritage, it was inevitable that Martha Wright should decide that she was going to do something significant with her life. She went to public schools in Pierce City and then to the University of Missouri, where she met Hicks Griffiths. They were married at the end of their senior year in college and together decided to go on to law school. Married graduates students were far less common in the 'thirties than they are today, nor was there any G. I. Bill of Rights to help the young Griffithses along as they worked their way through law school. They graduated together from Michigan Law School in 1940 and both worked for a short time in the legal department of the American Automobile Insurance Company until the war broke out, when Mrs. Griffiths joined the Detroit Ordinance District as a contract negotiator and her husband went to the Office of Price Administration.

At the end of the war Martha Griffiths opened her own law office; her husband joined the firm on the completion of his duties for OPA. In 1947 the firm was expanded to include a young Michigan lawyer who had worked with Hicks Griffiths at OPA. His name was G. Mennen Williams.

By this time politics had already become a factor in the Griffithses' lives. The possibility of a public career for Martha Griffiths had first been suggested a year earlier by one of Detroit's most eminent women lawyers, a one-time suffragette called — unforgettably — Phoebe Moneybean, who telephoned Mrs. Griffiths quite unexpectedly one day in 1946 and told her she must run for the state legislature. Astounded, Mrs. Griffiths demurred on the ground that she was not a Detroiter, that she was completely unknown to the electorate and that, besides, she was a Democrat. Phoebe Moneybean, a Republican, brushed aside all objections; she was interested only in getting qualified women into public office. Still Mrs. Griffiths said no, but when she reported the conversation to her husband, he thought otherwise. "Call her back right now and tell her you've just started running," he said.

Along with every other Democrat on the slate, Martha Griffiths lost the election in 1946. However, the defeat of the incumbents in the state legislature was considered good riddance by the rapidly growing group of Young Turks who, under the leadership of Hicks Griffiths, were out to pump new life into the Democratic Party. And by 1948 these reformers had the party well organized, with a candidate for every spot and a poll watcher for every precinct. Topping the ticket was the Griffithses' law partner, Soapy Williams, running for Governor.

Mrs. Griffiths maintains that she ran again for the state legislature in 1948 only to plug the name of G. Mennen Williams, and that she gave little or no thought to her own candidacy, although she was endorsed by the Democratic Party and by labor. A few days before the election, however, she realized that, whether Williams won or not, she was probably going to be elected to the state house of representatives. This meant that, with the state legislature sitting in Lansing, the Griffithses would face a change in their way of life.

When Martha Griffiths was elected, along with Mennen Williams, she spent much of her time in Lansing while her husband stayed in Detroit. Today the same *modus vivendi* prevails. While the Congress is in session, Mrs. Griffiths commutes to Detroit each weekend, or occasionally her husband comes to Washington instead, but in any case they are always together from Friday to Sunday.

The arrangement, except for the fact that it cost them $5,200 in airplane fares in 1967, works out very well, Mrs. Griffiths feels. She and her husband are both able to give full concentration to their demanding jobs during the week, and are thus free to enjoy each other over the weekends.

Mrs. Griffiths has the highest regard for her husband's talents as a politician. Although not given to much self-deprecation (most women in public office do not seem to be), she stated publicly at the time she and Williams were candidates in 1950, "My husband knows more about politics than either one of us. Soapy and I are the happy extroverts who run around shaking hands. My husband gets things done."

In 1952 Martha Griffiths made her first bid for the Congress of the United States when she ran for Representative from the Seventeenth District and lost by a narrow margin. Her contest was notable for one innovation; she campaigned from a house-trailer. The Seventeenth District is largely residential, composed mostly of single-occupancy houses with few convenient auditoriums or large meeting places where political rallies can be held. So instead Mrs. Griffiths worked out of her trailer. She and her four young girl assistants would park it in the middle of a residential block; the girls would then ring doorbells and invite the potential constituents to join them in the trailer for fruit juice and a visit with the candidate.

It was an appealing, neighborly, and essentially feminine approach. It is difficult to imagine a man candidate, especially a large man, appearing at his best in a cramped trailer, but for Mrs. Griffiths this proved a natural and effective way to meet the people of the district. Although she did not win in her first attempt, she has used the trailer for many subsequent campaigns with great success.

Shortly after her defeat in 1952, a judgeship opened up in Detroit and Mrs. Griffiths persuaded Governor Williams to appoint her to the post. She sat for ten months as a judge of the recorder's court and received so much favorable publicity that when she ran again for the House of Representatives in 1954 she won.

By this time a situation not unusual in politics developed within the local party structure. Factionalism grew, and with it came objections to Hicks Griffiths' leadership; his wife claims it was inspired by the CIO who wanted more control of local party affairs. In any case, although there was no overt break, the state Democratic organization did not endorse Martha Griffiths in 1954. In fact, it endorsed another candidate in the primaries, who, according to Mrs. Griffiths, turned out afterwards to be the head of the White Citizens' Council of Michigan. "And this," she says bitterly, "was the person whom the CIO and the Democratic Party were supporting."

Nonetheless, without party endorsement and without use of the ubiquitous green and white polka dots which had become the symbol of Governor Williams and of Michigan, Martha Griffiths won her seat to the House in 1954 and has held it ever since.

As a Congresswoman Mrs. Griffiths' committee assignments have been primarily concerned with fiscal matters. She started off on Banking and Currency (along with Government Operations) and moved upward in 1961 to the prestigious Joint [House and Senate] Economic Committee. Then, in 1962, she made an important breakthrough for her sex when she became the first woman ever to be elected to the all-powerful Ways and Means Committee.

Because it is such a key committee, Congressmen are not chosen for Ways and Means but are elected by the entire House. The Democratic members of the Ways and Means Committee in turn make the committee assignments of all the other Democrats in the House. (On the Republican side this job is handled by the Republican Policy Committee.) Martha Griffiths' election to this influential and sensitive position is a testament to the high regard in which she is held by her fellow Congressmen.

The Ways and Means Committee is responsible for framing the federal tax policy, which means that it often plays an innovative role in national affairs since, according to the Constitution, all financial bills must originate in the House. (Other bills may be introduced in either chamber.)

Shortly after she assumed her duties on the committee, Martha Griffiths initiated some permutations of her own in behalf of the country's self-supporting women. She had not, she says, been fully aware of the large number of legislative inequities which militated against the working woman until one day she sat at a Ways and Means Committee meeting listening to a discussion of social security payments. As she looked down at the figures, she was suddenly struck by the fact that if a man and his wife each earned $2,400 a year and each paid for social security throughout their working lives, they would jointly draw much less money on retirement than the man alone could claim if he had been the only breadwinner and had earned $4,800 a year.

Appalled by this blatant inequity, Mrs. Griffiths began checking for further disparities in benefits for men and women only to discover that, as she puts it, "the law is simply schizophrenic on this subject."

She found, for example, that if a man covered by social security should leave the labor force after having worked a sufficient time to qualify for a pension and then should die, his widow and children could draw indefinitely on his pension. But if a woman similarly covered should leave the labor force and then die a year and a half later, neither her husband nor her children could draw a cent.

She turned up similar injustices affecting civil servants throughout the government. In a statement to the House on May 17, 1967, she pointed out to her male colleagues that if she were to die while speaking to them, her husband could collect only that portion of her salary which she had paid in social security, whereas if one of them were to die while listening to her, their widows, beginning at nine o'clock the following morning, would receive pensions for life.

Early in her service as a Congresswoman she had signed up for a health plan and learned that to cover herself and her husband she was paying $2.50 more per month than a Congress*man* was paying to cover himself, his wife and two children.

"What that really meant," says Mrs. Griffiths, who has no children of her own, "was that I was taking care of at least one of that Congressman's children. And I wasn't even getting a Mother's Day card."

This particular inequity has since been corrected, but others con-

tinue to exist. A woman working for the State Department who
goes abroad has to pay to send her children to the Dependents'
School, maintained by the United States in all large foreign posts. A
man can send his children free. A woman marine who is married
and assigned to Parris Island must pay out of her own pocket for
quarters where she can stay with her husband. A man marine
is given an increased allowance for quarters where he and his wife
may stay.

The explanation, Mrs. Griffiths believes, is that there exists in
this country the "great myth that behind every woman from the
cradle to the grave is a well-heeled, loving man's support. And the
laws of the federal government reinforce that myth," she says. "Social security does, veterans' pensions do, and the working situation
within the government itself does. All of them are based on the fact
that the man supports the woman, but nobody looks at the fact that
there are millions of women supporting themselves." By the same
token, Mrs. Griffiths contends that the men who made the laws
looked kindly at the business of taking care of a widow and children.
But "they never thought," she says, "that really they were often
taking care of that widow and children by taking money away from
a working woman."

Early in the spring of 1967, Martha Griffiths introduced a bill designed specifically to correct inequities of social security benefits.
But the larger discriminations because of sex will, she strongly believes, only be corrected when, as she puts it, the Supreme Court
"finally gives way and recognizes that under the Constitution of the
United States a woman is a person and entitled to equal protection
under the law." Such a decision would automatically supersede the
individual states' legislation and thus knock out all of the so-called
protective labor laws for women.

Paving a way for a reversal of the Supreme Court's previously
held positions concerning the rights of working women is Title VII
of the Civil Rights Act of 1964, which provides that employers may
not discriminate on the basis of race, color, religion, national origins,

or sex. Inclusion of the word *sex* in the act caused much debate in the House and, in fact, on a number of occasions provoked open derision on the part of the male Representatives.

Martha Griffiths made one of the strongest arguments in favor of the inclusion of the word. One of the tenets of her case was that unless the word "sex" were added, a white woman who was discriminated against at the hiring gate could not invoke the act, whereas a Negro woman could. In a brisk colloquy with Congressman Emanuel Celler, Democrat from New York and chairman of the Judiciary Committee, who opposed the inclusion of the word "sex," Mrs. Griffiths postulated a hypothetical case of a qualified Negro woman applying for a job as a dishwasher in a restaurant that had previously employed only white male dishwashers. If the prospective employer refused to hire the Negress on the ground that he employed only *male* dishwashers, she could answer that he was refusing to hire her because he had only *white* dishwashers, and thus have a *prima facie* case to invoke the provisions of the Civil Rights Act; a qualified white woman under the same circumstances would have no case at all.

Although Mrs. Griffiths recognized that in actual practice cases militating against white women would be isolated ones, her argument was still a very telling one which she believes helped substantially to assure that the word "sex" be included.

The first case pertinent to Title VII likely to come before the Supreme Court and one which is being watched with particular interest, if from slightly different vantage points, by both Martha Griffiths and Esther Peterson, is Minglecoch vs. California. The plaintiff, Mrs. Minglecoch, who is the sole support of her three children, finds that her earning power is so critically curtailed by the California state law which prohibits women from working more than eight hours a day that she is willing to undergo the great and tedious hardship of challenging the law. Her case is now working its way up through the federal district courts.

Mrs. Griffiths is not very sanguine, however, about the Supreme

Court's decision on any case involving women; most of its previous opinions in this area, she feels, "sound as if they belonged in the Dark Ages." She is particularly vehement about a case that came up to the Court in 1948 from her own state, challenging a Michigan statute which said that a woman could not be a bartender — she could only be a bar*maid*, at lower pay.

While the minority opinion of the Supreme Court held that the equal protection under the law clause of the Fourteenth Amendment required lawmakers to "refrain from invidious distinction of a sort drawn by the statute challenged in this case," the majority opinion, which was written by Justice Frankfurter, upheld the statute, referred nostalgically to Shakespeare's bawdy barmaids, and ruled that the state had a right to determine how liquor was being served.

Citing this particular decision on the floor of the House during the Title VII debate, Mrs. Griffiths pulled no punches. "In the most vulgar and insulting decision handed down in this century by the Supreme Court, notable for its lack of legal learning as well as for its arrogant prejudice, the majority of the Supreme Court decided that it was well within the police powers of the state of Michigan for the legislature to draw the most arbitrary and capricious of lines as to who could tend bar in Michigan."

Perhaps one of the fringe benefits of being a lawyer herself is that it enables Congresswoman Griffiths to sound off so unequivocally against the highest court of the land. But she is never one to mince words nor to compromise her own strongly held views. On the floor of the House on June 20, 1967, she lashed out at certain of her colleagues who had spoken with grossly misplaced humor against a proposed forty-million-dollar rat-control bill:

> I should like to remind the Members who sit here in this body that . . . rats are a living cargo of death. Their tails swish through sewers and over that food we eat. Their stomachs are filled with tularemia, amoebic dysentery. They carry the most deadly diseases, and some think it is funny. Some do not want to spend forty million dollars.

Mr. Speaker, if we are going to spend seventy-nine billion dollars to try to kill off a few Vietcong, believe me I would spend forty million dollars to kill off the most devastating enemy man has ever had.

And in late 1967 she was one of the few Congressmen willing to air publicly her indignation over the fact that the expensive, sophisticated machinery which the Defense Department *gives* to American industry to enable them to produce essential military hardware is also used by many companies to produce profitable commercial items. As a purchasing agent for five years during the war Mrs. Griffiths could and did speak with authority. "No one knows better than I how stupid these military people can be," she was quoted in the press as saying. "This whole area of defense procurement and lack of control over government-owned property is a monstrous disgrace. The contractors, in my opinion, are stealing, they're cheating and they do this because they see that nobody in the Pentagon cares about it."

Though she of course makes enemies by being so outspoken, she also wins many admirers. India Edwards, former vice chairman of the Democratic National Committee, calls her "the most courageous woman in the Congress."

Mrs. Griffiths alleges to have declined an opportunity to run for the Senate on the grounds that, as a Senator, she would have had to travel all over the huge state of Michigan (it is further from Lansing to the Upper Peninsula in Michigan than it is from Lansing to Tennessee) and would therefore have had no home life at all.

Having thus foresworn the upper chamber, she is frankly partisan in favor of the House, "where all the real workers are," and opposed to the Senate, "which gets all the publicity." Martha Griffiths herself does not get much publicity; she is perhaps less well known as a national figure than the majority of her women colleagues. But with her two prime committee assignments, which she considers the best appointments accorded to any legislator, she represents the backbone, the hard-working hard core of the Congress.

Regarding her own position she says, "I like what I'm doing better than I could conceivably like anything in the Senate. I love the committees; the work is challenging, it's refreshing, it's stimulating and I enjoy it and find it more rewarding than I can possibly say."

If enthusiasm and dedication are the stuff of elective public officers, Congresswoman Griffiths plainly qualifies.

For Patsy Takemoto Mink there has been no single moment, no isolated event which marked a turning point in her career and propelled her into public life. Rather she has been a young woman whose destiny closely parallels the destiny of her state — Hawaii. When Mrs. Mink was elected to the House of Representatives in 1964, she was the youngest member of the Congress representing the youngest state in the Union.

Because of her youth and her background, her arrival in Washington was marked by more attention than is usually accorded to freshman Representatives. Universally described in the press as "petite and pretty," some writers also added the word "vivacious," probably because the name Patsy Mink somehow sounds so jaunty — almost like a drum majorette. Mrs. Mink belies the image of her name, however. Though she *is* pretty and she *is* petite, she is also a very serious and quite reserved young woman, articulate, thoughtful but hardly outgoing and not inclined to frivolity, at least in her public role.

It is possible that if Hawaii had already achieved statehood when Patsy Takemoto Mink came home to Honolulu after graduating as a Juris Doctor from the University of Chicago, she would have settled for a career as a successful practicing lawyer. But statehood was still seven years away in 1952; inevitably Mrs. Mink became involved in the fierce struggle to achieve this long-sought-after goal.

When the islands were first annexed to the United States in 1898 all Hawaiians became American citizens, but without representation in Congress; their single delegate had floor privileges in the House but no vote.

Beginning in 1903, when its territorial legislature first requested Congress to pass an act enabling it to enter the Union, Hawaii had made continued pleas, had in fact passed a statehood resolution at every session of its legislature. A total of forty-nine bills were introduced into the Congress of the United States and, although the first one was in 1921, no legislative action of any sort was taken until 1947.

It has often been observed that movements of rebellion only begin to gain real momentum when a chance of resolution is in sight. Thus, in a country like South Africa where no solution to the race problem is on the horizon, the vast black population is almost entirely dormant, while in the United States the Negro revolution gathered momentum only after the Supreme Court school desegregation decision in 1954.

So it was in Hawaii in the early 'fifties. With the first favorable legislation passed by the Congress on the long road to statehood, there was a growing indignation on the islands as demands for full citizenship became more insistent.

It was into this atmosphere of ferment that Patsy Takemoto Mink came home to Honolulu from law school with John Mink, an engineer from Jim Thorpe, Pennsylvania, and with her new baby girl, Gwendolyn.

At that time, in 1950, Hawaii was still, in effect, a one-party state; since its annexation, Republicans had entirely controlled the territorial legislature. But Patsy Mink and other young people, many of whom were returning from the mainland as she was with wider horizons, along with their professional degrees, were Democrats — young, idealistic, eager for reform, impatient for more recognition and a greater involvement in the affairs of state.

Although Mrs. Mink opened an office to practice law and accepted an appointment as a lecturer in business law at the University of Hawaii, the main thrust of her activity was political. She was so successful in organizing the Young Democrats of the territory into a strong forceful group that in 1954, partially through her efforts, the Democrats, foɪ the first time since 1898, gained control of the legislature.

In the 1954 campaign Mrs. Mink worked very hard running the headquarters, ringing doorbells, doing all the traditional party jobs. She got her feet wet in politics and liked it; the obvious next step was to be a candidate herself. In 1956 she decided to run for the territorial house of representatives. But, as Martha Griffiths had been fourteen years earlier, Patsy Mink was a political unknown to the electorate in Honolulu; her activity to date had been entirely behind the scenes within the Democratic Party structure. "I had no name, and no reputation," she says. "My family wasn't politically active; I was the first to venture forth."

Furthermore, she was not even a native of Honolulu; she was born and raised on the island of Maui, a hundred and fifty miles southeast of Oahu. Educated in Maui public schools, she was class valedictorian and president of the student body. "I didn't get to the big city [Honolulu] until I went to the University of Hawaii."

Patsy Mink's father, Suematsu Takemoto, is a civil engineer. Orphaned as a small boy, he worked his way through school, the Mid-Pacific Institute (then called Mills School), and graduated from the University of Hawaii in 1922. Mr. Takemoto was a surveyor with the East Maui Irrigation Company until 1945, when he moved with his wife, daughter, and son to Honolulu and set up his own land surveying business.

Mr. and Mrs. Takemoto were "quite thrilled" about their daughter's political ambitions and supported her initial try, both morally and financially. "But we didn't need a very large amount of money for that first campaign," Mrs. Mink says.

From the outset, John Mink was intensely interested in every step of his wife's public career. "I wouldn't have even tried except for the fact that he was always encouraging me to be active since he was confident that I had a contribution to make."

John Mink was no neophyte in politics; he had been active in the Democratic Party since the day he was old enough to vote.

Handsome, intelligent, and astute, with a distinguished war record,* he would himself have made an attractive candidate, but such a course has never tempted him. "Not with Patsy doing so well at it," he says and adds that the rewards come "because I am totally involved in her career myself, and I mean just as totally involved as any person who has his own professional life can be."

Patsy Mink won her first bid for elective office in 1954 and took her seat in the territorial house of representatives. In the same year she was also made president of the first Young Democrats Club of Hawaii, which she had helped to found, and in 1957 she led a delegation of ten Hawaiians to the Young Democrats convention in Reno, Nevada, and was elected national vice president of the Young Democrats Clubs of America.

Through this participation with mainland Democrats Mrs. Mink established what she refers to as a "wide spectrum of contacts" with leaders of the party.

In 1958 she ran again in Hawaii, this time for the state senate. She was in this office when the long-awaited statehood finally became a fact in 1959. At once the entire territorial legislature was dissolved; all offices both in Hawaii and in Washington were therefore up for grabs.

In that first year there was only one seat in the Federal House of Representatives and, of course, two in the Senate. The statehood bill passed late in March; potential office seekers had to make their decisions promptly, since the filing date was late May.

Patsy Mink announced at once for the House, and until two or three days before the May filing date she was the only Democrat seeking this nomination. What foiled her, at least indirectly, was an element rare in politics — sentimentality.

When Mrs. Mink announced for the House, one of her contempo-

* As navigator on a Flying Fortress he flew twenty-three bombing missions over Europe, including the first daylight raid on Berlin, and an additional sixty missions. For his service he received the Distinguished Flying Cross and the Air Medal with nine oak leaf clusters as well as five major battle stars in the European Theater of Operations.

raries, a young man named Daniel Inouye, whose career closely paralleled her own, announced for the Senate. Meanwhile, however, there was a growing feeling among the Democratic Party leaders that some of the older men who had devoted years of their lives to the struggle for statehood deserved the honor of representing Hawaii for the first time in the United States Senate. Persuaded by this argument, Inouye decided at the eleventh hour to relinquish his Senate race to one of his seniors and to file instead for the House of Representatives.

Inouye won the nomination and was subsequently elected. Mrs. Mink's defeat — her first — was, she says, a "maturing experience." Many people suppose that an unsuccessful candidate, having once tasted the excitement of a campaign, begins immediately, or perhaps after a brief vacation to catch up on lost sleep, to plan the next foray into politics.

Patsy Mink, for all her serious dedication to public office, did not bounce back so quickly. "A defeat is a repudiation, after all, and one loses the confidence to run again. I suffered through all the political analysis after the election. I listened to thousands of post-mortems."

Many voters thought she had been wronged by Inouye's unexpected last-minute switch, so gradually she began to realize that even in defeat she had not entirely lost her following.

Still it was not until 1962, three years later, and then only after very careful deliberation, that she decided to run for office again. Although a place in the House of Representatives was open that year, Hawaii having by then been accorded two seats, Mrs. Mink felt that she needed first to re-establish herself at home. She therefore chose to run again for the state legislature and won, leading the ticket. With her confidence thus restored and her political leadership secure, she was in a position, when a seat in the House unexpectedly became available in 1964, to make a successful bid for the Congress.

There were many reasons why Mrs. Mink's move from Honolulu to Washington was a greater upheaval for her than Martha Griffiths' move from Detroit had been ten years earlier or Margaret Heckler's from Wellesley would be two years hence. For, despite its statehood, Hawaii is not an ordinary state, and the mainland must often seem another world to Hawaiians, separated as they are from the Union to which they belong by 2,400 miles of Pacific Ocean. (Officially Hawaii is described as the first overseas and the second noncontiguous state of the Union.) The way of life in this so-called "Paradise of the Pacific," controlled by long established tradition, is less frenetic than in, say, Southern California or Florida; the mores of the Hawaiian Islands are more distinctly indigenous than they are in these, or in any of the other fifty states, with the possible exception of Alaska. Racially Hawaii is polyglot; its population is basically Polynesian but much intermingled with Japanese, Chinese, and Caucasian strains. Mrs. Mink is of Japanese origin; her husband is Caucasian.

For Mrs. Mink the distance of 5,000 miles between Honolulu and Washington precluded any reassuring preliminary trips to house-hunt, to look over office space, to get the feel of who was who around Capitol Hill, or even to figure out how to find her way through the complicated subterranean mazes connecting the three House office buildings to the House chamber. So, despite her extensive experience, her years spent on the mainland, and her "wide spectrum of contacts" within the Democratic Party, Mrs. Mink faced a formidable array of newcomer's problems when she arrived in Washington in December of 1964 to take her place in the 89th Congress.

"It was all very new," Mrs. Mink recalls, "and of course so different, and it seemed that everything needed to be done at once. I had to pick an office, get my furniture in, and hire a staff. I had to find out where things were and who people were that had responsibility for different things. In addition to that we had to find a place to live and get our daughter enrolled in a school. Then we had to buy a complete wardrobe for her and for me. We had no winter clothes of course."

For three months Mrs. Mink struggled to get these material aspects of their lives in order. The office arrangement alone would have been the despair of a less stout-hearted person. There are three House office buildings on Capitol Hill: the Rayburn, which was completed only in 1965; the Longworth, built in 1933 and referred to in the Congressional Directory as the New Building; and the Cannon (Old Building), which dates back to 1903. Although the Rayburn has been much criticized for aesthetic lacks and conspicuous waste (marble abounds), its three-room suites of offices are spacious, comfortable, and much in demand. The Longworth, where Representative Mink (she prefers the term Representative to Congresswoman) was assigned, has some pleasant offices; Martha Griffiths, with thirteen years' seniority, has one which commands a handsome view of the Capitol dome. But Patsy Mink's two-room suite on the sixth floor is dingy and overcrowded. The outer office is so cramped that when the eight staff members are at their desks there is literally no place for a visitor waiting to see the Representative to sit down. Mrs. Mink's own office, which is hardly better, is just large enough to accommodate her desk, chair, a couch, and a bookcase. Fortunately the Cannon Building is now being renovated and will be ready by the fall of 1969 to take some refugees from Longworth — Patsy Mink among them.

In one respect, however, Mrs. Mink feels that she is more fortunate than some of her women colleagues. Her husband is, she points out, "in a field that allows for mobility." As an engineer specializing in hydrology and geology, his services are in demand almost anywhere he chooses to live. In Honolulu he worked first for the Board of Water Supply. When his wife was elected to the House, John Mink accepted, from among numerous possibilities, an offer from Johns Hopkins University; he commutes to Baltimore and the Minks, after living for a year in Arlington, Virginia, have now moved to Silver Springs, Maryland, in order to make his driving time shorter.

Gwendolyn Mink, who is fifteen, goes to public school and has

Senator Margaret Chase Smith receives congratulations from Majority Leader Senator Mike Mansfield (left) and Minority Leader Senator Everett M. Dirksen (right), following the Senate Resolution, June 14, 1965, commending her 2,000th consecutive roll call vote since 1955.

Representative Frances P. Bolton, standing with
Secretary of the Interior Stewart L. Udall and Mr.
Turkey Tayac, a member of the Piscataway tribe.
This meeting on February 22, 1968, marked the
establishment of Piscataway Park across the Po-
tomac River from Mt. Vernon.

Right. Esther Peterson keeps a sharp eye on chain
store prices in her capacity as Special Presidential
Assistant for Consumer Affairs. (Dennis Brack,
Black Star)

Representative Martha W. Griffiths meets with
three young constituents from Michigan State University in the Rayburn Reception Room at the
Capitol, February 1968. The students had come to
Washington to study the President's Economic
Report and to attend hearings of the Joint Economic Committee.

Representative Patsy T. Mink addresses the Ladies' Auxiliary of the Veterans of Foreign Wars at their convention held in New Orleans, August 1967. On this occasion, Mrs. Mink stressed the need for women's greater participation in public affairs.

Above. At a luncheon seminar for new Republican members of Congress held in January, 1967, Representative Margaret M. Heckler is welcomed by an experienced colleague, Representative Frances P. Bolton, and Mrs. Gerald R. Ford. House Minority leader Ford is seated in the background (right).

Right. Representative Margaret M. Heckler talks with a constituent on the "hot line" from her Washington office.

Constance Baker Motley and James Meredith attend a Convocation of the NAACP Legal Defense and Educational Fund, Inc., May 1964. The meeting celebrated the 25th anniversary of the founding of the Fund and the 10th anniversary of the Supreme Court's historic decision in favor of school integration. (NAACP Legal Defense and Educational Fund, Inc.)

Ambassador Eugenie Anderson visits a collective
farm in Bulgaria during her term of office as
American Minister in 1963. (John Anderson)

Ann Uccello, Hartford's first woman mayor, takes her oath of office, December 5, 1967, in ceremonies at the Municipal Building. (Harry Batz, *AP Wire-photo*)

Left. Mayor Ann Uccello and Secretary of the State Ella T. Grasso appear at a symposium on Opportunities for Women sponsored by Hartford College, March 27, 1968. (Arthur Warmsley, *The Hartford Courant*)

Ella T. Grasso, Democratic floor leader, confers with Republican floor leader, Meade Alcorn (left), and State and National Democratic Chairman, John M. Bailey (right), during the constitutional convention in Connecticut, 1965. (*The Hartford Courant*)

Right. Senator Margaret Chase Smith, wearing her trademark, acts as hostess at a luncheon, August 20, 1965, in honor of the dean of Republican Senators, George Aiken of Vermont.

Esther Peterson presides with Eleanor Roosevelt at
the third meeting of the President's Commission on
the Status of Women, Hyde Park, June 16, 1962.
Mary Hilton, Deputy Director of the Women's
Bureau, is in the background.

made an excellent record thanks, in part, her mother believes, to the high standard of education in Hawaii.

Mrs. Mink does all of her own housework. She has not found it necessary, especially with her daughter's help, to have a maid, or even a cleaning woman. The larger problem for her is to find time to shop, to have her hair done, to attend to dry cleaning, laundry, and countless other household duties. But the Minks are a very organized family who have the routine chores of their lives carefully worked out. "You have to have a schedule, you see," says John Mink, ever the precise engineer. "You drop your clothes at the dry cleaners on the way to work. You know exactly where to park, and what day of the week is the best to leave them and what hour of the day to pick them up so you don't have to stand in line."

On Saturday afternoon, like many other American families, the Minks go together to the supermarket to buy groceries for the week. Saturday is also the only time Mrs. Mink has to buy clothes or to help Gwendolyn select hers. She fits in her weekly appointment at the beauty parlor at eight o'clock in the morning in order to get to her office by nine. "It's an ordeal sometimes," Mrs. Mink sighs, "but we've grown accustomed to it."

Since they have at least two or three official engagements a week, Mrs. Mink is very jealous of the limited time she has with her family and therefore seldom entertains at home. She does, however, invite many of her constituents for lunch in the Capitol Dining Room, or sometimes for dinner in town when John Mink can join them. Unlike businessmen, however, legislators have no expense account to take care of such entertaining.

In fact, Mrs. Mink finds that the popular conception of a Congressman's life is far removed from the reality of it. "People think we come here to Washington and have these lavish facilities, that we're waited on hand and foot and receive all sorts of privileges and perquisites. They just don't realize. . . ."

Congressmen (Senators and Representatives alike) receive a taxable salary of $30,000 a year. Their only perquisite is the four round trips which they are allowed to their home district each session; their only privilege is their franking, or free mailing permit.

But four trips a year do not begin to cover a Congressman's obligations to his district nor to keep him sufficiently in touch — and in favor — with his constituents.

In 1966 — an election year — Mrs. Mink made ten trips to Hawaii, six of which, at $340 a round trip, came out of her own pocket.

Without the franking privilege, it would be impossible for Congressmen to report regularly by mail to their constituents on their legislative actions in Washington. Six times a session Patsy Mink sends out a newsletter to approximately 50,000 constituents and the mailing costs would, of course, be prohibitive if she had to pay them herself. She does, however, pay to have the letter printed at a cost of $1,000 an issue.

Mrs. Mink's out-of-pocket expenses in an election year could run to $10,000, a third of her annual salary. It is not surprising, therefore, that she should be a strong adherent of the four-year term for Representatives. She believes many of her colleagues also favor a four-year term over the present two-year term, but so far there has been no substantial move toward a constitutional amendment, which such a change would necessitate.

Doubtless many legislators are reluctant to alter the intentions of the Founding Fathers, who designed the House of Representatives to be more directly responsive to the electorate than the Senate. Furthermore, the problem of whether elections in a four-year term would take place in a Presidential or an off-election year is widely disputed and remains unsolved.

Both as a candidate for re-election and as a legislator Patsy Mink is a solid Democrat; her record is, so far, unmarked by any deviation from the straight liberal line. On the A.D.A. voting record tally her so-called L.Q. (Liberal Quotient) was 100 in 1965 (the same year in which Frances Bolton's was zero) and 94 in 1966 when she was absent for one key vote.

Depending on one's point of view, Mrs. Mink is either in favor of everything good and against everything bad, or vice versa. But while her sincerity is not in question, she has a tendency toward generalizations and truisms in her public addresses. "Our greatest belief," she said in a 1963 speech, "is that legislation which most directly helps the common man to lead a better life today, tomorrow, and in his twilight years is the greatest responsibility of our government."

Or, in her civil rights speech at the Democratic Convention in 1960: "So long as there remain groups of our fellow Americans who are denied equal protection under the law . . . we must remain steadfast till all shades of man may stand side by side in dignity and self-respect to truly enjoy the fruits of our great land."

In private her speech tends to be slightly stilted and characterized by such words as "challenge," "interaction," "orientation," "motivation," and "commitment."

But, although her utterances are sometimes platitudinous and her views nearly always predictable, Patsy Mink is nonetheless an effective champion of the issues in which she believes.

As a member of the Education and Labor Committee she gave vigorous support in the 89th Congress to the Elementary and Secondary School Amendment Acts and in particular to the Higher Education Act, which incorporated a part of her own proposal for federal grants to teachers on sabbatical leave.

In addition to her committee work (she is also on Interior and Insular Affairs) and to her specific service to her constituents, Patsy Mink believes she has one further responsibility. "With so few women in the Congress, I feel an obligation to respond to the needs and problems of the women in the nation. Because I am so interested in getting more women active in politics and community affairs and in really fulfilling their civic responsibilities, I accept as many speaking engagements as I can to large gatherings of women, both in and out of Washington."

Mrs. Mink's normally restrained manner becomes markedly more animated when she speaks of women's potential as public servants. "The key, the only thing that counts, is whether a woman is genuinely dedicated to the ideal of doing something that will make a difference to her community and to her country. If she has this drive, if she's convinced she can make a contribution, if she's serious and has worked hard and shown the ability to take positions and to stand behind them, to fight for her beliefs, then she cannot fail at an election. I believe this totally."

She is also convinced that if more women succeed in elective office, whether county, municipal, state, or federal, more will be *appointed* to significant positions, both public and private.

Mrs. Mink readily concedes the built-in difficulties which women face in seeking a full-time life outside their homes. She does not, however, consider that the problems are any greater in the field of politics than they are in any other career.

"Being in public office doesn't involve any more inconvenience to the family than being a schoolteacher who has to get up early enough to be in school by 8:30, perhaps dropping her own children off on the way. I personally don't see any obstacles within the family that are so formidable that they can't be overcome with a little extra effort on the woman's part."

One might, of course, place husbands in the category of "formidable obstacles," but Patsy Mink, while recognizing her own exceptional fortune in having John Mink's unfailing support, scoffs at the idea that any *good* husband would stand in his wife's way or resent her involvement in politics.

"I hear that all the time," she says. "Women keep telling me their husbands would never put up with their running for office, but I think that's just a crutch they're using because they aren't really *motivated*. I think if the woman herself felt the necessity of getting involved, then her husband would be more than anxious to have her have this sense of participation. He may not give total encouragement at first, but if the wife is successful and recognized and elected, then I'm sure there are very few husbands who would not stand up and say they were terribly proud of their wives' accomplishments."

John Mink agrees.

Margaret Heckler ran for her first public office on her name, a name which, though totally unknown in politics, nonetheless served her very well during the campaign. Her slogan was: "You need a Heckler on the Governor's Council."

In Massachusetts the Governor's Council consists of eight members, elected from geographical districts throughout the Commonwealth; their function is to confirm the Governor's major appointments and to advise on judicial decisions, particularly in the field of paroles and pardons. As a thirty-one-year-old lawyer, mother of three, and housewife from Wellesley, Mrs. Heckler felt that she was well qualified to fulfill the office. The post was only a part-time job which she could successfully combine with her law practice and her home life. In every respect it seemed an ideal first step on a path she had only recently decided to follow.

A totally feminine conflict had crystallized her resolution to seek public office. In 1961 she and her husband bought a large, old, rambling house in Wellesley. It needed considerable renovation — the kitchen especially was very old-fashioned. With what she admits was a women's magazine concept of chrome, formica, and step-saving efficiency in mind, Margaret Heckler called in a contractor and outlined her ideas. The estimate for the dream kitchen she envisaged came to $10,000.

John Heckler demurred. It was one thing, he argued, to spend that money if his wife really planned to *be* in the kitchen very much. But did she? They had often discussed the possibility of her running for public office someday. Now was the time, he told her, to make up her mind. The new kitchen was a rallying point. Did she want it and a life centered around her home, or would she make do with the old-fashioned kitchen and set her sights toward a goal she had always had in the back of her mind? The kitchen remained old-fashioned.

In 1962, although the incumbent Governor of Massachusetts was a Republican, there was no Republican on the Council, nor was there a woman, nor a heckler, the latter being a conspicuous lack at a time when the Council was tinged with scandal and corruption.

Margaret Heckler determined to remedy this situation by running as a councilor. She met with considerable opposition from her own party however, not because the Republican leaders had anything against her — she had done good work on the Wellesley town committee and for various local candidates — but because she was a young, unknown, and inexperienced woman, far out of the political mainstream from which candidates for this particular office were usually plucked. In fact, the Republicans had already selected a well-qualified, well-known lawyer of twenty years' experience to run from the Newton-Wellesley district for the Governor's Council. Obviously Mrs. Heckler did not stand a chance of winning the primary against a man of such standing in the community, let alone of winning the election against the Democratic incumbent, an honorable man, who was widely considered to be one of the best on the Governor's Council. Given these circumstances the Republican party chiefs looked benignly on young Mrs. Heckler, and told her she was overreaching herself.

Young Mrs. Heckler thought differently. "Sometimes," she said recently, "I think the Republican Party loses sight of the fact that there are, after all, more Indians than chiefs. I didn't have the support of the chiefs, and I regretted it, but I decided to go after the Indians, the people of the district, and ask them directly for their support."

While her Republican opponent took off for the summer, secure in the knowledge that he was the party's nominee, Margaret Heckler, in a campaign reminiscent of Margaret Chase Smith's first senatorial contest in Maine, launched a grass-roots operation guided by her husband and assisted by a few friends.

On the Sunday before the primaries the Boston papers mentioned her name for the first time as an "also ran" who had no hope of capturing the nomination. Two days later she won the primary by a substantial majority.

With the first hurdle successfully cleared, Mrs. Heckler decided that her best strategy to win the election itself was to clutch firmly onto the coat-tails of Governor John Volpe, the Republican incumbent, who was running for his first re-election. Each time the Governor appeared publicly, Mrs. Heckler was right beside him, hoping that he would, as he often did, toss in the magic words, "You need a Heckler on the Governor's Council." Wherever the Governor went, she went — until election day. Then Margaret Heckler went on to the State House and John Volpe went down in defeat. She was one of two Republicans to survive in the state elections that year; the other was Edward W. Brooke, now the junior Senator from Massachusetts, who was re-elected state attorney general.

In Massachusetts, where shibboleths die hard, Mrs. Heckler had proved that one could win an election without the support of party leaders. Furthermore, she had disproved the belief that women will not vote for a woman.

As the only Republican serving on the privy council of a Democratic Governor, Mrs. Heckler was unusually free of political obligations, of the patronage and wheeling and dealing which dominated the actions of most of her fellow councilors. Although politicians are always fond of boasting that they "call the shots as they see them and let the chips fall where they may," few manage to be so independent and high-minded in practice — not and remain in public office. But Mrs. Heckler, who frequently found herself holding the key vote on a sensitive appointment, was able to vote her conviction without fear of disastrous consequence to her future political career.

During her first term the covert scandals about the Governor's Council became overt when three members were indicted and served time in prison. In 1964, when Mrs. Heckler was re-elected by a large majority, public disgust at the open corruption had erupted and the powers of the Governor's Council were substantially reduced. It was therefore time, Mrs. Heckler decided, to start looking for another office.

The Republican pundits thought she might run successfully for either lieutenant governor or secretary of state, both positions which had never been occupied by a woman in Massachusetts. But Mrs. Heckler was not intersted in "being the first or the last or the thirty-third woman to do something." She saw no reason to seek an office just because it might be considered a suitable one for a woman.

The district which she represented on the Governor's Council was a large one, roughly the size and shape of the Tenth Congressional District. The logical move, therefore, seemed to be to capitalize on the voter strength she already had in the area and run for the Congress of the United States.

Mrs. Heckler naturally puts it in more lofty terms, "I felt the Congress was the office where I could make the best contribution," she says. "I was really concerned about the issues of the day, not only in the traditional areas of education and consumer protection, though those are great interests of mine too, but in criminal justice, social security, conservation, air and water pollution. I also felt very strongly that there should be more women in Congress and that the government should be brought closer to the people."

Once again the ambitious young woman met with opposition at the top, policy-making level of the Republican Party. The resistance this time was for quite a different reason, however. The Tenth Congressional District was the bailiwick of Representative Joseph W. Martin; during the forty-two years he had represented it in Washington, he had been one of the most prominent Republican members of the House; he had been both Speaker and Minority Leader, he was extremely popular, and in general a great credit to the Commonwealth of Massachusetts. Although he was then eighty-two years old and in failing health, the sentiment among the upper echelon of the party was that until he announced his retirement no one should run against Joe Martin.

On the other hand, Margaret Heckler's own people — leaders in the cities and towns of her district, workers at the precinct level, those who had been largely responsible for her election to the Governor's Council — were all enthusiastically urging her to run for the congressional seat.

John Heckler was solidly in favor of his wife's making the try, regardless of Martin's intentions. But Mrs. Heckler says she had some "emotional difficulties" in making up her mind "because Joe Martin was such a sweet man." Some of her detractors may have questioned whether her misgivings were prompted by a sincere solicitude for the elder statesman, or by a concern for her own image if she chose to challenge the declining but beloved incumbent in a primary.

In any case, what finally clinched — or justified — her decision was her belief that at Martin's age and with the evident deterioration of his health, he would not be able to win the election; thus his seat would be lost — probably for a long time to come — to the Republican Party.

After Mrs. Heckler made up her mind to run, she still hoped that the "emotional problems" would be resolved by Mr. Martin himself deciding not to seek re-election. And indeed, a few days before she was scheduled to announce her candidacy, a testimonial dinner was planned for the Congressman at which Mrs. Heckler thought he would probably take himself out of the running.

Quite the reverse happened. Martin showed no inclination to step aside. To make matters worse for Mrs. Heckler, John Volpe, the titular head of the Republican Party in Massachusetts, who was running again for the office he had lost two years earlier to Governor Endicott Peabody, spoke at the dinner and firmly declared that no one should have the effrontery even to consider running against Joseph W. Martin for the House of Representatives.

Since there were no other Republican candidates for the office on the horizon, Volpe's unequivocal statement was clearly intended to rap the knuckles of the young pretender from Wellesley. "This was really a hard blow," Mrs. Heckler recalls. "I was crushed,

especially because I had been such a supporter of Governor Volpe's
— really a believer."

It was too late, however, for her to turn back, even if she had
wanted to, so, in announcing her candidacy at the scheduled press
conference a few days later, Margaret Heckler took the offensive.
Mincing no words, she hit back at Volpe for attempting to dictate
his views and thus to interfere with the right of the voters to express
their preference at a primary election.

Her bold, political riposte produced headlines, giving her a send-
off in the press which she might not have had if Volpe had not
sparked the controversy.

As in all such conflicts, there was another side of the coin, however. The full story, known to the regulars within the Republican
Party, explains Volpe's reluctance to endorse the candidacy of
Margaret Heckler. For years another Republican, a popular, able
state senator named John Parker, had been widely regarded as the
obvious successor to Joe Martin. Parker was a close friend of Martin's, so naturally he had never considered running against him.
Martin, of course knew this; he, too, wanted Parker to succeed him,
but in 1966 he had told him that, rumors to the contrary, he was
going to run one more time.

Meanwhile, Governor Volpe appealed to his trusted friend
Johnny Parker to take over the Republican State Committee chairmanship for a year or so to try to get the house in order. Believing
that he would have to wait for Martin's retirement in 1968, Parker
agreed. So when Mrs. Heckler announced her intention of running
for Martin's seat, Parker was locked solidly into his overriding party
obligations and could not contest her. Few people think Mrs. Heckler could have won the nomination against Parker. Some even
say that it was because she knew he was handcuffed for that particular election that she made her decision to run. Governor Volpe
obviously felt very sorry for having unwittingly put Parker in such
a bad position; hence he did everything he could to discourage Margaret Heckler. She herself does not mention Johnny Parker in des-

cribing her own conflicts at the time. But, in fact, there is no reason why she should, or why she should be faulted for seizing the moment that seemed the most propitious to her own interests. She, after all, owed little or nothing to the Republican hierarchy.

Meanwhile her candidacy received an unexpected boost. A letter came to her one day, written in a shaky hand, by a man who identified himself as the one-time administrative assistant to Congressman William S. Greene of Fall River, who had been Joseph Martin's predecessor in the House of Representatives. In 1924 when Congressman Greene was eighty-three years old, the letter said, Joe Martin, then a thirty-nine-year-old publisher and former state legislator, faced a situation identical to Mrs. Heckler's present one. Martin had resolved it by putting sentiment aside and contesting the old gentleman in the primary. The letter suggested that if Mrs. Heckler felt this little known historical coincidence might now be useful, she could verify the facts at the public library. In the *Fall River Herald* of July 23, 1924, she found Joe Martin's announcement of his candidacy:

> After very careful deliberation, I have decided to become a candidate for the Republican nomination for Representative in Congress. . . . The office of Congressman is one which presents an opportunity for real service to the people. . . . It is a position for one in vigorous health if the people are to be adequately served. . . . I am sure this is not a time for sentiment but the time to put on guard the men best capable of rendering efficient service. Too much is at stake to do otherwise. . . .

Martin's statement then went on to predict that his old and good friend President Coolidge would be triumphantly elected in November — which he was, by a 54.5 per cent majority.

Mrs. Heckler could hardly believe her good fortune at having this political bonanza fall into her lap; she exploited it fully, gearing her whole primary campaign to the stand which her opponent had taken forty-two years earlier.

Still she was by no means out of the woods. She had no ideological differences with Martin; there were no real issues. Any mention of Martin's age and general disability was taboo, since she realized the importance of treating her opponent with all the proper respect due him. She was, therefore, obliged to conduct a very mild, understated campaign, one which she feels would have been difficult, if not impossible, for a *man* to sustain. But as a woman she had the distinct advantage of being looked on as "delicate," when a man, in similar circumstances, would doubtless have been considered flaccid.

On the night of the primaries, early returns from Fall River, Martin's stronghold in the sprawling Tenth District, showed that Mrs. Heckler had made no substantial gains in enemy territory; the Congressman was far ahead of her. Once again Governor Volpe, who seemed singularly inept in his public utterances on the subject of Mrs. Heckler, said on television, when asked about her poor early showing, that he was not surprised, he had told Margaret she should not run and he did not expect her to win.

Most people in the greater Boston area — those who were not actually in the Tenth District — had been vaguely aware that a young woman from Wellesley was running against Joe Martin, but few had given the matter much thought. When they awoke on the morning of September 14, 1966, and found that Martin had been unseated they were stunned, and in many cases affronted. Who was this Margaret Heckler anyway? What had she ever done?

The plain fact was she had not done very much. True, she had been on the Governor's Council, but by 1966 that body had been so downgraded that membership on it hardly constituted a recommendation. And apart from that, Mrs. Heckler had had little or no experience to qualify her as a congressional candidate. Compared with Martha Griffiths and Patsy Mink at the time of their first elections to the House, she was a neophyte.

But Mrs. Heckler herself felt no sense of inadequacy as she faced the prospect of jumping from obscurity to the House of Representatives. For, if her public credentials were slim, her assets as a private citizen were not. Her home life was well organized. Her husband, an established stockbroker, was strongly in favor of her career. Her three beautiful children, aged nine, seven, and six, were well cared for by the Norwegian girls the Hecklers imported each year to live with the family and act as mother's helper. She had been a practicing lawyer for ten years, having established her own firm with some of her law school classmates when she discovered the paucity of openings for women lawyers in Boston's "best" and staid law firms. At Boston College Law School she had been editor of the law review and an active competitor in the Moot Court. She had studied for a year as an exchange student at the University of Leyden in Holland.

Perhaps the experience from her past that most buoyed her up as she faced her future was her participation, as an undergraduate in college, in the Connecticut Intercollegiate Student Legislature.

Many states have student legislatures which follow exactly the bicameral pattern of the regularly constituted state legislature. Connecticut has a particularly active and effective student organization. Delegates from colleges throughout the state are elected — 177 to the house and 36 to the senate.

In 1950 when Margaret O'Shaughnessy was a sophomore and a political science major at Albertus Magnus, a small Catholic women's college in Connecticut, she was elected a delegate to the student house. The following year, setting a pattern which she has consistently followed in her "real" political life, she decided to attempt the impossible and run for speaker of the house.

A girl had never been elected to that high office, and moreover, as a delegate from a very small college, she had far less home support than the delegates running against her from large, well-known institutions. But undaunted, Miss O'Shaughnessy, whose determinedly vivacious manner and tendency to chatter sometimes conceal her will of iron, campaigned at Yale, Trinity, Connecticut College for Women, Wesleyan — in fact at all the colleges in the state.

Her campaign manager, then a student at Fairfield University in Fairfield, Connecticut, was John M. Heckler.*

Meanwhile, in preparation for the duties of her office, Margaret set about learning *Robert's Rules of Order.* By the time she was elected speaker she had mastered the procedural complexities of her job so thoroughly that she was able to keep iron control over a "house" made up almost entirely of obstreperous male undergraduates. Indeed her initial session as speaker must have been eminently successful, for the *Hartford Courant* the next day ran a front-page story on the student legislature under the headline, "A Woman's Place is in The House."

So, in 1966, why not the House in Washington?

But first Margaret Heckler had to defeat the Democratic candidate from the Tenth Massachusetts District, no easy task as it turned out. Despite all her efforts to keep the tone of the primary campaign high, a residue of bitterness remained in the hearts of some Republicans, particularly in the Fall River area, where many staunch Joe Martin and Johnny Parker adherents simply decided to sit the election out, or in some cases to cross the line and vote in protest for the Democratic candidate Patrick J. Harrington.

Although politicians always like to build up the candidates they have defeated in order to make their own achievement more impressive, Mrs. Heckler did, in fact, have a formidable opponent in Harrington, who was a reputable, popular lawyer and had for many years been a county commissioner. "One of the worst handicaps I faced with him was that he looked so much like the image of a Congressman," she says ruefully. "He was tall and attractive and had white hair, although he wasn't too old, but just old enough."

Harrington exploited his mature, seasoned image in contrast to his thirty-five-year-old opponent's youthful looks, until finally Mrs. Heckler answered back. She did not think, she snapped, that can-

---

* Fortunately she married him, for in Massachusetts "You need an O'Shaughnessy on the Governor's Council" would have been advocating coals to Newcastle.

didates should be judged by the color of their hair. And for that matter, she added, her own hair might be just as silver as her worthy opponent's, but only her hairdresser would know it and her hairdresser was not telling.

Harrington, a strong Democratic Party man, was also receiving considerable help from the Kennedy organization in the state. By that time it was well known that Margaret Heckler's stock with the Republican Party leaders was not high, a circumstance which she exploited, playing up her underdog position. In effect, she campaigned against the smoke-filled-room-party-politician image, while skillfully (and truthfully) projecting herself as the proven choice of the people, not the ward heelers.

By a narrow margin she turned out, on election day, to be just that.

On January 10, 1967, she was sworn in as a member of the Congress of the United States, having never lost an election and having never received anything but discouragement from the Republican Party leadership.

As the somewhat implausible successor to Joe Martin, and as the only new woman member of the 90th Congress, Mrs. Heckler received more than passing notice from her colleagues in the House. Although she admits to some apprehensions about the sort of reception she would get in Washington, she did not make her entrance as a bashful freshman, feeling her way carefully along unfamiliar ground. She came in bustling, energetic, and, as is her wont, aiming high.

She announced that she hoped to be assigned to the prestigious Judiciary Committee, on which only one woman had ever served. "It's such an important committee," a Boston newspaper quoted her as saying, "and I'm the only woman lawyer." She was not, of course, the only woman lawyer. Nor was she appointed to the Judiciary, but instead to two committees more customary for freshman members — Government Operations and Veterans Affairs.

Even if Congresswoman Heckler was not exactly a retiring newcomer, she hardly expected to be called upon to deliver her maiden speech in the House only one week to the day after she was sworn in, nor to be involved, as she was, in a case that was making headlines throughout the nation.

One of her constituents, a Czech-born, naturalized American named Vladimir Kazan-Komarek had, in mid-November, been seized in Prague, charged with having engaged in subversive activities against Czechoslovakia. Kazan-Komarek, a travel agent who lives in Wellesley, had been returning from a meeting in Moscow when his Soviet plane detoured to make an unscheduled stop in Prague, where he was taken from the plane, arrested, and held incommunicado.

State Department officials were assisted in their efforts to obtain his release by the two Massachusetts Senators, Edward M. Kennedy and Edward W. Brooke, and by Mrs. Heckler, whose assignment was to keep in minute by minute touch with the anxious Kazan-Komarek family in Wellesley and to act as liaison between them and other participants in Washington. President Johnson, meanwhile, attempted to play as conciliatory a role as possible in order not to disturb East-West bridge-building efforts.

On January 17, 1967, the matter came before the House. Margaret Heckler, speaking on very short notice, called for strong action against the Czechoslovakian government for their patent violation of the human rights of an individual and for their disregard for the code of the community of nations.

Kazan-Komarek was released by the Czech government early in February and returned to the United States. This happy ending came about largely through the efforts of Senator Kennedy, but Mrs. Heckler, by her sympathetic and effective action, also contributed substantially.

In this realm, as servant of the people whose interests she is sworn to uphold, the young Congresswoman has, so far, shown up to her best advantage. Serving one's constituents is, as has been pointed out elsewhere on these pages, the most direct and rewarding performance of duty in which a Representative can engage. That it is also an indispensable tool for re-election does not downgrade the importance of the service *per se.*

Margaret Heckler has been quick to establish a rapport with her district. In the first summer of her first term she initiated a weekly telephone "hot line," a direct link between herself in Washington and her constituents in Massachusetts. On Tuesdays residents of the Tenth District may go either to Congresswoman Heckler's Newton or to her Fall River district office and wait their turn to air their grievances, or seek advice, counsel, or solace from their elected Representative, sitting in her Washington office, her ear attuned to the solution of their problems.

A family in Fall River hopes to bring over a sister from Lebanon; a remedial reading teacher in Taunton wishes to expand her project with Federal Title I or Title III Education funds; a town administrator wants to develop a local conservation project; a veteran needs housing for his parents. All these citizens queue up in Mrs. Heckler's district offices to telephone their problems to her. And she does more than just answer them well. She *acts* in their behalf.

By her imaginative response to the individual needs of her constituents, Margaret Heckler already appears to have mastered one important function of her office. In another sphere it is difficult, and perhaps unfair, after so short a time, to assess her grasp of the issues.

Her first vote of record, on the day she was sworn in, was her vote in favor of the ouster of Adam Clayton Powell. As a result of her experience on the Governor's Council in Massachusetts, she is very vocal (some have called it self-righteous) on the subject of ethics in government and on "the importance of opening the broom closet for inspection."

She thinks of herself as a moderate Republican and espouses the political philosophy of a distinguished fellow Massachusetts legislator, Leverett Saltonstall, who called himself a "liberal in human values and a conservative in fiscal policy."

Although she has often been spoken of as a hawk in regard to Vietnam, she clearly altered this impression during a television interview in February, 1968, when she came out with a hard-hitting blast at the administration and at General Westmoreland, who she said was "engaged in the vain art of self-delusion." She called for a "serious re-examination" of General James Gavin's enclave proposal. In the same interview she also surprised some political observers by stating unequivocally that Governor Rockefeller would be her party's Presidential candidate. Since she had previously expressed the view that Governor Reagan would make a good Vice President, she was apparently pushing the so-called "dream-ticket" for all it was worth.

Margaret Heckler has great admiration for Senator Margaret Chase Smith, and perhaps envisages her own career running along parallel lines. Already there are certain similarities, in addition to the first grass-roots campaign mentioned earlier. Mrs. Heckler, like Senator Smith, has never been a favorite of Republican Party leaders, nor has either woman lost an election. Mrs. Smith is a loner who keeps her own counsel. In some quarters, particularly as far as press relations are concerned, Mrs. Heckler is gaining a similar reputation of aloofness.

Her manner is very pleasant, as is Senator Smith's, yet neither woman gives the impression of candor. Evasiveness is not, of course, an unusual trait in politicians; in fact a certain overlay of cant is implicit. But in Mrs. Heckler the outward veneer is sometimes transparently thin. However, being the bright, clever, and resourceful woman that she is, she will undoubtedly learn to gloss it over more effectively as time goes on and her career moves onward and upward, as it is certain to do.

The talk in Massachusetts is that Margaret Heckler has well-laid plans to make an assault on the State House. Mrs. Heckler denies this. In addition to the usual protestations about wanting only to serve the people of her district and to make a meaningful contribution as a Congresswoman, she will admit to only one further ambition, and when she speaks of this her eyes sparkle with genuine enthusiasm.

"I have one daughter, my oldest child, who is superior in everything she does from athletics to academics. She's just a darling little girl. But the best thing she has is a great feeling for humanity and a heart that goes out to everyone. So, now finally I have found my ambition. I'd like us to be the first mother and daughter combination in Congress."

LET JUSTICE BE DONE

Constance Baker Motley

In JACKSON, MISSISSIPPI, the newspapers called her "the Motley woman." Constance Baker Motley had come to the state in the spring of 1961 as counsel for James Meredith in his fight to enter the University of Mississippi. She was then associate counsel of the NAACP Legal Defense Fund, second only to chief counsel Thurgood Marshall; she had, for the past twelve years, been directly involved with each of the Defense Fund's school and college segregation cases in the South; she had argued and won the first of her ten cases before the Supreme Court of the United States. Still, in Mississippi she was "the Motley woman." And in the courtroom, opposition lawyers called her either "Constance" or "Motley."

One such unreconstructed Southerner, with a name straight out of Faulkner, was Dugas Shands, the assistant attorney general of Mississippi. On one occasion, in the course of the twenty-two trips Mrs. Motley made to Mississippi for the Meredith case, she happened to meet Shands at the airport. He had been ill, and in her friendly, natural way, she went over to greet him and to inquire about his health. Unconsciously she extended her hand. Derrick Bell, Mrs. Motley's young associate in the Legal Defense Fund, was present. He recalls: "Her hand just sort of stayed out there. But Connie showed no embarrassment." She looked at Dugas Shands and then as casually as if she were saying, Oh, of course, I forgot, you don't take cream in your coffee do you? she said, "Oh, that's right, Mr. Shands. You don't shake hands with Negroes, do you?"

The line, especially as delivered in Constance Motley's flat, unemotional voice, must have rattled Dugas Shands. He turned quickly to Jess Brown, the local Negro lawyer associated with Mrs. Motley and Mr. Bell on the case. "Jess," he said, "you tell Constance that out here in public like this I can't shake hands with her, and I'm sorry."

With a forbearance which has been characteristic of the Legal Defense Fund staff, Derrick Bell explains the assistant district attorney's attitude. "Nothing in the Southern lawyers' background could have prepared them for Connie. To them Negro women were either mammies, maids, or mistresses. None of them had ever dealt with a Negro woman on a peer basis, much less on a level of intellectual equality, which in this case quickly became superiority."

By her superb preparation, by her persistence in the face of overwhelming obstacles, by her straightforward, courteous approach, and by never losing her cool, Mrs. Motley managed, throughout the fifteen years she tried cases in the South, to put the opposition at a disadvantage and thus to triumph.

Now she sits on the other side of the bench. Her extraordinary composure is today apparent when, as Judge Motley, she enters a courtroom in New York's Federal Building. One quickly senses the poise and intelligence of this tall, handsome, Junoesque woman, although her judicial role does not offer much opportunity for the lively grin and the cheerful humor which have so endeared Constance Motley to her family, friends, clients, colleagues, and associates. Even from the bench her serenity is manifest. She has the calm of a woman whose sense of purpose has been fulfilled.

For Constance Baker set her goal early. She was a high school girl in New Haven, Connecticut, in 1938 when the Supreme Court for the first time in the twentieth century ruled on a civil rights issue. The case concerned a Negro named Gaines who had applied for admission to the all-white University of Missouri Law School. Since the separate-but-equal doctrine required the state to offer equivalent education to Negroes and whites, the university refused him admission but met the problem, as they had met similar ones in the past, by offering to pay Gaines's tuition at any law school outside the state that would accept him. Gaines challenged the constitutionality of the University's action; when the case reached the Su-

preme Court it ruled, in a decision written by Chief Justice Charles
Evans Hughes, that the state of Missouri must provide an equal education for Negroes *within its borders.*

Constance Baker was an alert sixteen-year-old, curious, and interested in everything going on around her. Eager to learn, she
went to all the meetings and forums offered at the local community centers and Y's. One evening shortly after the Gaines case a
Negro lawyer spoke at the Dixwell community center on the significance of the Court's decision. Though hardly a revolutionary
judgment, it was considered a wedge which might eventually open
the way for application to racial issues of the Fourteenth Amendment's guarantee of equal protection under the law.

Listening to the talk that evening, Constance Baker made a decision about her future; she wanted to be a lawyer and to work
in the area of civil rights. It was one thing to make the decision,
however, and another to implement it. She was one of eleven children in a family of limited means; her father was a chef at Yale University whose salary could hardly be stretched to include college
educations for his numerous children.

When she graduated from high school, Constance decided to
work for a year or so in the hope of saving enough money to go to
college if she could get a scholarship. She made her first attempt to
find a job, and answered an advertisement for a dentist's assistant
which stipulated that no previous experience was required. She
phoned the dentist who told her to come right over for an interview. His office was three blocks from her house, and she left immediately. When she arrived he gave her a startled look; he was
sorry but he had just filled the position. Constance Baker did not
protest. She had hardly expected better, and, in fact, the only job
she was finally able to get in New Haven was one with the National
Youth Administration. Then, quite unexpectedly, after she had
been working there for a year and a half, the entire course of her
life changed.

One evening she went to a meeting at the community center in

Dixwell, the Negro section of New Haven. The center had been made possible in large part by an industrialist named Clarence Blakeslee, who was present that evening, since the meeting had been called specifically to discuss why the Negroes in Dixwell were taking so little interest in their center.

Eighteen-year-old Constance Baker thought she knew the reason why, and she got to her feet and gave it. Negroes took little interest in the center, she suggested, because they were given no responsibility for running it. All the members of the board were either from Yale or were downtown business people. All were white. Negroes could hardly be expected to care greatly about something which was not really theirs.

Many of those present that evening thought that the girl had been rude to attack their benefactor to his face. Fortunately, Mr. Blakeslee felt differently. He made inquiries and found, among other things, that Constance Baker had been an honor student in high school. The next day he sent for her. He had been very much impressed, he said, with the way she spoke last night. Listening to her, he had remembered that Abraham Lincoln once said that God's greatest gift to the nation was an independent voice. He was prepared, he told the astounded girl, to pay for her education for as long as she wanted, to college and graduate school.

Happily Clarence Blakeslee lived long enough to see the end of a chapter in history which his protégé helped to write. He died in 1954 at the age of ninety-four, just after the Supreme Court ruled in *Brown* v. *Board of Education* that segregation in public schools was unconstitutional.

Constance Baker decided to go South for at least part of her education. If she was to work for racial equality, she recognized that she would need to know and understand far more than she did about American Negroes. Her experience at the age of twenty was limited. The Negro community in New Haven was small, she had traveled very little outside the state, and, furthermore, her parents, who came from the island of Nevis in the British West Indies, reflected an outlook which was more European than American.

She chose to go to Fisk University in Nashville, Tennessee, because she had read that it was one of the best of the Negro colleges and one of the first to be established after the Civil War. At Fisk she had the opportunity to associate for the first time with middle-class Negro students. For a young girl who had known working-class people almost exclusively, it was a revelation to meet Negroes whose parents and grandparents had had the benefits of a college education.

At the same time she met a kind of hostility toward Negroes that she had never before experienced. In Connecticut there were certainly many whites who did not like Negroes and who refused to hire them, but the concept of the Negro as an inferior species of the human race was unknown to her until she went South, where vestiges of this nineteenth-century anthropological view still prevailed.

It was characteristic of the ambitious Miss Baker that, once on her way, she was determined to compensate for the time she had missed by working after her graduation from high school. She therefore elected to go to college the year round in order to complete her undergraduate program in two and a half years. She entered Fisk in February of 1941, remained until June, 1942, when she transferred to New York University and graduated from there in the fall of 1943 in time to enter Columbia Law School.

While at Columbia she met Joel Motley, who was studying law at New York University. They were married after her graduation, in August, 1946. During law school Joel Motley had been working in a real estate and insurance company; with marriage came the need to make a living, and he chose to remain in the real estate business. Today, he has his own company.

The Motleys live, with their teen-age son Joel, Jr., in a spacious apartment on West End Avenue in New York, and spend all their weekends in Chester, Connecticut, where they have recently acquired a charming eighteenth-century house set on a large, wooded piece of property which has a stream and two lakes — one for swimming, the other for fishing. Mrs. Motley is glad to be near her eighty-year-old mother, who still lives in New Haven, as do four of her five sisters and her two brothers.

Although she came of a large family herself, Constance Motley realized even before she was married that she could not be an activist in the field of civil rights and a busy mother as well. She chose therefore to have a small family and to organize her life so that she could devote all of her free time to her only child while he was growing up. Today Joel Motley, Jr., bears out the wisdom of his mother's choice. A poised, alert, attractive youngster, he was president of his class at the Dalton School in New York and is now a popular, successful student at Phillips Exeter Academy.

His mother made certain, however, that his relatively secure and shielded existence would not blind him to the realities of Negroes' existence elsewhere. She took him with her on one of her many trips to Mississippi where, for the first time in his life, Joel learned what it meant to be chased off a park bench in a white section of Jackson.

Constance Baker Motley started working as a clerk for the NAACP Legal Defense and Education Fund, Inc. (variously referred to as the Inc, the Fund, or the Inc Fund) while she was in her last year at Columbia Law School. After graduation she moved to a full-time position there, the first woman to join the staff, which at that time consisted of only three other full-time lawyers: Thurgood Marshall, now an Associate Justice of the United States Supreme Court, Edward Dudley, now a New York State Supreme Court justice, and Robert Carter, now general counsel for the NAACP. Although the NAACP is the parent body, it is quite distinct from the tax-exempt Legal Defense Fund, which serves not only the NAACP but other organizations and unaffiliated individuals as well. Since its inception in 1938 the Defense Fund has been widely regarded as the legal arm of the entire civil rights movement. Today it employs seventeen full-time lawyers, all experts in the laws of race relations. In fact, as Anthony Lewis of the *New York Times* once pointed out, "It might be more accurate to say creators of race relations law, for the Fund's lawyers over the years framed most of the civil rights cases that gave concrete meaning to the Constitution's generalities."

Remarkable timing seems often to have played a decisive part in Mrs. Motley's career. Her story during the seventeen years she served as a member of the Legal Defense staff is the story of the civil rights movement in America. In 1947 when Constance Baker Motley joined their staff, the Legal Defense Fund had just embarked on the Sweatt-University of Texas case, which was to mark the beginning of their program to strike down segregation at the graduate professional school level.

The Gaines case had established that the states must offer qualified Negro residents a legal education within their borders. Accordingly when Herman Sweatt, a Negro, applied to the University of Texas Law School, the state could not offer to send him to a university in another state for his legal education, nor would they admit him to the all-white University of Texas Law School. What they did was to set up a *separate law school* for him alone in the basement of a building in Austin, Texas.

The Defense Fund's argument in this case, supported by the Dean of the Harvard Law School and others, was that the University of Texas could not provide an equal education for Negroes in a separate and necessarily isolated situation, since the essential ingredient of a legal education was the opportunity for students to discuss the law with their peers and others with whom they would be associated professionally in later life.

In 1950 the Supreme Court upheld the Defense Fund's contention. It ruled that Sweatt had been offered separate but far from equal education. The decision, written by Chief Justice Fred M. Vinson, said that the white law school "obviously possessed to a far greater degree those qualities which are incapable of measurement but which make for greatness in a law school . . . reputation of the

faculty, experience of the administration, position and influence of
the alumni, standing in the community, traditions and prestige."

The Legal Defense Fund pressed on. From the graduate and professional schools they moved to the college level with cases in Dela-
ware and Maryland; then to the elementary school, filing briefs in
South Carolina, Virginia, and Kansas. These cases, designed to
challenge the separate-but-equal doctrine, and to test the constitutionality of segregation, led to the 1954 Supreme Court *Brown*
v. *Board of Education* decision.

In 1896 the Supreme Court had defined its position in regard to
protection under the law as it applied to Negroes in the precedent-
setting *Plessy* v. *Ferguson* decision. In 1890 the state of Louisiana
had enacted a Jim Crow transportation law. Shortly thereafter
Homer Plessy, who was part Negro, entered a railway car which
was reserved for whites only, took a seat, and was promptly arrested.
Plessy challenged the constitutionality of the state law, but when
the case finally reached the Supreme Court, it ruled by a vote of seven
to one that the statute was valid. The majority opinion, written by
Charles Evans Hughes, held that "the underlying fallacy" of
Plessy's argument was its "assumption that the enforced separation of
the two races stamps the colored race with a badge of inferi-
ority. . . ." Further, the majority held, "a statute which implies
merely a legal distinction between the white and colored races . . .
has no tendency to destroy the legal equality of the two races."

Only Justice John Harlan in his dissenting opinion foresaw that the
consequences of this separate-but-equal doctrine would arouse
racial hatred and "stimulate aggressions . . . upon the admitted
rights of colored citizens."

Fifty-eight years later Thurgood Marshall, who was one of the
lawyers arguing for the plaintiffs in *Brown* v. *Board of Education*,
called upon the Court to "meet the Plessy doctrine head on and
declare that it is erroneous. It stands mirrored today," Marshall as-
serted, "as a legal aberration, the faulty conception of an era dominated by provincialism." It was Constance Baker Motley's remark-

ably good fortune to have been associated with Marshall and with Robert Carter in the preparation of this historic case, which augured a profound change in American society.

On May 17, 1954, the Court handed down its unanimous decision. "We conclude," ran the key phrase in the opinion read by Chief Justice Earl Warren, "that in the field of public education the doctrine of separate but equal has no place."

The Supreme Court's decision was followed by its implementation decree, a gradualist document which stated that the federal district courts were to be guided by the principle of "practical flexibility" in enforcement of the desegregation decisions. Admission to public schools and colleges on a non-discriminatory basis was to proceed with "all deliberate speed."

The law of the land was now clear, but the phrases "practical flexibility" and "deliberate speed" were hardly designed to make compliance automatic. On the contrary, efforts toward enforcement met with open defiance in the South. Two forces epitomized the conflict: the National Association for the Advancement of Colored People on the one hand and the White Citizens' Councils on the other.

Paradoxically, it was the Negroes, with little or no reason to believe in our democratic system, who nonetheless clung firmly to the orderly *procedures* of that system in order to effect a change in their own way of life. The establishment, who represented organized society in the South, behaved in many instances with total disregard for law and order.

Constance Baker Motley's own faith in the system and in orderly procedures is fundamental. She was prepared to devote all her prodigious energies, her unyielding determination, and her wide legal skills to assure that the Merediths, the Hunters, the Holmeses, the Gantts, and all other Southern Negroes who came after them as test cases, would be adequately rewarded for their willingness to fight for their legal rights in a democratic society.

The first Negro to apply was a young girl named Autherine

Lucy, who tried to enter the University of Alabama. Mrs. Motley assisted Thurgood Marshall on the case, and eventully they gained a tenuous admission for their client. But when constant harassment of Miss Lucy gave way to bitter rioting, the University expelled the Negro girl as a "troublemaker." A federal judge ordered her reinstated, but by then the strain had proved too much for the girl. Marshall and Mrs. Motley took her back to New York for a rest. She never returned to Alabama; instead she went to Texas and married. Nevertheless, Autherine Lucy's name remains inscribed in the history of that decade as the first to have nudged the door open a crack.

For the next ten years, Mrs. Motley worked unceasingly to bring about compliance with the law in the South. In five states, Alabama, Florida, Oklahoma, Georgia, and South Carolina, she played a key role in opening the universities to Negroes. At the elementary school level she represented Negro children in twelve Southern and three Northern states. She worked in housing, transportation, sit-in cases, and protest demonstration cases throughout the South, representing, among other notables, the Reverend Ralph Abernathy, the Reverend Fred Shuttleworth, and the Reverend Martin Luther King, Jr., all of whom had been arrested in demonstrations.

During this period she was once introduced to an audience at Columbia University as a leader in the civil rights movement. When she rose to accept the introduction she began by saying, "I'm afraid I'm not really a leader in the civil rights movement. I'm just the one who gets the leaders out of jail."

Another woman lawyer and former municipal judge, Dorothy Kenyon, who was present that evening and is Constance Motley's admiring friend, wrote to her a few days later, "You get the leaders out of jail and their children into college."

Probably the case which brought Mrs. Motley the greatest renown was the admission of James Meredith to the University of Mississippi in 1962. In this trial, as in all others concerned with segregation, the law was perfectly clear and straightforward. Qualified Negroes had to be admitted to public institutions of learning. What the opposing lawyers sought to do was to interpose a stupefyingly large array of procedural and technical objections with a view to thwarting the obvious intent of the law.

In his brilliant decision reversing the lower court order and ruling in Meredith's favor, Judge John Minor Wisdom of the Fifth Circuit Court of Appeals wrote:

> A full review of the record leads the Court inescapably to the conclusion that from the moment the defendants [i.e., the University of Mississippi] discovered Meredith was a Negro they engaged in a carefully calculated campaign of delay, harassment, and masterly inactivity. It was a defensive designed to discourage and to defeat by evasive tactics which would have been a credit to Quintus Fabius Maximus.

Judge Wisdom then went on to detail the "defendant's Fabian policy of planned discouragement and discrimination" as evidenced by the correspondence between Meredith and the University. Meredith first wrote to the registrar at Ole Miss asking for an application form on the day after John F. Kennedy was inaugurated on January 20, 1961. His request was promptly and politely answered; an application form and instructions were enclosed.

At the time, James Meredith was a student in his second term at the Negro Jackson State College in Jackson, Mississippi. During nine previous years in the Air Force he had successfully completed numerous extension courses offered by various colleges for members of the armed services.

On January 31st Meredith submitted his formal application to the University of Mississippi. In a covering letter he stated that he was "an American, a Mississippian, and a Negro citizen," that he was sending transcripts of his grades from the other colleges he had attended and that he believed his application was complete, with one exception. He could not furnish the University with the names of six Ole Miss alumni who could vouch for him, since he did not know any graduates of the all-white University. In lieu of this requirement, however, he was submitting six certificates attesting to his moral character obtained from Negro citizens of the state.

Four days later Meredith received a telegram from Robert B. Ellis, the registrar, stating that "it has been found necessary to discontinue consideration of all applications for admission or registration for the second semester which were received after January 25, 1961. . . ."

Meanwhile, at the behest of the late Medgar Evers, who was then NAACP field secretary in Mississippi, Meredith had written to the Legal Defense Fund stating his intention to apply to the University of Mississippi. Shortly after he forwarded his telegram of rejection to the New York office, Constance Baker Motley was assigned to the case.

"Her assignment," wrote Meredith in his book, *Three Years in Mississippi*, "is the best possible thing that could have happened. I do not believe anyone else could have survived two and a half years of Mississippi courts."

In all of her Southern segregation cases Constance Motley operated on a seemingly simple principle: Make no mistakes, leave no loopholes, and you are certain to win since the law is plainly on your side.

Her correspondence with James Meredith reflects her rigid adherence to this rule. She had made a careful study of the catalogue of the University of Mississippi, she wrote Meredith in an early letter, and had noted on page 83 that his transcripts from the other universities he had attended must certify *both* honorable dismissal *and* eligibility for immediate readmission. She wished him to note carefully the residence requirements on pages 122 and 123. She called his attention to the requirement on page 82 which said that his letters of recommendation from responsible citizens must certify to his good moral character *and* specifically recommend his admission to the University. "I realize that you cannot comply with the requirements regarding certification from the alumni," she wrote, "and you have already so advised the registrar. We have already won a case in Georgia on the alumni certification point. But as to the other requirements it is absolutely essential that you comply with all of them prior to bringing suit. Otherwise the case could be dismissed. . . . This is the reason for my pressing you. . . . Please write me immediately, regarding these points. . . ."

Fortunately Meredith was both an orderly and a diligent young man. "I burned a little midnight oil," he wrote Mrs. Motley, "but I hope that the reward will be to furnish you with satisfactory answers to your questions."

When she was convinced that he had covered all the bases Mrs. Motley wrote Meredith that according to another page in the catalogue (which she must by then have memorized), the committee on admissions should, since he was a transfer student, provide him at this point with an evaluation of the credits acceptable at the University. "You should write the registrar immediately requesting him to send you this evaluation."

Meredith did so, and on May 9 the registrar, in his first communication since February 4, sent Meredith a letter stating that of the ninety semester hours he offered, forty-eight were considered acceptable. He was given no credit for his work at the Negro Jackson State College, which is part of the state's educational complex. The registrar was quick to add that his evaluation was in no way a final determination, but since forty-eight credits were more than enough to admit Meredith as a sophomore, Mrs. Motley considered that the letter clearly indicated he was officially qualified for admission.

But on May 25 Meredith received a letter which began: "I regret to inform you, in answer to your recent letter, that your application for admission has been denied." The letter then went on to give the alleged reasons. "The University cannot recognize transfer of credits from the institution which you are now attending, since it is not a member of the Southern Association of Colleges and Secondary Schools." No mention was made of Meredith's previously acknowledged forty-eight acceptable credits. "Furthermore," the registrar continued, "students may not be accepted from those institutions whose programs are not recognized." In effect then not only would Ole Miss not accept Meredith's credits from Jackson, but they would not accept *any* transfer students from this institution.

The fact that Jackson is a state institution, controlled by the same board of trustees that governs the University, makes this ruling an almost farcical travesty. A further irony was that the University, by its refusal to accept credits (or students) from the Negro college, was tacitly admitting to a separate but far from equal educational facility within the state. Under *Plessy* v. *Ferguson* this would have been unconstitutional. But with *Plessy* v. *Ferguson* overruled, the University was using the very unequality of their Negro facility as one of the alleged reasons for denying Meredith's admission to the white institution.

The second reason given by the registrar in his letter was that Meredith did not meet the requirements "because as I am sure you realize . . . your letters of recommendation are not sufficient." The registrar's final reason was no reason at all. "I see no need for mentioning any other deficiencies," the letter concluded.

Five days after James Meredith received this letter, Constance Baker Motley arrived in Jackson. The following day, May 31, she filed a complaint before Judge Sidney C. Mize in the United States District Court for the Southern District of Mississippi. Civil action on number 3130 was underway: "*James Howard Meredith,* on behalf of himself and others similarly situated, *Plaintiff* v. *Charles Dickson Fair,* President of the Board of Trustees of State Institutions of Higher Learning of the State of Mississippi *et al., Defendants.*"

In filing her first complaint, Mrs. Motley sought a temporary restraining order in behalf of the plaintiff, Meredith, in order that he could be admitted to the University's first summer session which was about to begin. This order was, as expected, denied, and on the plaintiff's motion for a preliminary injunction, which is the next step in the legal proceedings, the hearing was set for June 12, 1961 — four days *after* the beginning of the summer session.

Before this hearing, Assistant Attorney General Dugas Shands, who was to try the case for the defendants, took a deposition from James Meredith. This first encounter was in many ways a preview of what was to follow in the fifteen months of litigation. Shands's tone with Meredith vacillated between the patronizing and the insolent. Mrs. Motley's objections on the grounds of irrelevancy were all overruled by Judge Mize. Shands was given a free hand to give the plaintiff what Meredith calls the "Nigger treatment."

As the lunch hour approached on that day, Shands suggested that they take only a twenty-minute break in order to finish the deposition early in the afternoon. On the face of it this was an ordinary enough proposal, but the fact was that there was not a single restaurant anywhere near the courthouse where Mrs. Motley, her assistants, and her client could get a meal unless they were willing to go to the back door, as Negroes were required to do, and take away their lunches in a paper bag. Shands must have known this very well. Mrs. Motley asked him casually if he could recommend a nice restaurant nearby where they could have lunch and be back in time. The recess was quickly extended to an hour and a half to allow the prosecution side time to find a suitable Negro restaurant.

Perhaps it is worth pausing a moment to consider under what conditions Constance Baker Motley and Derrick Bell operated during the seventeen months that they shuttled back and forth between New York and Mississippi to fight the Meredith case. Apart from the constant difficulty of finding places to eat, they also had to find places to stay. In 1961 southern hotels were still segregated and Negro hotels as such either did not exist or were entirely unsuitable. The Defense Fund lawyers had to rely for their lodging on the generosity and bravery of local Negroes who opened their homes to them. Often the houses had to be guarded by other Negroes who took turns patrolling the area.

In Jackson, Mrs. Motley and Derrick Bell spent weeks at the home of a Negro named Robert Smith, who had been a stranger to them but who took them into his comfortable though small house because he cared about the movement and had faith in what they were doing. Since Smith would accept no money, Bell says that he and Mrs. Motley helped furnish his house in an attempt to repay him for his kindness; others in Jackson repaid him by throwing bricks through the windows of his grocery store.

In Biloxi, where the court also sat part of the time, Mrs. Motley had the use of a seashore cottage belonging to a friend. Here she, Bell, Meredith, and Jess Brown, the local attorney, stayed, and here she could indulge her fondness for cooking — and eating — by experimenting with all the fresh, and often quite unusual, seafood available in this Gulf town. "Some of that fish was pretty strange," Bell recalls, "but she'd make us eat it. Looking back on it though, I suppose we actually had a lot of fun."

Yet fear was always with them; everywhere, except in the courtroom, they were in danger. Walking from the car into the courthouse they were prey to a hostile crowd which surrounded them. Often they were subjected to verbal abuse which Mrs. Motley usually shrugged off with: "Just some kind of a nut." She was afraid, nonetheless. James Meredith said that she admitted as much to him when it was all over, but at the time, he said, she never showed it.

She would not let herself show it especially to Meredith, for she knew that if he, who lived in Mississippi, and thus did not fly back to the comparative sanity of New York between hearings, was willing to do what he was doing, she could do no less.

If fear was mercifully absent within the confines of the federal courtroom, frustration was ever present. From July 12, 1961, when the first hearing for a preliminary injunction began at Biloxi, Constance Motley was subjected to a staggering array of carefully planned obstacles, legal delays — euphemistically called continuations — and procedural contretemps, all part of the "calculated evasive tactics" to which Judge Wisdom referred in his final opinion. For a case of such obvious importance, for example, Judge Mize allowed only a half day on his June 12 docket for the preliminary hearing. The case was then continued until July 10, then until July 17, then until August 10, 11, and 12, and finally until August 15. For each continuance Mrs. Motley had to appear in court, often flying down from New York only to be confronted with another deliberate postponement.

In all she made fifteen different court appearances and faced innumerable legal obstructions. She was thwarted constantly in her efforts to take depositions from the defendants. On three different occasions her motion to inspect the records of students who *had* been admitted to the University of Mississippi was denied — an order which the higher court later labeled "manifestly erroneous."

Meanwhile Meredith's application to the University remained a continuing one pending the outcome of the trial. He could not, of course, enter the University in the middle of a semester, and somehow the legal continuances kept putting off decisive action until a new semester had either started or until registrations for it were closed. The net effect of the delays was that the two summer terms and the fall term of 1961 passed without the issue having been actually faced.

Judge Mize, complying with the "deliberate" but hardly with the "speed" of the Supreme Court's implementation order, took four months to render his decision following the preliminary hearing. Not unexpectedly he ruled for the University, finding that "the evidence overwhelmingly showed that the plaintiff was not denied admission to the University of Mississippi solely because of his race."

Mrs. Motley's appeal was denied by the Fifth Circuit Court. In an opinion which was sympathetic in tone, the court held that in order to "clarify the muddy record" a full-scale trial was required.

The trial, scheduled to begin on January 15, 1962, finally took place, after only three continuances, on January 24. On the stand the registrar of the University assumed a hurt posture; he was

"shocked," "surprised," and "disappointed" at the mere suggestion
that Meredith's application had been denied because of his race.
Other officials and members of the board of trustees, when examined
by Mrs. Motley, adopted the same line and firmly denied that a
policy of segregation existed at Ole Miss. In his book on the Meredith case, *A Past That Would Not Die,* Walter Lord writes:

> Constance Motley tried to pin them down. Asked if he had ever
> seen a Negro student at the University, Leston Lewis Love, Dean
> of Student Personnel, said he didn't really know "because I don't
> know the genealogical background of every person I meet."
> Asked if any had ever been admitted since his arrival in 1941,
> Vice Chancellor W. A. Bryant said he just couldn't tell — "I'm
> not an expert in the field of anthropology." Asked if he'd ever
> heard of a Negro there, Trustee Tally Riddell helpfully replied,
> "If you'll tell me what you mean by Negro, I'll try to answer it."

On the basis of such testimony Judge Mize, on February 3,
again found for the defendants and ruled against Meredith.

Time was now working in favor of the University, for at this
point Mrs. Motley faced a new dilemma for her client. In a few
weeks Meredith was due to begin his final term at Jackson State
College. Unless he could be admitted to Ole Miss for the February
term, he would graduate from Jackson in June, thereby making the
appeal of his case "moot." Mrs. Motley accordingly filed for another preliminary injunction pending the appeal, but the circuit
court, now undoubtedly even more conscious of the historic importance of the case, felt that it wished to render its decision on the
full record. It therefore denied the injunction with the suggestion
that Meredith "avoid mootness" by taking courses that would
not lead to his graduation. So, by studying such subjects as dairy
farming and animal husbandry, Meredith managed to stall off getting
his degree from Jackson while he waited for the decision from the
court of appeals.

Through all these months of harassment, Constance Motley held
to her purpose without gratifying the University's implicit hope

that she would become discouraged and founder, or that she could be trapped, through frustration, into making a mistake. On June 25, 1962, she and her associates and her client were rewarded. The Fifth Circuit Court of Appeals ruled that Meredith should be admitted to the University of Mississippi. "Reading the 1350 pages in the record as a whole," said the majority opinion, "we find that James H. Meredith's application was turned down solely because he was a Negro. . . . The judgment of the district court is reversed."

Although there was one further and very noisy legal skirmish in which Mrs. Motley was involved, she had won the battle; her major work was done, all of it accomplished before the Meredith "case" as such even became national news. And when finally the last legal bar to Meredith's admission was removed, Constance Motley could announce in triumph to the press, "This is the end of the road for the University."

But even she, with her intimate first-hand knowledge of how far Mississippians were willing to go to preserve their "sacred institutions," did not foresee the aftermath. For when the focus of resistance shifted to the state capital, the antagonists shifted too; no longer was it Meredith and the NAACP Legal Defense Fund versus Ole Miss, but Meredith and the federal government versus the sovereign state of Mississippi. Governor Ross R. Barnett's open defiance of the court order to enroll Meredith resulted in 23,000 federal troops being brought in to Oxford, Mississippi, to quell a bloody riot which lasted for fifteen hours. Three hundred and seventy-five persons were injured, including one hundred and sixty-six United States marshals. Two persons, a French newspaperman and a radio repairman bystander, were killed. All this before the rightful entrance of one slightly built, polite young Negro to the public, tax-supported university of his home state could be peaceably achieved.

A year later, when Mrs. Motley wrote a short article in *Crisis Magazine*, the official organ of the NAACP, on "Meredith in Retrospect," the aspect of his case which remained uppermost in her mind was that: "During our recent effort to secure Mr. Meredith's admission to the University of Mississippi *not a single public official of any description in Mississippi* called for respect for the law, let alone support of the integration orders of the federal courts."

Not only was there no respect for the law, there was no respect for the truth. Indeed it appears that at that time the Southern Universities' defense of their admission practices was based on the lie that no policy of segregation existed. University administrators, charged with molding both the intellectual and moral character of young students, all blandly conspired to further this lie by telling more lies.

At the University of Georgia, where Charlayne Hunter and Hamilton Holmes sought admission, the hypocrisy, while ultimately just as barefaced as it had been in Mississippi, was more subtle — or at least more complex in nature.

Arguing the case in behalf of Miss Hunter and Mr. Holmes was like putting together a jigsaw puzzle. "It's a long road with no heroics," Mrs. Motley has said. "You win by preparations and experience — that's all. Preparation and experience."

Charlayne Hunter and Hamilton Holmes first applied to the University of Georgia for admission in June, 1959, after their graduation from Turner High School, a Negro public school in Atlanta. Both had been honor students; Holmes had also been class valedictorian and a star on the football team. When they were rejected by the University, each asked that their applications be considered continuing ones pending admission at a later quarter. (The University operates on quarter rather than the semester terms.) Both students then enrolled as freshmen in other institutions; Holmes went to the Negro Morehouse College in Atlanta, and Miss Hunter to Wayne State University in Detroit.

Their status, when their case came to trial on December 13, 1960, was that both their applications as transfer students had been denied, Miss Hunter's because of the "limited facilities available," and Holmes on the basis of his personal interview during which he had, according to the University, been "evasive." The reason for the distinction in the two cases was that men were permitted to live off campus after their freshman year, so that the admittedly over-crowded dormitory conditions which served as an adequate bar to the admission of Miss Hunter would not apply to Mr. Holmes.

Since much had been made of Holmes's "unsatisfactory" inter-view, Mrs. Motley set about first to prove that the University's per-sonal interview requirement had been very loosely interpreted in respect to numerous white applicants. Armed with pertinent appli-cations culled from the 375 files she and her associate counsel, Don-ald Hallowell, had reviewed, Mrs. Motley questioned the registrar, Walter Danner, who was the named defendant in the case, about variations in the University's interviewing practice.

MRS. MOTLEY: I'll show you the interview sheet for William Robert Barbot, and the acceptance sheet for William Robert Bar-bot, and ask you if, according to the dates on these documents, Mr. Barbot was not first accepted, and then interviewed subse-quently?

MR. DANNER: The dates are Nov. 17, 1959, on the acceptance, and on the interview it is Nov. 20, 1959, and it is quite likely that you will find quite a few in our files, and if they were within two or three days even past a Tuesday we would date the applica-tion on the past Tuesday. It was our practice to mail, during most of the year, our acceptances on Tuesday of each week, and rather than waiting the following Tuesday, which would be predating it, and if a student wanted to know then we would date it back to the previous Tuesday.

MRS. MOTLEY: (To the clerk) Would you please read that answer. (Answer is read.) Mr. Danner, I frankly don't understand your answer and I would like to have you try again, if you will, to reply to that question. I'm sorry.

Being a very forthright and direct person herself, Mrs. Motley may well have been genuinely perplexed by the registrar's muddled response. She was also capable of using her bewilderment to good effect in showing up the woolly — or devious — thinking of the witness. Mr. Danner's second try was hardly more clarifying.

MR. DANNER: I don't know whether this Nov. 17th happens to be a Tuesday or not. I know that on a number of cases if a student comes in the office, we have had his application on file and say he would come in on Wednesday or Thursday, and he was acceptable and everything was in order except his interview, and he completed that that day, it is quite likely that his acceptance would be dated back to that Tuesday.

MRS. MOTLEY: What would be the purpose of that?

MR. DANNER: Well, if we did not date that one back a day or two it would be another five or six days before it would be mailed. I wouldn't want to mail one out dated — mail it out on Nov. 20 and date it Nov. 25.

MRS. MOTLEY: Well why would you want to date it Nov. 17, if he were not interviewed until the 20th?

Mrs. Motley let the registrar try to extricate himself as best he could, and then handed him various other files, including one which showed that one student had been interviewed over the telephone and another where the interview, which according to University policy could, in some out-of-state cases, be conducted by an alumnus, had been handled by the applicant's brother-in-law. Then she handed him another document.

MRS. MOTLEY: I'll show you Plaintiff's Exhibits 97 and 98. 97 is the interview sheet for Harriet Tisinger, and 98 is the acceptance. What is the date on the interview?

MR. DANNER: August 2, 1960.

MRS. MOTLEY: And what is the date on the acceptance for Harriet Tisinger?

MR. DANNER: May 31, 1960. . . .

MRS. MOTLEY: Now is there any Tuesday involved in here?

MR. DANNER: No, I don't think so. She was accepted pending the satisfactory interview when she came. Now she could have been accepted for June 13. It appears that she probably came the second term of summer school instead of the first . . .

At this point Judge William A. Bootle, the presiding district judge intervened.

THE COURT: What was the acceptance date?

MR. DANNER: June 13.

MRS. MOTLEY: No, the acceptance date was May 31, 1960, and she was interviewed August 2, 1960.

THE COURT: And then what was the June date?

MR. DANNER: That was the date she was supposed to arrive.

THE COURT: I see.

Having thus established that the University clearly did not rely to a very great extent on the personal interview as a criterion for admitting students, Mrs. Motley and Mr. Hallowell went to work on exactly what had happened in Hamilton Holmes's interview. It was anything but perfunctory. Three officials sat in on that occasion: Mr. Danner, his assistant Paul Kea, and an "admissions counselor," Morris O. Phelps. Apparently, as Judge Bootle was to point out in his opinion, the interview, which lasted for an hour, "was conducted with a purpose in mind of finding a basis for rejecting Holmes." The student was asked if he knew where the red light district in Atlanta was, if he had ever attended any tea houses or beatnik parlors, if he had ever been to a house of prostitution, or had ever attended any interracial parties. He was asked for his opinion on the school integration crisis and on the student sit-in movement. Finally he was asked if he had ever been arrested. He answered no, which was considered untruthful since he had once been fined for a speeding violation.

Although each person present at the interview testified at the trial that Holmes had answered all the questions put to him, the comment on his interview sheet was, "student was evasive with his answers. Some doubt as to his truthfulness, poor on verbal expression, and cooperativeness." *

Miss Hunter's interview, on the other hand, was stated to have been the model of cooperativeness. Although three persons were again present, she was asked more pertinent questions, and her responses were said to have been direct and polite. Clearly there was less at stake for the University in this interview, since they were confident of their ability to reject Miss Hunter as a transfer student on the grounds of "limited facilities."

Because of their overcrowded dormitory space, the University had adopted certain priorities in admitting transfer students. Category one included those students "who need a change in order to continue their academic program." Attempting to define this somewhat ambiguous guideline during the trial, Mrs. Motley asked Walter Danner, "So that, if the student is an applicant for the University of Georgia and is attending an out-of-state senior college, and cannot at that out-of-state senior college get a course which he might need to get a degree in forestry or journalism from the University of Georgia, that would be a student in this particular category, wouldn't it?" Mr. Danner agreed that it would be. Charlayne Hunter, however, was *not* considered to be in that category. Mrs. Motley's effort was therefore directed at studying the files of white applicants who *did* fall within the category to see wherein their qualifications differed from Miss Hunter's. A case in point was Miss Bebe Dobbs Brumby whose credentials — up to and including her delightful name — made her a perfect subject for comparison.

---

* It is a neat bit of irony that Hamilton Holmes's direct examination in the trial was conducted by a young Negro attorney named Horace Ward, who was an associate in Donald Hallowell's office. Ten years earlier Ward had been the first Negro to apply for admission to the University of Georgia Law School. He was denied on the grounds that he had been "evasive, inconsistent, and contradictory" in his interview.

By the summer of 1960 both Miss Hunter and Miss Brumby had completed one year's work at an out-of-state liberal arts college — Miss Hunter at Wayne State, Miss Brumby at Sophie Newcomb, the coordinate woman's college of Tulane University in New Orleans. Both young girls were interested in journalism, and although Wayne and Sophie Newcomb each offered degrees in journalism, both students wished to transfer to the University of Georgia. Both had been rejected by the University for the fall quarter of 1960 because of limited facilities. Here, however, the similarities ended. In December, 1960, at the time of the Holmes-Hunter trial, Miss Brumby, the daughter of a prominent Georgia newspaper man, was admitted to the University of Georgia for the upcoming winter quarter on the grounds that the change was necessary in order for her to continue her studies in journalism. The presumption was therefore that she could not get the courses at Sophie Newcomb that she would need as a prerequisite to her degree in journalism from the University of Georgia.

To establish that this was not in fact true, Mrs. Motley called Paul Kea, the assistant registrar charged with evaluating credits of transfer students, to the stand. Painstakingly, step by step, she led Mr. Kea through a comparison of the requirements for the degree in journalism at Georgia and Sophie Newcomb.

Mr. Kea began by being very flippant. It was not necessary, he insisted, for him to read from the University of Georgia catalogue that Mrs. Motley handed him. He could just say the requirements without reading. Would it be all right if he just held the book in his hand and then stated the requirements? Mrs. Motley calmly persevered ("What are the requirements for the degree, Mr. Kea, according to what it says in the catalogue, not to what you have in your head?") until she finally wrung from him the fact that eighty-five to ninety quarter hours of work were needed as a prerequisite for Miss Brumby to qualify as a candidate for the degree in journalism at Georgia.

She then handed him the Sophie Newcomb catalogue and established that Sophie Newcomb's prerequisite hours were also eighty-five to ninety quarter hours. By this time Mr. Kea was becoming noticeably less cocky. Still moving slowly, clarifying the requirements of the two institutions carefully, Mrs. Motley began to zero in:

> MRS. MOTLEY: I show you Plaintiff's Exhibit 22, which is your evaluation of Miss Brumby's transcript, and ask you to indicate which of these required courses for the degree of Bachelor of Arts in journalism she could not receive at Sophie Newcomb College. And I hand you the catalogue for Sophie Newcomb College in case you want to refer to it.

> MR. KEA: I would like to reiterate that this is generally the Dean's prerogative and this is strictly unofficial.

> MRS. MOTLEY: Yes, we understand that.

At that point Miss Hunter recalls she actually felt sorry for Mr. Kea. Faced with the facts which Mrs. Motley had methodically set up, he floundered. He could find only one single course, required at Georgia, which Miss Bebe Dobbs Brumby could not get at Sophie Newcomb — a course in the history and constitution of the state of Georgia.

Shortly thereafter Charlayne Hunter was called back to the stand and asked by Donald Hallowell:

> MR. HALLOWELL: Miss Hunter, can you get a course in Georgia history at Wayne State University, as required by those who are seeking to take journalism at the University of Georgia?

> MISS HUNTER: No, I can not.

It was on such miniscule, niggling little points, skillfully exploited by Mrs. Motley, that the color line was finally broken at the University of Georgia.

Opening universities and schools to Negroes was, of course, only one prong of the Legal Defense Fund's thrust to end segregation in the South. In the early 1960's Mrs. Motley was also deeply involved in numerous protest demonstration cases, the most notable ones being in Albany, Georgia, in 1962 and in Birmingham, Alabama, a year later.

The Birmingham protest was one of Martin Luther King's most impressive non-violent demonstrations; more than any other single action it was believed to have led directly to the passage of the Civil Rights Act of 1964. For many people Birmingham is perhaps best remembered as the place where City Commissioner of Public Safety Eugene "Bull" Connor unleashed his dogs and fire hoses against the Negro demonstrators.

Yet, despite the terrible provocation to retaliate, Dr. King and the Reverend Fred Shuttleworth managed to control their forces through five weeks of the integration drive, until the Birmingham Board of Education, a body which had been appointed by Bull Connor, acted to exacerbate a situation already stretched to the limit of tension. On May 20, 1963, the Board summarily arrested and then expelled or suspended 1100 Negroes from school for "parading without a permit."

The Negro community rose up in revolt, and Dr. King, faced with losing all that had been accomplished in five weeks, called in the Legal Defense Fund. Brought into the eye of the hurricane, Constance Baker Motley was presented at once with an ultimatum from the Negro leaders: "Either get our kids back to school or we'll tear up the city."

Mrs. Motley went to one mass meeting after another, assuring the infuriated Negroes that the lawyers would take immediate court action. It was May 21, and the school term was to end just ten days later. Prompt reinstatement was mandatory if the high school seniors, who had been expelled outright by the Board of Education, were to graduate on May 31 and the younger children who had been suspended were not to lose credit for the entire second term of school.

Mrs. Motley, with two Birmingham lawyers, appeared before Federal District Judge Clarence W. Allgood to file a complaint against Dr. Theo R. Wright, the superintendent of schools, and to seek a temporary restraining order against him, which, if granted, would have permitted the students to return to school the next day.

Leroy Clark of the Legal Defense Fund, who was present on that occasion, recalls that Judge Allgood first called the lawyers to his chambers to negotiate. He began by trying to engage them in a little homely conversation; he had been talking with his Negro yard boy about the whole problem, and his yard boy had told him he thought what the demonstrators were doing was wrong because it was causing everyone so much anguish. Turning to Mrs. Motley he asked, "Now do you yourself think what they're doing is right?"

Mrs. Motley, who does not react favorably to being dealt with in a patronizing manner, said coolly, "We're not here to discuss the wisdom of their actions, we're here to discuss the constitutionality. And if we can get on with it now, I think it will be better."

Judge Allgood set the hearing for the next day, May 22, at which time he refused to grant the temporary restraining order. The next step would have been for Mrs. Motley to file for a hearing on a preliminary injunction, but there was obviously no time for that procedure, which, under the best of circumstances, would have taken four or five days. So, on that same afternoon, Mrs. Motley flew from Birmingham to Atlanta to plead her case before the Fifth Circuit Court of Appeals. Six hours after Judge Allgood had denied "relief," the higher court reversed his decision. Chief Judge Elbert P. Tuttle sharply rebuked Judge Allgood for his failure to recognize that the students had been illegally arrested for exercising their constitutional rights and granted Mrs. Motley's injunction. The suspensions and expulsions were canceled. The students returned to school on May 23 to finish their school year; the seniors graduated with their class on May 31.

The Birmingham case was one of the last that Mrs. Motley argued before the Fifth Circuit Court of Appeals. For fourteen years she had devoted almost all of her prodigious energies to fighting open defiance of the law in the South; she felt that she had accomplished virtually everything she could through the courts. Though the problems still remained, most of the Southern states had complied with at least token desegregation.

By 1964, when the focus in the struggle for racial equality shifted to the North, Constance Motley, her career always following the trend of the civil rights movement, now began to turn her attention nearer home to some of the ills which confronted her race in the vast urban centers. But here, she soon realized, the problems of the ghettos, of de facto segregation and inadequate schooling, poor housing and unemployment could best be dealt with by legislative rather than judicial means.

Once again, fortune guided her own particular star. In January, 1964, James L. Watson, the Negro state senator from Mrs. Motley's district, was appointed to the New York Civil Court and resigned his post in Albany. The local Democratic club in the Twenty-first Manhattan District, which covers the Columbia University area and about one-third of central Harlem, had decided they wanted to run another Negro to fill the vacancy, but had selected a man who was poorly qualified. Later it was discovered that he had been convicted three times for his connections with the numbers racket. Learning of their choice, J. Raymond Jones, the acknowledged Negro political leader in New York, objected strenuously. Jones, a city councilman, who was shortly to become head of Tammany Hall, told the Twenty-first District leaders frankly that they would have to go out and find themselves another Negro candidate if they wanted his support.

Meanwhile two women lawyers, both active in local party affairs in the Twenty-first District, who had studied at Columbia with Constance Motley and knew that she had been considering a try at politics, put the vacancy and the woman together. Mrs. Motley was nominated and then elected in February, 1964, to become the only woman serving in the legislature in Albany and the first Negro woman ever to serve in that capacity.

She was obliged to run twice for the post in the same year, since the February election had been to fill a vacancy. In November she was elected to a regular two-year term, defeating her Republican opponent, also a Negro woman, by a seven to one majority.

Four months later, before Senator Motley could really get her feet on the ground in Albany, a new but similar set of circumstances made her the leading contender for the office of President of the Borough of Manhattan. She was nominated by the committee on vacancies to replace Edward J. Dudley, a one-time Legal Defense colleague who had been appointed to the state supreme court.

Her jump from the relative obscurity of the state senate (during a period when the Republicans controlled the legislature) to the high visibility post of Borough President came as a surprise not only to most New York politicians but to Mrs. Motley herself.

Once again J. Raymond Jones had a hand in the proceedings, and once again he fixed upon Constance Baker Motley as a compromise to block the appointment of another candidate — a bitter political foe whom Mayor Robert Wagner favored for the position. The Mayor agreed to accept Mrs. Motley, however, and when Governor Rockefeller intervened to swing the two Republicans on the city council to her side, she was elected by a five to three vote. She became the first woman President of the Borough of Manhattan, thus adding one more to her notable list of firsts.

At the time the press reported two interesting reactions to her selection: Adam Clayton Powell announced that he was not in favor of her taking the job, and, in a sense, Mrs. Motley agreed with him. Powell's objections appear to have stemmed from the fact that she had not worked her way step by step up the Negro political ladder as he had done, but had won her $35,000 position from the white establishment on the basis of past non-political accomplishments.

Mrs. Motley's reported misgivings about assuming the post were of a very different nature. On February 19, 1965, the *New York Journal American* ran a picture of Senator Motley captioned, "The Lady Protests." The text ran that "as soon as Constance Baker Motley learned that there would be a good chance that she would be elected to the Borough President post, she phoned Mayor Wagner and bluntly told him, 'Mr. Mayor, you are ruining my chances of becoming a federal judge.'"

The story is somewhat difficult to credit, for reluctant as Mrs. Motley may have been, it hardly seems her style to bandy about her own ambitions or publicly to weigh her chances of one office against another. Far more characteristic is a later statement of Mrs. Motley's concerning her possible appointment to the federal bench: "I feel it is improper to discuss the problem at this time."

It was true that Mrs. Motley was well aware that she had been proposed for a federal judgeship by Senator Robert F. Kennedy and that she was being considered for this position, which she very much wanted, at the time she was first appointed Borough President. Her appointment to the bench was still pending — was in fact an even stronger possibility — when, six months after her interim appointment, she had to run again for the Borough Presidency. This time there was an even louder hue and cry in the press that Mrs. Motley was acting in bad faith, that she would quit right after her election to accept the federal appointment, that she was in fact only running to keep the seat warm for another Democrat.

However, Mrs. Motley kept her own counsel and went ahead with the campaign. She won the primary fight, after which she was endorsed by the Democratic, Liberal, and Republican Parties for the final election. It would have been difficult not to win under the circumstances; she was re-elected on September 12, 1965.

On January 25, 1966, as had long been anticipated, she was named a federal judge. "There was a great and general sigh of relief in many city agencies yesterday," the *New York Times* noted. "Constance Baker Motley, a single-minded woman has been selected as a federal judge and the hope was that the government boat she had been rocking since she became Manhattan Borough President would sail on calmer waters."

If boat-rocking meant refusing to accept the status quo, the term was certainly applicable. Although the Borough President is a member of the Board of Estimate, the governing body of the city of New York, the position, which had once carried considerable power and responsibility, had deteriorated, since the reorganization of the city under Mayor Wagner, into a more or less ceremonial, window-dressing office. The fact that it was nonetheless a very high-paying job caused many critics to suggest that the post be abandoned altogether. Politicians, on the other hand, were very reluctant to give up such a lucrative plum.

As soon as Mrs. Motley was appointed to the job, she at once set about trying to find a new and significant role for the Borough President to play. She soon saw an opportunity in Manhattan's twelve community planning boards whose members, appointed by the Borough President, were citizens interested in city government and community improvements. The planning boards could be as strong as the Borough President chose to make them. Their effectiveness also depended on the President, who was in a position to reflect their views and fight for their interests on the Board of Estimate.

To the irritation of the politicians who had been accustomed to paying only the necessary lip service to these grass-roots groups of "do gooders," Mrs. Motley became their spokesman and champion.

A perfect example of enlightened, intelligent coordination between citizens' groups and public officials resulted in a radical revision of the Morningside Heights urban renewal plan to incorporate amendments offered by the West Side Community Planning Board. The residents in the area had bitterly opposed the original plan on the grounds that it gave Columbia University far too much leeway for expansion at the expense of much needed low-income housing. Mrs. Motley arbitrated the town and gown conflict; she was the architect of the compromise plan which, also through her good offices, was approved by the Board of Estimate.

Not unexpectedly, much of Borough President Motley's attention was directed at issues directly concerned with the Negro community and with civil rights. In her first public speech she castigated the construction unions and others for their discrimination against minorities: "There remain a considerable number of unions and business enterprises which are making little or no progress toward recruitment policies which conform to the needs of our times."

On several occasions she filed charges with the police department's hack bureau against taxi drivers who refused her as a passenger because she was a Negro. To revitalize Harlem and to strengthen the local banks she advocated that certain key municipal projects be located there. At the same time she vigorously resisted moves which would downgrade the area. When a cement company threatened to relocate in Harlem she announced: "I have not become President of the Borough of Manhattan to preside over the destruction of the Harlem waterfront by cement mixing plants unwanted in other communities." Plain talk from a plain-spoken woman.

Mrs. Motley continued in office as Borough President from the time of her February nomination as federal judge until August 24, 1966, when her appointment was finally confirmed by the Senate. Senator James O. Eastland, Democrat from Mississippi, chairman of the Judiciary Committee, had blocked her nomination for as long as he could.

When she took the oath of office to become Judge Motley on September 7, many of her friends viewed the ceremony with mixed feelings. Would not the civil rights movement suffer from the loss of one of its most effective activists? Judge Motley's own view, as quoted in the Negro press, was: "It will help overcome discrimination if the majority of the community has an opportunity to see Negroes in positions of power and of equality. So, in that sense, I think I serve the civil rights cause."

That she also gives the community an opportunity to see a woman in an office of high trust is of only secondary importance to Constance Motley. "I have been too busy eliminating discrimination against race to fight discrimination against women," she has said.

Still, the fact that she is one of only three women out of 245 federal district judges makes her appointment a significant breakthrough for both minorities to which she belongs.

As one of twenty-three judges in the busiest federal district in the country, Constance Baker Motley hears a full range of cases, many dealing with undramatic commercial transactions far removed from the fields with which she is familiar. Obviously no judge can be an expert in all spheres of the law, and Mrs. Motley must stop to do her homework, read the latest cases covering areas in which she is not conversant. But the basic capacity for understanding and interpreting the law is there. She is essentially both a good and an imaginative lawyer according to Robert Carter, general counsel of the NAACP, who has known her all of her legal life. Furthermore, she brings even to corporation cases a fresh point of view, backed by intelligence and by what Mr. Carter calls the "greatest capacity for sustained work" he has ever seen.

But inevitably the cases closest to Constance Motley's heart are those more directly concerned with the rights of people, not only Negroes but members of all minorities, as well as the poor whites who are caught up in problems of city living. Significantly her most important, and most controversial, decision in her first year on the federal bench involved such a right — the right of a pupil, suspended from public school, to be represented by counsel at a hearing before the Board of Education. The case in point concerned a fourteen-year-old Puerto Rican boy named Victor Madera. Following his suspension from school on February 2, 1967, his parents (his mother speaks no English) were advised to appear at the district superintendent's office for a hearing at which Victor's educational fate would be decided. As soon as they received the notice, Victor's parents secured a lawyer through Mobilization for Youth, Inc., but the counsel was not permitted to be present at the hearing under the Board of Education's "no attorney" clause.

When the case came before Judge Motley, she ruled that the denial of Victor's right to be represented by counsel was a violation of the due process clause of the Fourteenth Amendment.

Her decision, handed down on April 10, 1967, met with a clamor of protests from secondary school educators. Many feared that the aura of the courtroom would be cast over the school environment, that school authorities would be intimidated, that there would be no discipline over "hostile, violent pupils." "Apparently Judge Motley misunderstands the nature of the hearings," said the High School Principals Association.

Judge Motley, in her lengthy opinion, makes it clear that far from misunderstanding, she understands all too well the potential damage inherent in the nature of the hearings. For as a result of what occurs in the "guidance conferences," as the hearings are somewhat euphemistically called, a child can be excluded from school for a month, a year, or forever, while waiting for a place to become available in the severely limited facilities of New York's special day schools for maladjusted pupils. And in more severe cases, the recommendation resulting from the hearing may be that the child be institutionalized in a treatment center or psychiatric hospital. Parental consent is necessary before such recommendations are acted upon, but if that permission is not forthcoming the parents are in jeopardy of a civil action against them for neglect of parental duties. Since the vast majority of pupils suspended from school come from what is politely called "multi-problem families," parents and the child are almost always ignorant of the issues, confused by the proceedings, and intimidated by the punitive atmosphere engendered, though perhaps not deliberately, at guidance conferences.

Judge Motley held that to deny the "proper safeguards of procedural fairness" in cases where "serious consequences flow for the juvenile involved," was "constitutionally repugnant." Although certain educators denounced her decision in the Madera case, many civic agencies hailed her finding as a landmark which would move civil rights another step forward on the road to full equality.

For Mrs. Motley herself, *Madera* v. *Board of Education* represents a full cycle. As a lawyer in the civil rights movement she helped to formulate laws for the protection of individual rights which, as a judge, she is now charged to uphold.

MADAM AMBASSADOR

Eugenie Anderson

EUGENIE ANDERSON has the distinction — rare among politicians — of having moved into public life from the comfortable shelter of an ivory tower. Until she was twenty-eight years old, neither Mrs. Anderson nor her husband had paid more than passing heed to the trend of events in the world around them. John Anderson was a painter; Eugenie Anderson was a musician, a pianist so devoted to the work of Johann Sebastian Bach that she named her daughter Johanna after him.

Unfortunately the Andersons lived in a decade when such single-minded preoccupation with aesthetics was not possible. By the late 1930's isolation was no longer just a way of life, but an international philosophy. The distinction was underscored for Mrs. Anderson when she and her husband made their first trip to Europe in 1937. Adolf Hitler by then had annexed the Rhineland, the *Anschluss* of Austria was in the making, and the Third Reich seemed unalterably committed to war.

Though an inexperienced observer, Mrs. Anderson was not a blind one. In Germany she clearly saw and was chilled by the portents of what lay ahead. Hers was not a gradual realization. Having read the signs correctly, she knew at once that she could not remain a passive observer; she must train herself to become an activist.

The Andersons had been living in New York while completing their studies, but had recently moved back to John Anderson's family home in Red Wing, Minnesota. On her return there in 1937 after her European trip, Eugenie Anderson at once joined the League of Women Voters. Her action was not merely symbolic; she immersed herself in League activities, learning all that she could about her own country, its government, and its relation to the shrinking world. By the time World War II began she was a committed internationalist.

Throughout the war, as her knowledge and understanding deepened, a determination to make her convictions politically effective crystallized. The prospect of a United Nations organization based on the ideology of the Atlantic Charter was for her a tangible hope. As the war drew to a close she felt, with a growing sense of urgency, that the United States must take the lead in creating a permanent international peace organization. Yet, as a private citizen, she was being represented in Congress by a man who was an intransigent isolationist.

This conflict led her to decide that the time to enter partisan politics was at hand. The League of Women Voters had served its purpose. For Mrs. Anderson, as for many similarly placed women, it had proved an invaluable internship in public affairs. But because of the League's basic non-partisan policy, women who wish to become active participants in a particular political party must move out of it.

Mrs. Anderson was fortunate that when the moment came in 1944 for her to take her stand, a new party in the state of Minnesota, fusing the existing Democratic and Farmer-Labor Parties, had just been formed under the leadership of a young man named Hubert Horatio Humphrey, who was then a professor at Macalester College in St. Paul. Humphrey was a dynamic, exciting, young idealist, an intellectual, who attracted many others like himself into the fold.

Mrs. Anderson's first action, consistent with her reason for having entered partisan politics, was to serve as chairman of the campaign committee for the Democratic-Farmer-Labor candidate from her own First Congressional District. Her candidate, a professor from St. Olaf College in Northfield, Minnesota, lost, which was not surprising, since the district was heavily Republican. But Mrs. Anderson was satisfied, in her initial political venture, to have sparked an anti-isolationist protest.

Although she could not have known it at the time, in casting her lot with the Minnesota Democratic-Farmer-Labor group, Eugenie

Anderson did more than simply join a party. She became a charter member of a dynasty, one of a hard core of twenty-five or more dedicated, talented, young liberals, many of whom were to play an important role on the national scene. The group that Hubert Humphrey referred to as his "diaper brigade" included Secretary of Agriculture Orville Freeman, Senator Eugene McCarthy, Mayor Arthur Naftalin, of Minneapolis, Evron Kirkpatrick, director of the American Political Science Association, Dorothy Jacobson, Assistant Secretary of Agriculture. The other incumbent Senator from Minnesota, Walter F. Mondale, though too young to have been in the original group, was involved in the party's early days as a student of Humphrey's at Macalester College.

But before the "Humphrey crowd" could emerge triumphant, they had to engage in and win a bitter internecine fight within the Democratic-Farmer-Labor Party, a fight which was Eugenie Anderson's baptism of fire and in which she played a key role.

Minnesota, though essentially Republican in character, has always been something of a mugwump state, prone to third parties and independent political factions. In the late nineteenth century the Anti-Monopolists and the Greenback Party exerted considerable pressure on state politics. In the twentieth century the dominant voice of protest was the Farmer-Labor Party. During the depths of the depression in the 1930's, this populist group, which was openly committed to left-wing radicalism, rose to its greatest power when their leader, Floyd B. Olson, became Governor of the state.

Governor Olson was able to keep the most radical elements of his dissident party in hand while he was Governor, but when he died in 1937 and was succeeded both as Governor and party leader by Elmer Benson, the fortunes of the Farmer-Labor Party began to decline sharply. In 1938 a relatively unknown Republican named Harold Stassen, charging corruption and widespread Communist infiltration in the Farmer-Labor Party, swept them out of power and took over the State House.

Meanwhile the Democrats, who were a decided minority in the

state, realized that their only hope of gaining a majority was to pick up the pieces of the Farmer-Labor group and unite them with the Democratic Party. The uneasy marriage lasted from 1944, when the fusion took place, until 1946, when the Communist element led by Benson made a successful bid to take over the entire Democratic-Farmer-Labor Party.

By that time Hubert Humphrey was mayor of Minneapolis and one of the most popular figures in the state. Yet he and his cohorts were effectually routed at the 1946 state convention of the Democratic-Farmer-Labor Party by Elmer Benson and the Communists. (Orville Freeman says that Benson was not a card-carrying member himself only because he had always managed to gyp the Communist Party out of their dues.)

In retrospect Mrs. Anderson is able to regard the take-over by the Communists as a "very educational experience." At the time though, she says, it was "a terrible experience for someone who had never really encountered any Communist organization before. I had not realized that this was even possible in a democratic country."

Both Eugenie Anderson and Orville Freeman agree that their group was not sharp or alert enough to see in time how completely they were being absorbed by the Communist faction, and when they did realize it, they were not sufficiently determined or experienced or organized to combat their adversaries effectively. They therefore faced the classic dilemma: whether to get out of the Democratic-Farmer-Labor Party altogether or to stay in and fight to regain control. Humphrey strongly urged that they must stay and fight from within.

The Benson group, in an effort to make use of what they called the "right wing" and to give the semblance of a unified party, made Orville Freeman secretary to the party (they had first suggested that he be treasurer, Freeman says, but since there was no money in the treasury he demurred and finally settled for the equally perfunctory but less fraudulent post of secretary). Eugenie Anderson was made vice chairwoman.

The Humphrey crowd began at once to regroup their forces and, with the 1948 elections as their goal, to dig in for a long fight. Meanwhile, in January of 1947, a new national organization called the Americans for Democratic Action came into being. The Minnesota crowd saw in this liberal, New Deal organization, whose ideology was entirely consonant with their own, a perfect vehicle to serve their interests in the state. By associating with the A.D.A. they would gain the leadership of Eleanor Roosevelt, and a national identity which was very important to them. Furthermore, by forming a Minnesota A.D.A. chapter to which they all belonged, they could effectively hold their own private caucuses instead of holding them, as they were obliged to do, only within the framework of the Democratic-Farmer-Labor Party. Accordingly, in the spring of 1947 they joined the A.D.A. and elected Eugenie Anderson chairman of the chapter.

The Benson-Communist forces in a parallel move polarized around the National Citizens for Political Action Committee, whose spokesman was Henry A. Wallace. The battle lines were thus drawn. Unless the Humphrey forces could recapture the Democratic-Farmer-Labor Party by 1948, Henry Wallace's name would appear on the ballot as the party's Presidential nominee instead of Harry S Truman's.

All this was very heady stuff indeed for the young housewife from Red Wing whose sole ambition ten years earlier had been to become a sufficient master of the pipe organ to perform the works of Johann Sebastian Bach.

The *Minnesota Leader* was the journal for the pro-Wallace-Benson-Farmer-Labor Association forces;* what they had to say about the A.D.A. sounds more like what might be written today about the John Birch Society. In an open letter to Mayor Humphrey, the *Leader* scored him for his "association with the unsavory Americans for Democratic Action, created nationally to serve as liberal window

---

* Dr. G. Theodore Mitau's article, "The Democratic-Farmer-Labor Party Schism of 1948" (*Minnesota History*, Spring, 1955) has been a valuable source for this chapter.

dressing for the Wall Streeters and militarists behind Truman. . . ."
The A.D.A. was charged with red-baiting, with giving support
to Winston Churchill's foreign policy, with backing the Marshall Plan — all evidence of the organization's "reactionary" purpose.

The Humphrey-A.D.A. forces, convinced that the Benson-
Wallace third-party movement was part of a Communist-inspired
pattern to "confuse honest liberals and hobble the function of democracy," struck back in their official organ, *The Minnesota Outlook*, stating unequivocally their determination to remove from the
Democratic-Farmer-Labor Party "all those who have aided and
abetted the program and tactics of the Communist Party."

As Mrs. Anderson points out, "This all happened just at the time
when the Communist Party in the Soviet Union changed its line
from the wartime cooperation of the United Front to a policy of
world-wide aggression. First we had to learn to recognize Communist tactics and to see how they worked and succeeded. Then
we had to learn how to outstay and out-organize and out-idea them."

Finally, to outmaneuver them, the A.D.A. chapter began at the
lowest level of the party structure — the town and county committees. They went to every precinct caucus held in every little red
schoolhouse; Eugenie Anderson was responsible for the counties
around her home territory south of Minneapolis. In Minnesota not
only party workers but any Democratic-Farmer-Labor voter is eli-
gible to attend caucuses, so, in effect, she and her colleagues took
their case directly to the people.

The result of the caucuses gave the Humphrey crowd a three to
one majority over the Benson faction — a victory which they as-
serted to gain a majority of the delegates, first at the county convention and then at the all-important state convention where
their claims were loudly protested by the opposing forces. The
Benson dissidents countered by holding a rump meeting on the side-
walk outside the convention hall. Hastily they organized a convention of their own in Minneapolis and presented to the secretary
of state *their* slate of candidates, headed by Henry Wallace, claiming

that their group was the true Democratic-Farmer-Labor Party. It took the Minnesota supreme court to rule their claim fraudulent and to uphold the right-wing slate as representing the clear will of the party.

The A.D.A. chapter, in effect, now became the top echelon of the Democratic-Farmer-Labor Party; Hubert Humphrey headed the slate of candidates as the nominee for Senator, Eugene McCarthy was nominated as Representative from the Fourth Congressional District, and Eugenie Anderson was elected the National Committee-woman.

At the 1948 Democratic Convention in Philadelphia, Mrs. Anderson was one of a small group who worked with Hubert Humphrey to bring about a strong minority plank on civil rights. Another of their company was James Loeb, then executive secretary of the A.D.A. and the first member of that organization to have journeyed to Minnesota to meet the Humphrey crowd. Loeb, who is now publisher of the *Adirondack Daily Enterprise*, says, "Eugenie is really a very sharp gal politically. It was her stroke of genius that made victory possible, because she suggested that our minority plank include specific language mentioning Truman's Civil Rights Commission. The inclusion of Truman's name made it impossible for some delegates to vote against us."

The outcome of the election was equally triumphant. The Democratic-Farmer-Labor Party captured three congressional seats, including McCarthy's, from Republican incumbents, Hubert Humphrey defeated his opponent in a resounding victory, and President Truman carried the state with 692,966 votes while Henry Wallace garnered only 27,866.

A long, exhausting, and exceedingly rough fight was won. Through it all Eugenie Anderson had been in a top strategy position, working as hard and determinedly as any of her male colleagues. Orville Freeman says of her, "Not many women are emotionally constituted to be on the prime firing line and to be totally effective. But Eugenie is. She held her own very well in the smoke-filled rooms, she kept cool and she also remained a lady."

Being a lady, which seems as natural to Eugenie Anderson as breathing, could have presented no problem, but finding the time and energy during four years to have devoted herself so single-mindedly to her purpose was another matter. She did, after all, have two young children and a husband. Fortunately, as she is quick to point out, her husband was extremely interested and understanding. "John is a theorist," Mrs. Anderson says. "He isn't concerned with the practical application of politics, but he recognizes the importance of it, and looks on it as something I could do but he couldn't. But his very detachment has always been particularly helpful to me. And he has a wonderful sense of principle and also of humor — both things you need in politics."

John Anderson's father was a food technologist and, among other things, the inventor of Puffed Wheat and Puffed Rice. Old cold-cereal lovers will doubtless remember the copy on the Quaker Oats boxes proclaiming Professor Anderson's unique "shot from a gun" technique for achieving the puff. The laboratory in which this extraordinary process took place was part of an experimental farm called High Tower, where John and Eugenie Anderson have always made their home. During the time that Mrs. Anderson was so busily occupied with Democratic-Farmer-Labor Party politics, her husband, whose work as an artist and photographer permitted him to be at home, was able to keep an eye on the two children, Johanna and Hans.

After the successful 1948 elections, Mrs. Anderson says she looked forward to settling down again at High Tower and resuming a more or less normal life with her husband and children, although whether she would ever have been satisfied, having been an activist on the "prime fighting line," to be an observer on the sidelines is questionable.

As it turned out, she had little opportunity to test her capacity for passivity. In January, 1949, just after President Truman's inauguration, the telephone rang at High Tower. It was a Presidential advisor, calling from Washington to ask her if she would be interested in having her name proposed for an ambassadorial post.

The suggestion was so utterly unexpected that Mrs. Anderson says she could not at first seem to take it very seriously. She remembers that when the call came she and her husband were just about to leave for a short trip — her husband was already in the car waiting for her — and that she reported this sudden turn of events to him laughingly, almost as if it were a joke.

It was not. The call had come from India Edwards, who was then the executive director of the Women's Division of the Democratic Party. As Mrs. Edwards recalls it, directly after the 1948 election, President Truman, always a man who staunchly remembered loyal friends, had asked India Edwards, who certainly qualified as one, what post she wanted in the government. She wanted no job at all for herself, Mrs. Edwards told the President, but instead she wanted "a lot of jobs for a lot of women."

Truman was quite willing to consider a qualified woman for any post, always provided that the Cabinet member whose department was involved would agree. Mrs. Anderson's name was one of the first put forward by Mrs. Edwards.* Dean Acheson, the Secretary of State, required little selling on the idea of a woman ambassador, although there had never been one before — the three women previously appointed as heads of missions had all had the rank of minister.

In Red Wing, Minnesota, John Anderson did not need to be sold either. He liked the idea at once. His own profession made him al-

* Another was Georgia Neese Clarke who was at that time the president of a bank in Richland, Kansas. Mrs. Edwards suggested to Truman that she would make an excellent Treasurer of the United States, a post that had never before been occupied by a woman, but which has often been since. When India Edwards called to ask her if she would be interested in the job of Treasurer, Mrs. Clark's first reaction was favorable. Then she demurred. She was also the Democratic National Committeewoman for Kansas and she wondered how her opposite number, the National Committee*man* would feel about it. "First I'll have to call and clear it with him," she said. "Nonsense," Mrs. Edwards snapped, "Would he call you?"

together mobile; in fact, with his increased interest in photography the change of scene was desirable. The experience of living abroad would, he felt, be exciting and beneficial for the children. For his wife, he knew that a diplomatic appointment would be gratifying, and that, furthermore, she would do the job well.

Eugenie Anderson herself was more skeptical. In the first place it seemed to her very unlikely that she would ever really be chosen. Although she had worked hard for the party, she had never given it any money apart from buying occasional tickets to hundred-dollar-a-plate dinners; high diplomatic posts, she reasoned, traditionally went to substantial contributors. She knew that Hubert Humphrey would be her strong supporter, but he was, after all, just beginning his first term in the Senate; would not others, with longer service, have prior claims? And finally, she wondered if she could even do the job if it were offered.

During the winter months of 1949 she was twice called to Washington for interviews at the State Department and the White House. In between there were long periods when nothing whatsoever seemed to be happening. In the spring she was told that she was one of several candidates being considered for a Scandinavian post. She began reading books on Denmark. Then, at one point during the summer, it looked as if her appointment was not going to come through after all, for when the Danes heard that the United States was considering appointing a woman to their country, they feared a Call Me Madam situation and objected. But Dean Acheson had Mrs. Anderson meet with the Danish Ambassador in Washington, after which his doubts were completely dispelled. On October 12, 1949, Eugenie Anderson was officially named Ambassador to Denmark.

After her early misgivings, Mrs. Anderson's faith in her ability to represent her country abroad had soon been restored as she thought of other ambassadors — political appointees with no previous diplomatic experience — who had handled their assignments successfully. A genuinely modest woman, she none the less has a quiet self-confidence which permitted her to face her new responsibilities with equanimity.

Because she had always, as she says, worked in politics "at the man level of the party," she felt no anxiety about becoming a woman ambassador. And because she knew that at least one-third of our ambassadors are political appointments, she felt no uneasiness at the prospect of heading a large mission composed almost entirely of experienced career diplomats.

"I have always believed," she says, "that if you approach your job seriously and if you have an attitude of respect towards the people you work with, you will have no trouble in getting their cooperation."

It would be difficult to imagine anyone not wanting to cooperate with Eugenie Anderson. There is every reason to believe that she is just as nice a person in fact as she seems to be. Soft-spoken, clear and direct, she radiates an aura of warmth and sincerity. She is unpretentious yet dignified, approachable yet with a degree of reserve that does not encourage overfamiliarity.

Characteristic of Eugenie Anderson, the ambassador, is the first party she gave after she and her family arrived in Copenhagen. As Dean Acheson was later to write, "It [the party] was not as the conventional or the readers of society columns might suppose for officialdom. It was given for the workmen and their wives who had worked so hard to prepare the residence for her arrival. From that day on the Danes opened their hearts to her."

From the outset, Mrs. Anderson's aim was to reach the Danish people directly, not just through their government. A broader, person-to-person approach was, she felt, a vital part of modern diplomacy, and one which seemed to her especially important at that particular juncture in Danish-American relations.

Denmark, a neutralist country by tradition, had recently joined with the United States and eleven other countries in the newly formed North Atlantic Treaty Organization. The Danes, knowing that their fate was now closely tied to that of NATO's most influential participant, the United States, looked with greater interest, and perhaps with a need for reassurance, to the American ambassador.

To win the people, Mrs. Anderson had to be able to talk with them in their own language; she therefore set out, immediately after her arrival in December, 1949, to learn Danish. Fortunately, being a musician, she had a good ear; without it and without her iron determination she could never have accomplished what is still regarded as one of her finest diplomatic coups.

Although all American ambassadors abroad traditionally give large Fourth of July parties, Denmark is the only country in Europe that celebrates the day on a gigantic scale. The ceremonies are held on the sloping greens of Rebild Park in Aalborg. Thirty thousand people were present in 1950 to see the new American ambassador. Mrs. Anderson had been in the country and studying the language for only six months. She stood before them and gave her first speech in Danish.

"I'll never forget how scared I was," she recalls. "Of course I knew the speech by heart, and I had the text in front of me so I could read it, but for the first few seconds I really didn't know what I was saying. And then when I finished, for a moment there wasn't any sound at all from the audience. I thought for one dreadful minute that maybe they hadn't understood me. But they had. Because then there was just a deafening applause. I think my speaking in Danish came as a complete surprise to them."

If the Danes had opened their hearts to her after her first embassy party, they gave their hearts to her outright after the Fourth of July. Suddenly it seemed to Mrs. Anderson that everybody in Denmark wanted her to come and speak to their organization, visit their town, or open their local fair. "It was a very heartwarming experience," says Mrs. Anderson. "I felt as if I had got off to a good start."

It was providential that Mrs. Anderson established such rapport with the Danes just when she did. Late in June — in point of time only ten days before her July 4 speech — the Communist forces had crossed the 38th parallel in Korea and hostilities had begun. As the situation in Korea worsened, tensions in Europe increased. Denmark, a small country, close to the Soviet Union, had gone through a harrowing occupation during World War II, and thus felt particularly vulnerable. NATO, her only defense, was still too new and untried to inspire total confidence among the Danes. As someone explained to Mrs. Anderson, "Every Dane believes that every war begins in Kongens Nytorv (the King's Square) in Copenhagen."

As 1950 drew to a close, Mrs. Anderson sensed that more and more the Danes were focusing on her, watching her for overt signs which would indicate that the Americans were expecting the Korean war to spread to Europe. The key question was what she would do about her two children, Johanna, sixteen, and Hans, twelve. If she sent them back to the United States it would be a clear omen that the Americans were anticipating trouble in Europe.

Outwardly Mrs. Anderson maintained a steady, business-as-usual comportment, but behind her calm she struggled with the nagging conflict between her duties as a representative of her country and her growing concern for her children. As an ambassador receiving daily communications in the diplomatic pouch from Washington, she knew how grave the situation was. Already in her possession was a detailed evacuation plan for the embassy staff in case of hostilities. Could she continue to expose her young children to the potential dangers of living in a small country whose fate depended entirely on others coming to its defense?

"Almost every evening my husband and I would talk about whether we should send the children home. And then every morning I would decide we couldn't possibly do it."

The children remained. Quite apart from all the implications, they would have hated to leave; they were having a wonderful time in Denmark. Both were in Danish schools, both had already far surpassed their mother, with the maddening ease that young people have in acquiring languages, in their command of Danish. Hans was particularly favored. The Danes naturally assumed that his middle name was Christian. Could a boy named Hans Anderson have any other middle name?

As a slight concession to her anxieties during the critical period, Mrs. Anderson permitted herself one womanly, non-ambassadorial action. She sent home, with a friend who was returning to the States, a suitcase containing especially treasured family possessions — photographs, heirlooms, her mother's wedding ring. Clearly recognizing how illogical her sentimental gesture was, she none the less felt better for having made it.

Early in 1951 fears in Europe began to be allayed. General Dwight D. Eisenhower was named head of NATO's military arm, SHAPE (Supreme Headquarters Allied Powers in Europe), giving the mutual defense organization a shield of strength and its member countries a sense of confidence and hope. Eisenhower's first act as soldier-diplomat was to travel to all the NATO countries; he went to Denmark in January, 1951. His visit, Mrs. Anderson says, marked the turning point. The crisis had been surmounted. Eugenie Anderson could now begin to solidify her gains.

As an ambassador she had two objectives: to represent the best of America and Americans to the Danes, and to promote the interests of the United States in Denmark. In the first area, her almost legendary popularity with the Danish people brought enormous credit to her own country. Furthermore, she and her husband rendered a notable service in dispelling some widely held myths: Americans were uncultured boors. Yet the American Ambassador was a musician and her husband an artist. Americans cared nothing about things of the mind. Yet the Ambassador's husband, the son of a scientist, found a common ground with Denmark's most eminent atomic scientist, Niels Bohr, and ultimately became his close friend. America was a capitalist country whose politicians cared only about money. The Ambassador, with her strong ties to the liberal wing of the Democratic Party in Minnesota, was able to demonstrate to the leaders of the Social Democrat Party of Denmark (then the majority party) that many politicians in her own country also cared about the welfare of the people.

Her excellent relations with the top officials of the country helped Mrs. Anderson to fulfill her other ambassadorial duty: to further the interests of her own country in Denmark. In 1951, when she concluded a Treaty of Friendship, Commerce and Navigation with the Danish government, she became the first woman to sign a treaty in behalf of the United States. Later in the same year she signed the Fulbright Agreement, permitting the exchange of students and scholars between the United States and Denmark. A more complex diplomatic achievement was her negotiation of the Greenland Treaty, which provided for the joint defense by Denmark and the United States of Greenland, permitted the Danes to take over the Gronnedal Naval Station, then operated by the United States, and established mutual aid for surveys and meteorological research.

"In the field of intergovernmental relations," wrote Secretary of State Dean Acheson to Senator Hubert Humphrey, "Mrs. Anderson handled for us matters of the greatest difficulty and importance with firmness, tact, and efficacy."

The Secretary of State's letter was written to be read at a dinner Humphrey was giving to honor Eugenie Anderson at the conclusion of her service as Ambassador to Denmark. "If you seek the ideal ambassador," Acheson ended his letter, "I say to you, look at your guest of honor."

One of the disadvantages of politically appointed ambassadors is that their service, no matter how successful, is subject to abrupt termination when the party in power changes in Washington. Had Eugenie Anderson been a career diplomat her outstanding usefulness to her country could and probably would have continued without interruption. But as a Truman appointee she was obliged to offer her resignation to President Eisenhower and to return to private life in February of 1953.

Her leave-taking from Copenhagen was marked by a profusion of tributes, the most impressive and memorable being offered by

King Frederick IX, who decorated her with the Grand Cross of the Order of Dannenborg in recognition of the esteem and affection in which the Danish people held her. It was the highest honor ever accorded to a woman in Denmark's history.

Fortunate as she is in many respects, Eugenie Anderson does not seem to be blessed with the luck of being the right person at the right time. In 1953, fresh from her triumphant tour of duty in Denmark, she was manifestly the right person to continue public service in some new capacity. But — also manifestly — it was the wrong time for her. A Republican administration in Washington precluded any possibility of an appointive office commensurate with her proven abilities.

An elective office therefore seemed indicated, and, as time went on, Mrs. Anderson began to look with growing interest toward the Congress of the United States and the possibility of joining her friend Hubert Humphrey there as the other Senator from Minnesota.

The seat, then held by Republican Edward J. Thye, was due to be contested in 1958, and the auguries for a Democratic take-over seemed favorable. Eugenie Anderson was by this time very well known throughout Minnesota; she was unquestionably the state's outstanding woman public figure, and was, in fact, referred to familiarly as Eugenie wherever she went. In every way, she seemed an ideal choice to be the Democratic nominee.

There was only one drawback. Another one of the original Humphrey crowd also had his eye on the Senate seat. Just when Mrs. Anderson's prospect seemed the brightest, Eugene McCarthy, then serving his fourth term in the House, made known his intention of running for the Senate in 1958. The situation posed an acute dilemma for Senator Humphrey and for Orville Freeman who was then Governor of the state. In point of fact, both men were closer to Eugenie Anderson than they were to McCarthy, who had always been something of a loner. But though they may have preferred Mrs. Anderson, neither man felt it possible to block McCarthy, who was beyond question well qualified for the post, who had solid backing from labor, and of course very strong Catholic support in the state. They, therefore, maintained a strict hands-off policy which, Freeman admits, irked Mrs. Anderson at the time. In any case, Freeman does not believe that even if he and Humphrey had openly endorsed Eugenie Anderson they could have successfully wrested the nomination from McCarthy, who had far too much political strength to be turned back. Though Mrs. Anderson was not convinced of this, she has harbored no bitterness toward Humphrey or Freeman; they remain close friends. Her feeling for Senator McCarthy, on the other hand, is somewhat less than warm.

Mrs. Anderson would undoubtedly have made a very good Senator; it is unfortunate in this instance that she happened to come from a state which has such a plethora of political talent. With the Senate closed to her, many of her friends urged her to run for the House. Although her district was and always had been a conservative Republican one, her enthusiastic supporters told her she was the one Democrat who could be elected. But she herself was not so convinced. Furthermore, the prospect of having to campaign every two years to hold her seat if she should be elected, was very unappealing both to her and to her husband. And finally, she did not feel that in the House she could play as significant a role in foreign affairs, which was her main interest, as she could have done in the Senate.

So for the next few years Mrs. Anderson remained a private citizen, though by no means an idle one. She was appointed to the Zellerbach Commission to study the problems of refugees from Iron Curtain countries, she worked actively with Mrs. Roosevelt, whom she knew and revered, in the American Association for the United Nations, and of course she campaigned extremely hard for Hubert Humphrey in his unsuccessful primary fight for the Presidential nomination.

Shortly after Kennedy's election in 1960, the Andersons started off on a trip around the world. Their ultimate objective was India, where their daughter, who had married an Indian Fulbright student, was living, and where Mrs. Anderson was scheduled to give a series of lectures under the sponsorship of the Indian Council of World Affairs.

While she was in New Delhi, she received word that the Kennedy administration was prepared to offer her a diplomatic post if she were interested. She was, and on her return to the States she met with Presidential Advisor Ralph Dungan and with Senator Humphrey to consider possible assignments. Hubert Humphrey had an idea that Mrs. Anderson would be particularly effective in an Eastern European country; as he expounded on her first-hand experiences with Communists and their tactics during the Farmer-Labor days, Dungan was at once interested. He indicated that he thought President Kennedy would react favorably to the suggestion, although it had been customary to send only career diplomats to represent our country behind the Iron Curtain.

That the Kennedy administration finally chose to assign Eugenie Anderson to Bulgaria demonstrated their confidence both in her courage — for certainly this qualified as a hardship post — and in her diplomatic skill. Bulgarian-American relations, which had been non-existent for ten years and had only recently been resumed, were still extremely tenuous.

Mrs. Anderson's arrival in Bulgaria in May of 1962 was in marked contrast to her first days in Denmark. Instead of the cheerful, attractive, newly redecorated residence in Copenhagen, the residence that greeted her in Sofia was a large, gloomy, red brick building that looked like a prison on the outside and was in a dreadful state of disrepair inside. "I must say," Mrs. Anderson confesses, "that when I first walked into it I felt like crying." It was one of those moments when she must have wondered why she had ever given up playing the pipe organ. To get the residence in agreeable shape took almost a year; Mrs. Anderson's efforts in this regard, incidentally, point up one of the minor drawbacks of being a woman ambassador. Men ambassadors have wives to take care of refurbishing rooms and running a household, but Eugenie Anderson had to carry on all the usual womanly chores along with her official duties as head of the mission. She is quick to point out, however, the advantages she had from her husband's many supportive activities in her behalf, as well as from his keen intelligence and widespread interests.

The Andersons had to learn quickly just how one lived as representatives of the United States behind the Iron Curtain. In the privacy of their own apartment they could permit themselves only the blandest, most mundane conversations. The only way they were able to talk freely together was to take long walks in the country, and even then they were warned to check their clothing carefully for hidden listening devices. In her office at the mission in downtown Sofia, Mrs. Anderson never dictated to her long-time secretary and close friend, Vivian Meisen, but wrote out every letter in long-hand; in fact she and Mrs. Meisen conducted most of their "conversations" by writing notes. Although the mission was equipped with a so-called "safe room," an electronic room within a room which defies bugging, Mrs. Anderson used it infrequently and then only for large staff conferences.

Not long after her arrival, the new minister had an opportunity to test her mettle against Bulgarian officialdom. At Plovdiv, one hundred and fifty miles southeast of Sofia, a large trade fair took place every other year; this year, for the first time since diplomatic ties with Bulgaria were severed in 1950, the United States was to have an exhibition. Because she hoped that our exhibition would symbolize a new era in relations between the two countries, Mrs. Anderson had planned the displays with great care and also had arranged for a descriptive pamphlet with a picture of President Kennedy and a friendly greeting from him and from her, to be distributed to everyone who visited the exhibition. As with all publications or public utterances behind the Iron Curtain, the text of the pamphlet had to be cleared by the regime; it had been edited and re-edited numerous times until finally the appropriate minister in Sofia had officially approved it.

The weekend the fair was to open the Andersons went to Plovdiv to help put the finishing touches on the United States exhibition. Mrs. Anderson was delighted with the whole result; ours was one of the most attractive exhibits at the fair, and much more effective than the Russians', she thought. Apparently the Bulgarians thought so too and they were not happy about it. They were even less happy that the obviously favorable impression made by the United States was to be heightened by a free brochure which people could take home and study.

The day before the opening, the Andersons were sitting in a café with Alex Bloomfield, the cultural affairs officer and interpreter of the mission, when the president of the Bulgarian chamber of commerce stopped at their table. Bloomfield introduced him to Mrs. Anderson. After only the barest civilities, the Bulgarian told her flatly that he understood she was planning to distribute a pamphlet at the trade fair which she had no right to do without permission. She was, in fact, going to be stopped, he said.

Eugenie Anderson, whose gentle manner can turn to ice if the occasion demands it, said that on the contrary she *did* have permission; the pamphlet had been approved by the proper officials and if there were now further objections these officials would have to come to her office in Sofia and specifically state them. Meanwhile the pamphlets would be distributed as planned.

In recalling the incident, Bloomfield points out that fortunately he had already paid the bill so that, following Mrs. Anderson's strong exit line, they were able to sweep majestically out of the café leaving the president of the Bulgarian chamber of commerce glaring after them.

A very considerable war of nerves, occasionally reaching almost James Bond proportions, ensued. The Bulgarians threatened to seize and destroy the 150,000 pamphlets stored in boxes at the American exhibition. The Americans had to move them to the comparative safety of the trade fair manager's locked office. The maintenance crew at the fair, apparently under orders, struck and refused to work at the American exhibition. Members of the mission staff had to be rushed from Sofia to Plovdiv to help out.

At the opening of the fair when the Prime Minister and his party arrived to visit the United States exhibition, Mrs. Anderson was there to greet them, pamphlets in hand. Ingenuously she pressed one on Premier Todor Zhivkov. "You might be interested, Mr. Prime Minister, in reading this little pamphlet which explains some of the displays." Zhivkov and the other officials had no choice but to accept graciously.

Outside, however, the police were intimidating the crowds lined up waiting for the doors to open and, when finally the public was admitted, there was a stampede for copies of the pamphlets. "You would have thought we were passing out dollar bills," Mrs. Anderson chuckles. If the police could not stop people from going in, they tried to grab the pamphlets from them as they came out, and the more apparent it became that the regime did not want them to have the perfectly innocuous little brochures, the more people were determined to have them. In a few hours a brisk black market in pamphlets was already flourishing.

The police-state tactics continued for almost a week while Mrs. Anderson remained in Plovdiv firmly holding the line. Then suddenly the Bulgarian resistance collapsed. Ruefully the minister of foreign trade told Alex Bloomfield, "We underestimated the determination of your minister. We didn't know the Americans could be so tough."

Gratified as she was with this victory, Eugenie Anderson generally prefers quiet persuasion to the hard line in diplomatic relations. She wanted to reach the people and she was aware that the greatest single factor which had made this possible for her in Denmark was that she had learned the language. Now in Bulgaria she must do the same thing; but here she set herself an incalculably more difficult task, as anyone who has ever studied a Slavic language knows. Again she made the Fourth of July her goal and on that day, fourteen months after her arrival in the country, Eugenie Anderson appeared on television and radio speaking in Bulgarian.

Looking back on it, Mrs. Anderson feels that her real achievement was not so much having learned enough Bulgarian to give the speech, but having persuaded the authorities to allow her to do it. For months before July 4, Alex Bloomfield and others on the United States staff had been trying, without success, to get permission for the American Minister to speak. One day Mrs. Anderson had an opportunity to bring the matter up herself with the deputy foreign minister who had recently been Bulgaria's ambassador to the United States. Pointing out that he had spoken to the American people several times during his tour of duty in Washington, Mrs. Anderson suggested that he owed her the same reciprocal courtesy. His case was quite different, the deputy foreign minister said loftily. In America he had spoken in English. Mrs. Anderson had him just where she wanted him. "Well, if I speak in Bulgarian will you let me do it?"

Since he doubtless considered that a very large "if," the deputy foreign minister agreed, and Eugenie Anderson became the first Westerner ever to appear on radio or on television. She did not miss the opportunity to point out that the Bulgarians, who had for so many years been under the domination of the Turks, must well understand, "why we Americans prize our national independence and our individual freedom. On this day — July 4 — we Americans celebrate freedom, peace, equality, democracy, and justice," she said. "These are the great ideals on which America was founded and by which we still live. These are the blessings which all mankind longs to enjoy."

When Mrs. Anderson returned to the residence after her speech had been telecast, one of the Bulgarian women on her household staff rushed forward to congratulate her; she managed only a few words before she burst into tears and fled from the room, leaving Mrs. Anderson herself dissolved. This was the first intimation of how responsive a chord she had touched in the hearts of the Bulgarian people, not only by her words, and by the fact that she had spoken to them in their language, but by her own gentle, calm, warm, and somehow reassuring presence.

From that moment on the American Minister was recognized

and welcomed everywhere she went. She was permitted to speak again a year later on July 4, 1964, and also on November 23, 1963, just after the news of President Kennedy's assassination reached Bulgaria.

"The reaction to the President's death," Mrs. Anderson says, "was just as it was in every other part of the world, only I think more intense." And that very intensity was of great significance, for although she had had numerous indications of the Bulgarians' friendly regard for the United States, Mrs. Anderson had not realized the depth of their feelings until the moment when John F. Kennedy was killed. She had put a notice on the window of the mission in downtown Sofia saying that she would be at home at certain hours to receive persons who wished to pay their respects. It is customary at such times for officials to go to the residence to write in the book; Mrs. Anderson had not anticipated that any ordinary citizens would come. But to her astonishment literally hundreds of people arrived — people from all walks of life, showing great courage since certainly their presence at the American Minister's residence was noted by the regime — all expressing not only their love for Kennedy but their warmth for his country.

Over and above her quite special brand of people-to-people diplomacy, Eugenie Anderson had a major substantive assignment to fulfill in Bulgaria. Because of the ten-year break in diplomatic relations, a backlog of old problems between the two countries remained unsolved, the most pressing being the financial settlement of World War II claims. Since 1960, when relations had been resumed, sporadic negotiations on this question had been carried on in Washington between the State Department and Bulgaria's minister to the United States. Because the talks had so far been almost entirely fruitless, Mrs. Anderson persuaded the State Department to reverse the pattern and, as she puts it, "to let me take a whack at it in Sofia."

Accordingly, with the Department's blessing, she began negotiations in February, 1963, and here, sitting around a bargaining table with members of Bulgaria's Politburo, Eugenie Anderson's early experiences with the Communists in Minnesota stood her in good stead. Her relations with Premier Zhivkov were by that time very good, and his obvious respect for her undoubtedly was reflected in the attitudes of other officials with whom she dealt on the war claims problem. But Mrs. Anderson was not deluded into thinking that friendly acts toward her meant she had won a victory; because she knew so well the undulations of Communist strategy, she was wary and alert for traps, for small concessions on their part which would lead to larger demands. On the other hand, she was also quick to recognize the moment to agree when finally it came. By May of 1963 the claims were settled and the agreement completed. In four months of talks in Sofia Eugenie Anderson had accomplished what had not been done in over two years of talks in Washington.

Relations between the two countries, which had been improving anyway, now took a decided turn for the better. For most of 1963 there was a real *détente*. Then, in December of that year, the upward curve suddenly plummeted when a former member of the Bulgarian delegation to the United Nations, Professor A. H. Georgiev, was accused of having spied "for capitalist interests" in 1956. Georgiev quickly confessed, allegedly admitted to having received $200,000 from the CIA which he said he spent on "loose living." The State Department denied any knowledge of the charge, and the CIA refused comment.

In retaliation a mob in Sofia stormed the United States mission, smashed windows, overturned cars and roughed up several members of the staff. Mrs. Anderson happened to be in Washington for consultations at the time; her second in command, Richard Johnson, handled the official protest in Bulgaria. By the time Mrs. Anderson returned to Sofia early in January everything had changed, a solid freeze in relations had set in which took some six months to thaw. Meanwhile the United States mission suffered two more unpleasant demonstrations.

However, by July of 1964 the climate was sufficiently restored for Mrs. Anderson to be permitted once again to make a Fourth of

July speech on Bulgarian television; she continued to be recognized and warmly welcomed wherever she went, from schools to official occasions to collective farms around the countryside.

But the difficulties of living in a police state, the sense of isolation, the constant awareness of surveillance and of the need even in private always to think before speaking, took their toll of both Eugenie Anderson and her husband. She had served her country magnificently for almost two and a half years; late in 1964 she wrote to President Johnson that she wished to resign.

It has been said that in doing so she made one of her few diplomatic gaffes. She should properly have told the President that she wished to resign at his pleasure; instead she specifically asked that her resignation be effective at the end of the year 1964.

Mr. Johnson is not a man to overlook even such a mild impropriety; Mrs. Anderson had some quick fence mending to do on her return to the States. She did so, however, with her usual tact and skill, thus paving the way for the assignment she wanted next as Representative to the Trusteeship Council of the United Nations with the rank of Ambassador. This post was previously held by another woman, Marietta Tree, and in fact, largely through the precedent first set by Mrs. Roosevelt, women have always held one of the top positions in our mission to the United Nations.

Although Mrs. Anderson's title implied that her work on the Trusteeship Council would occupy a major portion of her time, in fact the Council meets only for one month of the year to consider problems connected with the few remaining trusteeship territories in the world. The United States trust territory consists of three major archipelagoes in the Pacific: the Carolines, Marianas, and Marshalls. These islands had been under Japanese mandate until during and after World War II, when they came under United States concession. Among the islands, Saipan and Kwajalein are the names most familiar to Americans as scenes of bloody battles, and Bikini and Eniwetok as the distant atolls where nuclear bomb tests were held.

Shortly after her appointment to the United Nations, Ambassador

Anderson led a congressional delegation on an official tour of all the major islands in the United States Trust Territory. As a result of her many recommendations the Congress increased certain appropriations to provide greater social and economic aid, and over 500 Peace Corps volunteers were sent to the islands. Her conviction that the people's movement toward self-determination and self-government should be strongly encouraged gave impetus to the White House proposal that a Presidential Commission be constituted to draw up plans leading to a plebiscite in the Territory.

The greater part of Mrs. Anderson's two years at the United Nations was spent on consideration of African questions both as a member of the Fourth Committee of the General Assembly and as a member of the Committee of Twenty-Four, which is a special body of twenty-four countries that meets when the General Assembly is not in session to consider problems of decolonization. In the course of her duties on the Committee of Twenty-Four, Mrs. Anderson made a five-week tour of Africa in 1966 as chief United States delegate and was a valuable and convincing spokesman for the cause of racial justice in Rhodesia, Mozambique and Angola.

She made a significant contribution in African affairs as a member of a special ad hoc committee which was created in 1966 to try to establish some sort of U.N. control in Southwest Africa. Mrs. Anderson worked very hard, negotiating with members of other missions, primarily African, to draw up a resolution of the General Assembly stating that South Africa had forfeited its mandate over Southwest Africa and that the United Nations would therefore assume responsibility. In 1966 the United States signed the resolution which Mrs. Anderson among many others had helped to prepare. In 1967 she again worked on a new resolution which went further toward more specific proposals, but which the United States, while sympathetic, felt might force a confrontation and therefore did not sign.

During her tenure at the United States Mission Mrs. Anderson also traveled extensively within this country, speaking at many important gatherings to publicize the activities of the United Nations.

One of her most important official trips in recent years, however, was one made, not as a U.N. representative, but as a member of a three-woman special Presidential mission. On Friday, November 24, 1967, Eugenie Anderson took off on very short notice for a trip to Vietnam; her traveling companions were Anna Lord Strauss and Dorothy Buffam Chandler. Miss Strauss is an eminent public figure, a former president of the National League of Women Voters and a lineal descendant of the famous suffragist, Lucretia Mott. Mrs. Chandler, a prominent Californian, is the publisher of the *Los Angeles Times*. The women flew to Saigon with Ambassador Bunker and his wife, Ambassador Carol Laise, and in the course of their flight encountered perhaps the most dangerous moment of their trip when one of the motors of their huge C-142 caught on fire. Fortunately they had just taken off from Japan and were able to return safely and transfer to another aircraft.

In talking about her trip, Eugenie Anderson makes two points very clear: first, that she supports the war in Vietnam. "I believe it is important that we're there," she says simply. And second, she emphasizes that she was only in Vietnam for nine days; in such a short time one can only make observations. With this qualification established, she says that her dominant impression was of the "absolutely superb caliber of performance of the Americans, both military and civilian." She felt that the vast majority of Americans she talked with — not including representatives of the press — believed fully in the United States effort, and she was struck by the number who had re-enlisted for a second tour of duty.

The South Vietnamese that she met seemed to her surprisingly hard working — she had expected them to demonstrate the slow motions, the languor typical in a warm, damp climate. She says, however, that she did not talk with enough ordinary South Vietnamese citizens to be able to grasp how deep their commitment was to the war.

Mrs. Anderson did not ask for interviews with either President Thieu or Vice President Ky. At the suggestion of Hubert Humphrey, however, she did request a meeting with Prime Minister Nguyen Van Loc, whom she found articulate and willing to talk. She also thought that Foreign Minister Tran Van Do, who gave a dinner for her, was an exceedingly acute, shrewd and sophisticated man.

But the South Vietnamese who impressed her the most was Major Be, the man who heads the Revolutionary Development program, as the Vietnamese effort to clear the National Liberation Front out of the countryside is called. One of the reasons Mrs. Anderson wanted to go to Vietnam, she says, is that she had long felt that American reporting was not putting enough emphasis on this and other purely political activities managed by the South Vietnamese themselves, and she wanted to see for herself what was happening in these areas. She therefore concentrated on learning as much as she could about the Revolutionary Development program.

As reported in *The Economist* of January 13, 1968, the tasks of the RD teams operating in the hamlets include "identifying and isolating the local Vietcong; identifying corrupt local officials; organizing local elections; establishing farm co-operatives; setting up teaching programs aimed at removing illiteracy and . . . show-[ing] the villagers how to protect themselves. . . ."

Before the Tet offensive on January 31, there were 645 such teams operating throughout the countryside and approximately seven thousand young people undergoing the thirteen-week training course at the Revolutionary Development School at Vung Tau under the vigorous leadership of Major Be. More than any other factor, Mrs. Anderson says, this operation gave her an increased confidence in the basic commitment of the South Vietnamese and in their determination to fight for their independence.

Mrs. Anderson left Vietnam in December, 1967, believing that although there were evidences of massive problems, there were also many evidences of clear progress throughout the country. "I had the feeling that things were going very much our way," she says. Then, in common with every other American, she was shocked and saddened by the Tet offensive, the more so because of her close identification with the country and with the people she had so recently visited.

But neither the Tet offensive, nor any subsequent events* have shaken her quiet conviction that the United States is following the proper course by being in Vietnam. In general Mrs. Anderson's hews closely to the Johnson administration line. She considers that we have treaty obligations which it is imperative to honor; our failure to do so would, she believes, bring into question our treaties with other countries in Europe as well as Asia. While she admits that the domino theory may be an oversimplification in terms, she subscribes to the fact of it, convinced that by our presence in Vietnam we are "buying time" for the other newly independent and still unstable countries of Southeast Asia, who are threatened by internal subversion and external aggression.

Mrs. Anderson side-steps all questions about de-escalation, about cessation of bombing in the North, or ending search and destroy missions, as matters of military strategy which she does not feel qualified to answer. She wishes that we had done far more, however, in the line of economic assistance before we got so heavily involved militarily in Vietnam. Still, she feels strongly that there is no other country but the United States which has the power — and therefore the responsibility — to try to halt the expansion of Communism. And she is convinced it must be halted at any cost.

Her strong anti-Communist sentiments, Mrs. Anderson concedes, are very subjective ones, based on her own bitter experiences during the Democratic-Farmer-Labor struggle in Minnesota, and more importantly on her life behind the Iron Curtain in Bulgaria. "I'm sure I have a more intimate and, I think, a deeper awareness than most people who haven't had these experiences," she says. By the same token one may argue that her consciousness of what happened in the past blinds her somewhat to the realities of the present. Both in Minnesota and in Bulgaria success meant triumphing over

* As of April 1 when this book went to press.

the Communists, and perhaps this pattern had become so much a part of Eugenie Anderson's thinking that she is reluctant — or unable — to accept new circumstances and to adjust to what President Kennedy once called the "surprising changes in the relations between nations."

Mrs. Anderson's position is a lonely one for a liberal of such long standing. The woman who helped push President Truman toward a more progressive civil rights plank in the 1948 platform now finds herself alienated, on the issue of Vietnam, from most of her old liberal friends. Not, however, from all of them; her closest political ties have always been to Hubert Humphrey and they remain so today. In fact there are those who submit that if circumstances were different, as they might so easily have been had Johnson chosen another Vice President, Humphrey might well be leading the movement against the administration's Vietnam policy and Eugenie Anderson might well be supporting him.

Somehow this postulation seems unlikely. For Eugenie Anderson's convictions appear to stem more from her deeply ingrained hatred of Communism than from her unwavering admiration for Hubert Humphrey. However, these two strong sentiments of hers have, at least indirectly, brought about a change in her career.

On her return from Vietnam, Mrs. Anderson did not go back to the United Nations. She took a long leave of absence and then early in the spring of 1968 she resigned from the United States Mission. On April 1 she moved to the Department of State as a special assistant to the Secretary. She retains the rank of Ambassador in her new position, and her responsibilities place her on the level of an Assistant Secretary of State.

The press release announcing her appointment in Washington described her duties as "flexible." Whatever they are, Eugenie Anderson may be counted on to perform them conscientiously, intelligently, and with the high sense of purpose that has characterized all her public service.

TWO FROM CONNECTICUT:
CITY HALL AND
THE CAPITOL DOME

Ann Uccello and Ella T. Grasso

THEY ARE NOT Connecticut Yankees, but because their names end in a vowel they represent an important segment of Connecticut's electorate. Both are Italian-Americans; both hold key positions in the state. Otherwise the two women have little in common.

Ella T. Grasso, a Democrat, is an established political figure. As Secretary of the State she is the highest woman officer in Connecticut; she is also one of the top vote-getters. A keenly intelligent woman with great legislative experience and skill, she plays a significant role in the hierarchy of the state Democratic Party, which automatically means she is close to the state's omnipotent Democratic boss, John M. Bailey. Early in Mrs. Grasso's career Bailey recognized her talents; and for the past fifteen years she has been an increasingly valued and influential member of his brain trust.

Ann Uccello, the newly elected mayor of Hartford, is a political unknown, a Republican who seems to have come from nowhere to capture the top spot in Connecticut's heavily Democratic capital city. In a sense Miss Uccello's sudden political fame is also closely bound to John W. Bailey, since her upset victory is all the more astounding and newsworthy for having taken place — as the press is fond of putting it — "in John Bailey's backyard."

Many straws in the wind and many ironies led to Mayor Uccello's assumption of her office on December 5, 1967. In fact, the changing structure of Hartford's municipal government within the past thirty years is a testament to the dynamic forces which sometimes operate to make American politics responsive to the will of the people. In 1946 their will was for reform in the city of Hartford. A group of public-spirited citizens, weary of what they considered the evils of the spoils system, joined together under the leadership of the Chamber of Commerce to rid the city of its existing political bosses. They formed the Citizens Charter Committee and, to the outrage of Hartford's long-time politicians — some Republican but mostly Democrat — created a non-partisan, city-manager form of government. Nine councilmen, running without party labels, were elected to the city council; the one who received the highest number of votes automatically became the ceremonial mayor. The council then hired a city manager who was the municipal chief executive.

In 1946 John Bailey, to whom non-partisanship had always been a dirty word, had just become chairman of the Democratic State Committee. Though already powerful, he did not yet have quite enough strength to stop the Citizens Charter Committee. But by 1953 he was ready, as he puts it, "to take back Hartford," and to put politics back where he strongly felt they belonged — in city elections. During the previous seven years under the CCC, any person who wished to and who could garner a mere two hundred and fifty signatures could enter the primaries for the city council. The top eighteen candidates who made it through the primaries were then listed in alphabetical order on the ballot from which nine were chosen, the electorate voting for six. Of the eighteen, the CCC endorsed six.

In 1953 Bailey announced that the Democratic Party also intended to endorse six candidates. In the hue and cry that followed his partisan proposal, the head of the Republican State Central Committee announced in shocked tones that "John Bailey had violated the moral principles of the Hartford charter system with his outrageous action." * Bailey responded with some well-aimed thrusts at the CCC which he said was a mere Republican puppet, "self-righteously labeling itself the good government party." In the election that followed, five of the endorsed Democrats won places on the nine-man city council. The CCC was all but finished, and John Bailey was back in business.

* Lieberman, Joseph I., *The Power Broker*. Boston, Houghton Mifflin Company, 1966, pp. 161-2.

What he really wanted, however, was a return to the strong mayor form of government in which, assuming a Democratic mayor (an apparently safe presumption in Hartford with its three to one Democratic majority), the party would control the patronage.

Bailey was greatly assisted in his purpose by members of the Greater Hartford Chamber of Commerce, who had in twenty years come full cycle and were now regarding *partisan* elections as the will of the people. In 1967 the Chamber and Bailey achieved their ends when the electorate voted a new charter which provided that in the next — the 1969 — election, candidates for the mayoralty would be nominated by each party and would run for office in a direct election. Meanwhile, until the new charter went into effect, the old system would remain, and in 1967, for the last time, the person receiving the most votes for councilman would be mayor. The Democrats saw to it, however, that during this final term the mayor, while not strong, would not be quite as weak as he had been. He would be privileged to nominate, subject to council approval, members of various "policy-making and quasi-judicial boards and commissions." Previously he had served without financial compensation. Now he would receive an interim salary of $10,000.

The only things that went wrong from the Democrats' point of view was that the "he" turned out to be a "she" and, far worse, not a Democrat but a Republican. Antonina P. Uccello, a quiet, unassuming two-term member of the city council, who worked as a minor executive at Hartford's famous department store, G. Fox, calmly swept into office on November 7, 1967, with the most votes and picked off the prize the Democrats had so confidently set up for one of their own.

An accident, John Bailey calls it ruefully, and indeed one can hardly imagine a more unlikely person to have achieved such a stunning upset.

Ann Uccello looks much younger than her forty-five years; she is pretty and can be extremely photogenic; she is unmarried. To the voting public she appears sincere, modest, fresh, hard-working, honest, and naïve. She is, in fact, all these things with the possible exception of the last. Certainly she is politically unsophisticated, but there are some who feel that she clings deliberately to a quality of wide-eyed innocence to preserve her image as the good little girl who foiled the big bad politicians.

The Democratic top echelon, to a man and woman, regard her as pure but vacuous, and thus as here today and gone tomorrow. Yet behind their quick dismissal one senses a bit of whistling in the dark. She could be trouble, she could be formidable; even John Bailey concedes that "she's a good piece of merchandise."

Another national chairman, Meade Alcorn, who led the Republican Party during the Eisenhower administration and who lives in Hartford, recalls the first time he met Ann Uccello in 1956. "She looked like a frightened fawn," he says.

The occasion was a meeting of campaign workers for Edwin H. May, a new face in the Republican Party who was making his initial bid for the Congress. "Ann seemed genuinely in awe of the important personalities who were there that evening," Alcorn says. "She was very unobtrusive."

Undoubtedly this was her introduction to the political big time which, in Connecticut, if only because the chairmen of *both* national parties live there, is rather bigger time than in most states. But if Ann Uccello was shy and retiring, she was also determined and quietly ambitious.

"I always knew that someday I would like to run for public office," she says, "but just how I would go about it and how it would happen was very vague in my mind."

Ann Uccello (she pronounces her name with the soft "c") is the second of five daughters of Salvatore Uccello, an immigrant shoemaker. Both her parents came from the same small town in Italy. Her mother's family was the more prosperous; they were active culturally, socially, and civically; in fact her mother's uncle had been mayor of the town, and, from a ninety-four-year-old aunt, Ann recently heard that her great-great-grandfather had also been the mayor in his time. Ann's parents are still living in Hartford; she makes her home with them and with her unmarried sister, Vinnie, who is a painter and a professor of art at St. Joseph's College in East Hartford, Ann's alma mater. Her married sisters, Jill, Nellie, and Carmella, all live nearby.

Although Ann had hoped to go on to law school in 1944 after her graduation from St. Joseph's, she had to defer to the financial needs of her three younger sisters, who also wanted their chance at a college education. She therefore accepted a teaching position at a high school in nearby East Hampton, but she soon found the school's "progressive system of education" incompatible with her own strict parochial school and Catholic college training. Furthermore it was wartime and the feeling of unrest, particularly among her older students, frustrated her attempts at maintaining the discipline she considered suitable.

Ruefully she recalls asking one of her strapping seniors a question about Alfred the Great. "Who the hell cares," the boy answered. His twenty-two-year-old teacher sent him from the classroom and then watched out the window in despair as he stepped into his car and drove off in high dudgeon. Then and there Ann Uccello decided that the life of a schoolteacher was not for her. Looking back now, she realizes how immature she was and how unrealistic. "After all, I should have understood that a youngster, facing the prospect of going to war, couldn't have cared less about Alfred the Great."

At the end of the school year she took a job at G. Fox and Company. She had worked there summers during her high school days and had been mildly intrigued by the mechanics of a large department store. Because she was shy and not very easy with people, she knew that she wanted a non-selling position. Accordingly she started in Unit Control, where her duties were to compile data and figures on the movement of merchandise — in short, to keep track of what was selling and what was not.

It soon became evident, according to the assistant general merchandise manager of the store, that Ann Uccello was "a very, very good organizer, strong on details and office work." She became supervisor of Unit Control and also took charge of all of the clerical and secretarial personnel working in the backstage area of the store.

Miss Uccello found her job absorbing and stimulating but by no means a full outlet for her interests and energies. "I gave it my all while I was there," she says, "but at six o'clock when I put my foot in that elevator I had another life completely." Her after-hours life polarized around a newly formed organization called the Catholic Graduates Club, composed of Catholic men and women who were college graduates, though not necessarily graduates of Catholic colleges.

In part, Ann's interest in the organization was frankly social. She had gone to a women's college and, because of the war had not had many opportunities to meet young men. The Catholic Club offered dances, picnics, ski weekends, all extremely agreeable for an attractive, spirited young girl. But her interest was practical as well. If she were to run for public office, she knew how important it was to become well known in her community.

The founders of the Catholic Graduates Club realized from the start that in order for their organization to endure, it would have to make a significant social service contribution. The club started the Catholic Activities Program, and Miss Uccello soon became chairman, a position which gave full rein to her gifts as an organizer and to her instincts as a do-gooder (if this phrase can be considered in the non-pejorative sense). The projects which she initiated included a tutoring program at the House of the Good Shepherd, a home for wayward girls, diapering babies at the St. Agnes home, planning programs for belated vocations at a men's seminary, starting a book cart at the St. Francis Hospital, raising money for scholarships for three new Catholic schools being built by the archdiocese. "I had the nerve to undertake a black-tie dinner at twenty-five dollars a person at the Statler," says the Mayor of Hartford. "It was really very, very successful. We raised almost two thousand dollars for scholarships."

During this period the energetic Miss Uccello also helped form an alumnae association of her alma mater, St. Joseph's College, which had been founded only in 1932 and as yet had no formal organization. Miss Uccello printed the first alumnae directory, helped to write and publish an alumnae newsletter and bulletin, organized chapters in other cities, and subsequently became the president of her own Hartford chapter. In this capacity she successfully promoted a huge outdoor pop concert at the college by the Hartford Symphony Society for the benefit of the St. Joseph library fund. The more she did, the more her services were in demand by other Catholic organizations.

Ann Uccello enjoyed her many activities, and, if she was driven by a motive beyond mere social service, at least it was not an ulterior one. She was unabashedly inching her way toward her goal of public office in the only way she knew how and via the only route that seemed open to her.

Still she had never quite abandoned her feeling that the law would be important, perhaps even indispensable, to her career. In 1953 she finally decided to give it a try. She enrolled in the evening division of the University of Connecticut Law School. Though "evening division" sounds more civilized than the old phrase, "night school," by any name the routine is a punishing one for the working person who is obliged to get an education after hours. Miss Uccello of course had to drop all her outside activities. She would leave the store at six o'clock, rush to get a milkshake and a sandwich, then catch a bus (she did not even drive a car then) in time to be in class by seven. She took three courses and somehow found the stamina to study, to brief cases, to learn and to survive. She was one of sixteen students, out of forty-nine, who qualified for the second year. She then had to decide whether or not she really wanted to continue.

Should she commit herself to three more years of the night-school grind and then be faced with the uncertain prospect of having to earn her living as a woman lawyer? Or should she remain at G. Fox, where she now had a better position as head of Comparison Shopping, even though she knew the store's policy of discouraging its employees from participating in local politics?

She concluded finally that three more years of enforced isolation from all her community activities might lose her more than she would gain by pursuing the law. At the very worst, she told herself, she might have to wait until she retired from G. Fox after thirty-five years of service before making her bid for elective office. Meanwhile she could work behind the scenes in the Republican Party and she could try to revitalize her local town committee.

There was never any question in Ann Uccello's mind that she was a Republican. She belongs to that school of thought which believes that the best government is the one that governs least. Her philosophy at twenty-one, when she registered as a Republican, was that the government should do for the people only what the people could not do for themselves. Basically, she says, this is still her philosophy, although today she recognizes the need for the government to take the lead in certain areas, such as equal opportunities for minority groups. She once would have regarded such activity as dangerous big brotherism. But though she has learned to "bend" toward a more progressive view on occasion, she still speaks of "*extreme* liberals" in a tone of shocked disparagement second only to "card-carrying Communists," a phrase which also finds it way into her lexicon from time to time. She is outspoken in her belief that the poor are often tools of the Communists and that all race riots are Communist-instigated.

During the late 'fifties and early 'sixties, when Ann Uccello became more involved in party affairs, it is doubtful if she thought in any but the broadest terms about her philosophy of government, however. She was primarily concerned with the ineffectuality of the Republican Party in Hartford, Connecticut. And indeed she had reason to be.

The Republicans had never been able to recover, as the Democrats had, from the city's non-partisan elections in which they, as a party, played no role. When the Democrats made their comeback in 1953 and began endorsing a slate of six candidates for the nine spots on the city council, the Republicans did not follow suit. They stayed with the Citizens Charter Committee whose endorsed candidates were largely, though not entirely, Republican. When the CCC was eventually dissolved, the Republicans endorsed no candidates of their own for the council and, of course, elected none.

The Republican town chairman, overwhelmed by the better than three to one odds against him, accepted the inevitable and did nothing. The Democrats, to assure the Republicans' continued inactivity, obligingly threw a little patronage their way.

By 1963 Ann Uccello and a group she refers to wryly as the "overgrown Young Republicans" decided that the time had come to take matters into their own hands. The town chairman would have to go. There would be no more of the take-it-lying-down attitude. *They* would be the new Republican Party of Hartford; they would run a slate of candidates for the city Council. They hoped for the maximum of six, but could find only three capable and willing men. The new activists begged Ann Uccello to join them and make a slate of four candidates. She was sorely tempted, but haunted still by the bugaboo of G. Fox's policy regarding their executives' participation in local politics, she declined. She was single, and entirely self-supporting; under no circumstances could she afford to lose her job.

The three candidates announced without her. Just before the filing date a friend suggested to Ann that she might try actually asking her employers directly what their attitude would be if she were to run for the city council.

The president of the store and daughter of its founder is Beatrice Fox Auerbach. A forceful woman, and still very powerful today at eighty-one, she had already demonstrated an interest in women's affairs by creating and supporting the state-wide Service Bureau for Women's Organizations. In the course of Miss Uccello's duties as head of Comparison Shopping, she had often reported directly to Mrs. Auerbach; she went to her in September of 1963 on the matter of her political future. To her amazement, Mrs. Auerbach gave her blessing.

Jubilant, Miss Uccello called "the boys." A period of momentary consternation ensued: would Ann's entrance into the race at the eleventh hour give the public an impression of disorganization and indecision among the new Republicans? Strategists and participants "caucused" that evening and quickly decided that the advantages of her presence on the ticket would far outweigh the disadvantages of her slightly tardy arrival at the starting line. It was all very breathless; she had until four o'clock the following afternoon to file her petition papers complete with two hundred and fifty signatures. She arrived well before the legal deadline with eight hundred signatures; already her loyal friends from the Catholic Graduates Club had swung into action to take her petitions all over the city to be signed.

The Republican town committee financed the campaigns for their slate of four candidates, but from the first it was clear that Miss Uccello's strength was coming from outside the party, from her many Catholic friends, most of whom were Democrats, who speedily fanned out to rally more Democrats to the support of their Republican candidate. The high Catholic population of Hartford had heretofore been dominated politically by the Irish. In 1963 the Italians turned out in strength to vote for Ann Uccello and her fellow Republican, Ted di Lorenzo. Both were elected; in the primary Miss Uccello came in ninth; in the election she moved up to seventh place and di Lorenzo took the ninth spot.

Very little newsprint was used up on Ann Uccello during her first term on the Court of Common Council, as Hartford's city council is officially called. As one of two Republicans on the nine-man body she did not have a great deal of political muscle. Her election had been impressive, but still, in such a Democratic stronghold, her future appeared limited, and the press saw little reason to build her up. In fact, she probably received the most public attention for an event which was more in line with her old Catholic Graduates Club activities than with her new duties as city councilwoman. The two fountains in front of the Municipal Building had long been inoperative. When Ann Uccello discovered that seven thousand dollars was needed to refurbish them, she organized a Fountain Ball, which was held in the atrium of the Municipal Building, to raise the necessary revenue.

She was made chairman of the Finance and Personnel Committee of the council, which was considered a dog job, and spent many of her evenings and all of her Mondays (when G. Fox is closed) at City Hall poring over pension benefits and reclassifications of city employees' wage scales. ("I'm the conscientious type, I'll admit it," says Miss Uccello.)

In the 1965 election she won fourth place on the council, and with her came three other Republicans, a rather considerable progress for the supposedly dormant Republican Party. As the top vote-getter among the minority members, Miss Uccello now began to raise her voice. More and more she emerged as an individual, a common-sense, down-to-earth public servant who spoke her mind freely because she was not a party pawn. And if her grasp of the complexities of city problems was not profound, neither was that of the ordinary voter who identified with her.

When she ran fourth in 1965 with almost no campaigning, a thought seemed to strike a number of people simultaneously. Ann Uccello, herself, George Ducharme, the assured young man who was her unofficial campaign manager, and the Republican State Central Committee all decided that if she could do that well with so little effort she might, with some real exertion, achieve the top spot in the next election and with it the mayoralty.

In the fall of 1967 Ann Uccello asked for a six-week leave of absence from G. Fox and took to the hustings. The state committee, participating for the first time in Hartford's campaign, gave her all-out backing, and George Ducharme now came into his own as her campaign manager. An amateur strategist who had also once worked at G. Fox, Ducharme had no previous political experience and no significant connections — in fact he did not even vote in Hartford. But he knew his candidate and how best to promote her. "Look at her," he would say, waving her particularly saintly-looking campaign picture. "You may wonder what someone so clean and wholesome and nice is doing in the dirty world of politics. But I say if this kind of person really wants a chance, you've got to give it to her."

The backbone of her organization continued to be the friends — now more numerous and more zealous — from the Catholic Graduates Club who had first put her into office. The four Uccello sisters, equally clean, nice, and wholesome, enthusiastically shook hands at bus stops, street corners, and factory gates and were often mistaken for the candidate herself. Through it all, Ann Uccello, who is not a glad-hander nor even a very outgoing person, behaved with a natural and disarming simplicity which endeared her to the voters.

In contrast to this refreshing political purity, the Democrats were appearing at their shabby worst. With the new charter in sight, the mayoralty now loomed as an office worth having, in terms of power. The Democrats were noisily engaged in sordid in-fighting as they struggled among themselves for the chance to win this new prize.

Many Democrats (among them Ella Grasso) felt that if John Bailey had stayed home and tended to business, instead of moonlighting in Washington on his "other" job as National Chairman, he could have knocked a few heads together and straightened matters out. Too late Bailey himself realized what was in the wind as one after another of the party faithful said to him, "John, I'll vote for five of ours but you've got to let me have one of my own."

That Ann Uccello was the "one" was clearly demonstrated on primary day when she came in first. The only question was whether the voters would stay with her through the election, knowing that if they did they would be making a woman their mayor.

Uccello in Italian means bird. On November 7, 1967, the *Hartford Courant* announced on its front page that a Lady Bird was now the mayor of the city.

National interest in a woman mayor had centered that day in Boston, where the controversial Louise Day Hicks was finally defeated in her mayoralty race. Suddenly the press woke up to the fact that ninety miles south of Boston another woman had not only won but her race had passed a milestone.

Ann Uccello was the first woman ever to be elected mayor of a capital city; of America's hundred largest cities, only Hartford (seventy-seventh), currently has a woman mayor. In Connecticut, which can sometimes be rather insular, Miss Uccello was heralded simply as the first woman ever to be elected mayor in the *state*.

The Republicans were, of course, triumphant. For years Ella Grasso had dominated the state on the distaff side. In fact, the GOP had not had a woman of importance in their ranks since Clare Boothe Luce left the House of Representatives in 1947. Now they had Ann Uccello.

But the fact that the mayor of Hartford was a woman was just an added fillip to her party; what was important was that she was a winner — new timber for the Republicans in a state in which the Democrats hold five of the six congressional seats, both of the Senate seats, have absolute control of the state house, and a majority in both of the state legislative bodies.

Ann Uccello was inaugurated as mayor on December 5, 1967. At a testimonial dinner given for her shortly afterwards, she was presented with a large, beribboned pink and blue rolling pin to wield over the heads of the Democratic majority on the city council. Then, almost before she had had time to have the shabby leather couch in the mayor's office recovered in a bright chintz, there was talk that the Republicans were thinking of running her for Congress in the 1968 elections. Although she would be opposed in Connecticut's First District by the very strong Democratic incumbent,

Emilio Q. Daddario, there was always a chance — so the reasoning went — that a Rockefeller sweep might carry her into office. If not, even running well in defeat would strengthen her politically.

Asked in January about the rumor, Miss Uccello said that she was so busy trying to learn the ropes of her job as mayor, she had not even considered the possibility of running so soon for another elective office. Her response was a standard political gambit, which in this case, also happened to be very close to the truth. At the time Ann Uccello's outstanding achievement, if not her only one, was to have got herself elected. People on both sides of the political fence in Hartford were now watching her and waiting for her to back up her victory with solid performance.

The new mayor proceeded with caution. When some of the top Republican brass, feeling that she might be a little short on political know-how, urged her to appoint a kitchen cabinet of professionals to guide her, she declined, apparently recognizing the value of keeping her amateur standing untarnished.

She may have been right. "Connecticut," says Meade Alcorn, "is the kind of state where professors get elected." When Mr. Alcorn says professors in this instance he clearly means amateurs, and he is thinking of one of the state's most famous professors, Wilbur Cross. Shrewd "amateur" that he was, Wilbur L. Cross, dean of the Yale Graduate School, managed to capitalize on his naïveté to such an extent that many believe the people elected him Governor of Connecticut largely because they wanted to protect the old gentleman (he was then sixty-eight) from the "pols." But whether they kept electing him (he served four terms) for that reason is another question.

There was an obvious parallel in Ann Uccello's situation. Still, though she may have lacked a keen political insight, she showed in her first weeks in office that she could grasp situations very quickly and that she was capable of using political tools effectively when they were provided for her.

Ironically, her opponents did most of the providing. The six

Democrats on the city council who, by their own divisive tactics had helped Ann Uccello win the mayoralty, seemed bent on assuring her success in office. At her first council meeting as mayor, for example, the Democrats made not the slightest show of cooperation "for the good of the city." Instead they voted in a block against her first resolution, a procedural matter about which they might easily have been gracious with no loss to their own prestige or integrity. Furthermore, they treated her with a studied flippancy, tripping over the proper form of address: Mrs. Mayor, Miss Mayor, and even Mr. Mayor before arriving at what they must have known, or should have known, was the correct, Madam Mayor. "It was all a little bit of a production," says Miss Uccello.

Immediately the press slapped the Democrats' hands. Jack Zaiman, Hartford's top political columnist, reminded the Democrats in the *Courant*:

> In politics public sympathy nearly always flows to a woman official engaged in combat with a man or group of men on the other side of the political fence. A woman smart in politics usually seeks to put herself into a role where she can be a defender of the public against the rough tough male politicians.

Miss Uccello got the message, but apparently the Democrats did not. Shortly thereafter they handed the Mayor her first potential political gain.

Hartford is one of sixty-three American cities chosen for the Model Cities program. The federal directive called upon the recipient cities to appoint a City Demonstration Agency which would first devise the plan for a massive renewal effort in the disadvantaged urban areas and then administer the entire program. The agency (CDA) was to be primarily a citizen-oriented body and to include numerous residents from the "target areas."

The initial designation of Hartford as a demonstration city was made in November, 1967. On January 22, at Mayor Uccello's second council meeting, the six Democrats in a surprise move, which the three Republican members were powerless to stop, voted to make the city council *itself* the interim City Demonstration Agency. And having thus designated themselves as the "local instrumentality," the Democratic majority, without consulting the Hartford city manager, who is still the city's chief municipal executive, proceeded to hire a Model City program director of their own choosing. Their action was at the very least unprecedented and contrary to the federal directive, and at the worst illegal.

Ann Uccello took steps; she got on a train and went quietly to Washington to lodge a complaint with the Department of Housing and Urban Development (HUD). As a result, the "proceed letter" to Hartford was held up pending an inquiry. At best, however, the Mayor's victory was a Pyrrhic one, for, as the experienced Meade Alcorn points out, a Republican complaining in Democratic Washington, D.C., about some fractious Democrats in Hartford, Connecticut, is hardly likely to have very far-reaching consequences.

A more hard-headed politician would have stayed home and created as loud a ruckus as possible. Had Miss Uccello at once called a large press conference and played the game by denouncing the patronage-hungry Democrats for their power grab, she might have got an outraged citizenry behind her. Then, as a final gesture, she could have flounced noisily off to Washington to perpetuate her image as the champion of the city's moral rectitude, thereby getting the most possible mileage out of her opponents' strategic gaffe.

As it was, the Democrats could and did argue to the HUD investigator that they had only constituted themselves a *temporary* agency, that the wider, citizen-oriented agency was in the making, and that their action was merely a stopgap measure to get the Model Cities program started faster. If their purpose was, in fact, to get control of the program away from the city manager and into their own hands, this was certainly none of Washington's concern.

Further difficulties underlying the conflict in the city council stemmed from the wide difference in ideology between the Democrats and Miss Uccello. At least one Democrat claimed that he and

his colleagues were forced to take their precipitous action because
the Mayor herself was basically opposed to *any* citizen participation in the City Demonstration Agency. Miss Uccello denies that
she is against citizen *participation* but concedes she is against citizen
control — which may amount to the same thing. In this regard she
shows her strong conservative side. She resists giving "the poor"
from the disadvantaged "target areas" a real voice on the CDA because she believes that they are not qualified by education or experience to make final determinations on the Model Cities program,
even though it is designed to benefit them.

The political atmosphere was thus marked by unusually sharp
dissension when, four months after Ann Uccello took office, the
inevitable partisan fight over the annual budget began heating up.
The city manager had presented his budget to the council in January; as expected it was very high. The council had a month to work
over it, making what cuts they could agree on before the final budget
meeting was held on the last Monday in February.

All through the month, Mayor Uccello called unofficial meetings
of the Committee of the Whole in order that the nine councilmen
could deliberate together. As she had anticipated, the Democrats
gave her "the business" and declined to attend. When George B.
Kinsella, majority leader of the council, called on her to state publicly which cuts, if any, she would make in the city manager's rec-
ommended budget, she snapped that if Kinsella had attended any
one of the five council meetings she had called to discuss the budget
he would be well aware of her views. "The Mayor is becoming
shrill," responded one pained Democrat.

The final budget meeting took place on February 26. According
to law, if the city council did not vote an amended budget by midnight of that date the budget as initially proposed by the city manager would automatically be adopted and a sky-high tax rate, the
dread of all politicians, would result.

Public interest in the meeting was unusually high since, for the
first time in sixty-three years a Republican, one of three minority

members, and a woman to boot, was in the chair trying to control six Democrats. The council chamber was jammed, not only with the curious, but with those persons who had a personal stake in the outcome of the budget.

What the spectators saw was a tug of war, a game that is being played, with some variations, in council chambers throughout the country. The rules were as clearly prescribed as in any organized sport. The strategy of each team was to maneuver itself into the position of public-spirited savior, while forcing the opposition to play as spoilers and selfish misanthropes. Thus, before the Democrats voted a pay raise for the firemen, they had to make speeches to insure that the firemen would be well aware of whom they had to thank for more money in their pockets.

The Republicans did not have the votes to put through any resolutions of their own; they had to make what political capital they could out of their opponents' mistakes. When the Democrats cut $200,000 from the snow-removal account, the Republicans saw to it that the voters would know who to blame when the next blizzard came — and stayed.

The Cinderella deadline offered an opportunity for each team to score additional points by making it appear that the other side was delaying the proceedings and would therefore be responsible for the higher taxes if the reduced budget were not voted by midnight.

From her exceedingly vulnerable position at the head of the council table, Ann Uccello handled herself with commendable *sangfroid*. She was scrupulously correct: "What is your pleasure, gentlemen?" She resisted delaying tactics: "Read the next resolution please, Mr. Clerk." She dodged attempts to ensnare her in procedural traps: "I declare passage of the resolution."

She was willing in several instances to take unpopular positions regardless of whose toes she stepped on, although the opposition was quick to impugn her motives: "Madam Mayor is singing this song because she wants to make headlines."

She showed restraint and authority when, on one occasion, the acerbity went beyond the bounds of normal partisanship. Democratic Councilman George Ritter, irritated to the point of indiscretion by what he apparently considered a particularly self-righteous statement of Miss Uccello's, flared: "I would like to remind the little girl mayor that she has only one vote on this council." Ann Uccello banged the gavel down hard. "You are out of order, Councilman Ritter."

She kept her cool as the hands of the clock approached midnight, and even managed to provide the spectators with a photo finish. At one minute before the witching hour the city council voted a budget reduced by $800,000 and a tax increased by 14.3 per cent; the new rate was $59.50 for every $1,000 worth of property. Both sides had previously pledged that the tax would not go above $60 per $1,000.

In her first real public test, Ann Uccello thus came through unscathed, possibly with even an added luster. At least her opponents would think twice before again calling her a little girl mayor. Somehow she had emerged as Madam Mayor grown-up, and perhaps none too soon.

Ella Tambussi Grasso won her first elective office in a year when any victory by a Democrat was news in Connecticut. In the 1952 Eisenhower sweep, the Republicans captured five out of six congressional seats, both Senate seats, the state house and the state legislature. Mrs. Grasso's successful bid to become the Democratic representative from Windsor Locks to the state house of representatives was certainly an upset, though hardly one to be heralded in the national press, as Miss Uccello's was sixteen years later. On the other hand, it is unlikely that observers in either party ever regarded Mrs. Grasso as a mere transient on the public scene; from the first she impressed her colleagues in the legislature as one who was there to stay.

She came to office superbly prepared. Her academic career had been distinguished. She was an economics and sociology major at Mount Holyoke College, elected to Phi Beta Kappa in her junior year, and graduated magna cum laude in 1940. Two years later she received a master's degree from her alma mater, having also been a teaching assistant in the department of economics and sociology while completing her graduate studies. Her master's thesis was on the Noble and Holy Knights of Labor, a secret and pioneer organization of American workers, founded in 1868, the precursor of the AFL and the CIO.

In 1942, just after Ella Tambussi received her master's degree, she came home and married Thomas H. Grasso, a schoolteacher, whom she had known most of her life. The couple settled down to live in Windsor Locks where Ella was born, where her parents, who are both immigrants from Italy, had first met, where her father had for years been a baker, where the Grassos and their two children and the elder Tambussis still live today, and where Mrs. Grasso says, God willing, she hopes to die.

Windsor Locks still has a very close-knit Italian community. Many of the older people came from the same village in Italy and transported much of their way of life to this New England town. Ella Grasso, who has a warm and earthy humor, delights, when going "down the street" to shop, in stopping to pass the time of day, in Italian, with old cronies of her parents.

Although her academic background was important in shaping her ideas, Mrs. Grasso credits the League of Women Voters with having truly prepared her for her role in public life. "I can't imagine a better apprenticeship," she says. "The League is a perfect training ground. It teaches you to understand issues, to formulate programs, and to learn legislative procedures. However," she adds, "when the time comes that you want to translate legislative programs into action, then you have to learn to work within the political structure."

When that time came, as it did for Mrs. Grasso in 1952, her primary objective as a member of the Connecticut General Assembly was to project the League of Women Voters program into the platform of the Democratic Party. In her first session she pushed hard for many of the League's progressive measures, notably a reform of the court system and elimination of county governments. With the Democratic fortunes at a low ebb, her suggestions reached John Bailey's sympathetic ear. Bailey, who cared less for the substance of a program than for its vote-getting appeal, saw in the issues that Mrs. Grasso was raising a chance to arouse public interest and make political gains for his party.

The minority leader of the house was Connecticut's present Governor, John Dempsey, who was also fired by Mrs. Grasso's ideas and helped to present them effectively to the legislature. The Democrats' forward movement during the 1953 session gave added impetus to the election, in 1954, of a liberal Democratic Governor, Abraham Ribicoff. By that time Ella Grasso had won her spurs; she was on the inside of the Ribicoff campaign from the beginning, sitting in on all strategy conferences, working on every major speech. She herself was easily re-elected to the house, and during the 1955 session was appointed floor leader. She became the chief architect of the Democratic platform and at the 1956 state convention was made chairman of the state platform committee, a position she has held ever since.

At that same convention she was also elected Democratic National Committeewoman, and therefore did not run again for the next legislature. This was unfortunate for her party, which suffered one of its worst defeats at the polls in 1956; only five Democrats were elected to the state senate and only thirty to the house, the smallest return in thirty years. As a result, twenty-six vetoes of Governor Ribicoff's were overridden during the session and it was clear that the Democrats needed every friend they could find. Ella Grasso stepped into the breach as a volunteer worker. "I had to," she says. "I had to watch out for my platform and try to keep alive those issues that I thought were so important."

As for her position as National Committeewoman, Mrs. Grasso

says she did not distinguish herself; in fact she alleges to remember very little about what she did in that capacity. "I went to the convention in California in a DC-3 which was exciting," she says, "and I know there was a terrible row over something, but I can't remember exactly what." Clearly she does not regard the job, which is much sought after by many, as having been important in her career, for she does not even list it in her official biography. In any event, she was National Committeewoman for only two years; she resigned the post in 1958 when she was elected to her first term as Secretary of the State. Although it was not mandatory that she resign, John Bailey left her little choice. Ever mindful of spreading his plums as widely as possible, he needed the position of National Committeewoman for someone else. Ella had her reward as Secretary of the State.

Connecticut and the state Democratic Party were also rewarded by having Mrs. Grasso firmly ensconced in her spacious first-floor office at the Capitol in Hartford. For in 1958, the year of her election as Secretary of the State, the pendulum swung hard in the Democrats' direction. Ribicoff, who had been an enormously popular and effective Governor in his first term, set the pace with a tremendous victory, and swept into office with him every one of his party's candidates for state and federal office. Furthermore, the Democrats not only won control of the state senate, but achieved what had been considered the impossible because of inequitable legislative apportionment: for the first time in sixty-three years, and by a majority of three votes, they won control of the house of representatives.

Joseph Lieberman in his book, *The Power Broker*, a biography of John M. Bailey, records the Democratic boss's reactions on the night of the great 1958 victory:

He seemed at once delighted and dubious. . . . It was a very big win; and he liked to win. Yet he knew that each political victory brought with it responsibility as well as glory and since this exceptional victory brought with it exceptional responsibility, he was dubious. The 1958 Democratic platform — as most party platforms before it — had admittedly contained pledges Democrats thought they would never have to fulfill.

But now they were faced with having to live up to their platform, for now, despite the "terrible apportionment" problems about which they had complained continually, the Democrats were in the majority; they no longer had an excuse. Ella Grasso was one of the first to remind the party of its commitments. As John Bailey puts it wryly, "she shrill-voiced it to us continually." So, in addition to her official positions as Secretary of the State and as chairman of the Democratic platform committee, and to her unofficial one as brain truster to John Bailey, she assumed a new role. She became, according to one of her colleagues, the "conscience of the Democratic Party."

"It was an exciting time," Mrs. Grasso recalls. "There was the challenge and the opportunity and we Democrats had to keep faith with all the things we had said. We had called county government obsolete; now we had to do away with county government. We had said the court system — especially the municipal plan with judges going in and out of office according to which party controlled the executive branch of government — should be replaced with a permanent system. Now we had to do something about it."

Governor Ribicoff was entirely committed to court reform and to the abolition of county government. John Bailey was said to have grumbled a bit about these reforms which he regarded as "good-government moves," dear to the hearts of liberals, intellectuals, and editorial writers, but conspicuously less so to the regular organization politicians. Had he been more the prototype of the rascally big-city boss, he would have resisted — especially the court reform which cost him 500 patronage judgeships. But Bailey is not an ordinary political hack; the mere fact that he surrounded himself with intellectuals of the caliber of Mrs. Grasso and of two gifted young lawyers, C. Perrie Phillips and Jon Newman, and that he sought not only their advice but their approval, is proof of his own high intent.

Moreover, Bailey relishes nothing more than a good fight, and with a Democratic majority of only three in the house, his enjoyment was guaranteed for the 1959 session. Ella Grasso, he says, was invaluable in rallying the troops, skillful at keeping the Democrats in line while also wooing enough Republicans to assure a majority when, inevitably, certain Democrats defected.

Though Mrs. Grasso's most important qualification as a public officer may well be what one local observer calls "her habit of being right," she is also adept at winning others over to her point of view. In the first place she is a good politician, voluble, warm, friendly, capable of cheerful glad-handing, and able to tailor her arguments to her listener. (While not quite in John Bailey's class as a persuader, she has acquired at least one of his notable characteristics: his habit of shoving his reading glasses up onto his forehead when talking.)

The Secretary of the State is short, with cropped blond hair, regular features and a lively, twinkling smile. She is an attractive though not a fashionable woman — Bailey and Perrie Phillips get after her frequently to smarten up her casual manner of dress. She has a natural political know-how and an understanding of the fundamentals of political organization. She is, however, primarily concerned with issues, and is both articulate and well informed in talking about them. Above all she is enthusiastic. "Exciting" is one of her most overworked words, but she uses it so sincerely that one could well imagine her convincing a legislator whose brother-in-law was a county commissioner and about to lose his job that the abolition of county government would be of great benefit to the people of Connecticut — an *exciting* step forward.

During the 1959 session these talents of Ella Grasso's, coupled with John Bailey's wider variety of blandishments, produced spectacular results for Governor Ribicoff. The legislature voted his court reform and his county abolition bills; they voted for a major reorganization in the department of health, and for the creation of a department of consumer protection. The last was a particular project of Mrs. Grasso's. Also, largely through her vigorous sponsorship, Connecticut became one of the first states to pass a housing law banning discrimination on the basis of race, religion, or nationality.

While accomplishing all these great reforms in the state, Ribicoff and Bailey were, at the same time, casting their eyes beyond Connecticut's borders toward the national scene. At the 1956 Presidential convention they had strongly backed John F. Kennedy in his bid for the Vice Presidency; Ribicoff made the nominating speech and Bailey was one of Kennedy's floor captains. For the next four years both men continued to support the young Massachusetts Senator — in fact the Kennedy-for-President bandwagon really started from Connecticut. Faithfulness and hard work paid handsome dividends after Kennedy's election; Ribicoff went to Washington as head of the Department of Health, Education and Welfare, and John Bailey became National Chairman of the Democratic Party.

Bailey, however, continued in his role as state chairman. Although he spent much of his time in Washington, he had two extraordinarily capable and loyal women minding the store for him in Connecticut. Katherine Quinn, whom Mrs. Grasso describes as the "great lady of the Democratic Party," and who had long been Bailey's second in command at headquarters, took charge of all party matters and kept in the closest touch with the Boss, often speaking to him five or six times a day. At the state Capitol Ella Grasso became the overall legislative field commander, concerning herself as always with the substantive issues, but now acting for Bailey as the grand strategist in the General Assembly.

The two Bailey alter egos were close friends, worked well together, and served each other's interests smoothly. Miss Quinn, who has never had the least desire for elective office for herself, "protected Ella's flank with the women" according to Bailey. That she did so very successfully was demonstrated in the 1962 election when Mrs. Grasso was the state's top vote-getter with a plurality over three times that of Abraham Ribicoff, who had resigned his

Cabinet post to return to Connecticut and run for the United States Senate.

When Bailey became National Chairman, there was much speculation around Hartford as to who would be plucked from the Connecticut political scene to go with him to the nation's capital. Bailey in fact took no one to Washington; he had no intention of decimating the state party by taking any talent away from Connecticut. However, Ella Grasso wrote most of the speeches he gave in his national capacity. As a reward for her services, he asked the President to appoint her to the Board of Foreign Scholarships, and this appointment marked her first appearance on the national scene. Of far greater importance to her political future, and also considerably more commensurate with her abilities, was her selection as co-chairman of the Resolutions Committee at the Democratic National Convention of 1964. Publicly acknowledging her services in this capacity, Carl Albert, Democrat from Oklahoma, said: "The chair will take this opportunity to express his personal appreciation to his co-chairman who has done so much of the work — the honorable and gracious Ella Grasso. Mrs. Grasso has been my able and strong right arm and has brought to the rostrum a charm which has made the hearing a pleasure for each of us."

Privately Mr. Albert, who is the House Majority Floor Leader, was said to have told Mrs. Grasso that if she ever decided to come to the House of Representatives in Washington he personally would see to it that she got a top committee assignment worthy of her talents. The Majority Leader's promise did not come right out of the blue. By 1964 the idea of running Ella Grasso for Congress had occurred to many prominent people — including Mrs. Grasso herself.

But first there was important work to be done on the home front. Connecticut calls itself the Constitution State, the reason being that the document which marked the beginning of Connecticut as a commonwealth, the famous Fundamental Orders of 1639, was the first written constitution of the Western world. In 1964 Connecticut's constitution, albeit updated slightly from the Fundamental

Orders, had become perilously obsolete. Because of disproportionate legislative representation, "rotten boroughs" existed throughout the state in the many small towns and rural areas which had excessive voting powers.

In most states the courts have been reluctant to take positions on reapportionment problems, excusing themselves on the grounds that the question is political rather than legal. The federal district court of Connecticut did not dodge the issue, but stepped squarely into it, and in 1964 declared the state constitution null and void, since its provisions for legislative representation were inconsistent with "one man one vote." Furthermore, the court prohibited any further legislative elections until the current procedures were revised; accordingly the 1964 legislature had to be held over.

No one could have been more exercised than Mrs. Grasso was over this "absolutely shameful" situation in the Constitution State, and no one could have been better qualified by experience, knowledge, and temperament to bring about a change in the old order.

In response to the edict of the courts, the lawmakers enacted legislation calling for a constitutional convention; they decreed that fourteen persons from each of the six congressional districts would be elected as the delegates. Governor John Dempsey then appointed Mrs. Grasso to the Commission to Prepare the Convention; members of the commission voted her their chairman. She was subsequently elected as a delegate from the Sixth Congressional District, and when the convention convened she was named Democratic floor leader.

Meade Alcorn was elected the Republican floor leader. He and Ella Grasso have high regard for each other's abilities; each speaks of the other with a warmth not usually expressed in this highly partisan state toward a member of the other party.

The convention met on July 1, 1965, to try to revise an instrument of government that had been adopted forty years after the signing of the Declaration of Independence. The Constitution of

1818, which replaced the Charter of the Colony of Connecticut, provided in its article on the legislative department that "Every town which now contains or hereafter shall contain a population of five thousand shall be entitled to send two representatives." Every town incorporated after 1818 was to be allowed only one representative until it reached 5,000 inhabitants — a population growth which may well have seemed about maximum probability to the 1818 constitutional framers.

The result in twentieth-century terms was a classic situation which permitted a town such as Avon, Connecticut, with 5,263 inhabitants, the same representation as the city of New Haven, with a population of 152,048.

In 1901 another constitutional convention had tried to grapple with the problem only to have their recommendations for a new constitution roundly rejected by the voters because, as Ella Grasso points out, "The small towns felt they were being cheated and the larger communities knew they were."

The ghost of that 1901 convention haunted the delegates in 1965. Furthermore, they were aware that many other states facing reapportionment, which automatically means a reshuffle of power, had been forced into a stalemate by conflicting groups struggling to stay on top of the pack. "But in Connecticut," Mrs. Grasso boasts, "we proved that we could get things accomplished. We just sat down on the first day of July, 1965, and by the end of October, 1965, we had finished our work."

The new constitution replaced the provision of one or two representatives for every town with a far more equitable representation on the basis of population. There would be one and only one representative for each assembly district; numerous small townships were grouped together to form a district.

For many towns the loss of their individual representation (and in a sense their identity) was a bitter pill to swallow. Ella Grasso had keen sympathy for the residents' feeling of disenfranchisement. Indeed her personal position was at times quite ticklish. Not only did she herself live in a small town, but she had been the first *second* representative to the General Assembly of that town when, in 1952, Windsor Locks reached a population of 5,000. Had *her* new constitution been in effect at the time there would have been no second representative and she might never have been elected to office.

Still, to all the doubters and even to those whose vested interests were threatened, Mrs. Grasso could and did argue with her customary conviction that the "greater good" was being served by a stricter adherence to "one man one vote" and that government in Connecticut must move forward to "meet the challenge of the times."

While the electorate accepted the new constitution on December 14, 1965, there is some question whether all the voters knew exactly what they were voting for. To save the face of the diehards and to make reapportionment sound less like a millennium from which there was no retreat, the language, as concocted by Ella Grasso and Meade Alcorn was deliberately vague. "The establishment of districts in the General Assembly shall be consistent with federal constitutional standards," read the key passage.

When the first legislature under the new constitution convened in Hartford following the 1966 election, there were 177 representatives instead of the previous 294. In the same year Ella Grasso was re-elected Secretary of the State, this time leading the ticket with an even larger plurality than she had had four years earlier. One further item of significance in the 1966 election: In the Sixth Congressional District the Democratic candidate, Bernard Grabowski, the incumbent Congressman, was defeated by his Republican opponent, Thomas J. Meskill. Windsor Locks is in the Sixth Congressional District and all signs, including the finger of John Bailey, pointed to Ella Grasso as the candidate most likely to recapture the seat for the Democrats two years hence.

For the next eighteen months Mrs. Grasso's candidacy was widely regarded as a foregone conclusion. But then, late in 1967, rumors began to circulate that she might not run. By February of 1968 she was under a mounting pressure to declare her intentions since the only spot still in doubt on the Democratic ticket for 1968 was the Representative from the Sixth Congressional District.

John Bailey said plainly that he wanted her to be the nominee, and it was clear that he was giving her his all-out support, not merely to reward her for her years of service, but because he considered her to be the best candidate, if not the only one, who could defeat the Republican incumbent in November. He also had full confidence in her ability to be an effective, useful Congresswoman, and he believed that Ella, who, he points out, is "not one to hide her light under a bushel," shared his confidence.

In her years in Connecticut politics, Mrs. Grasso had always respected the discipline of the party, stronger in her state than in most. But in 1968 she was for the first time reluctant to do her party's bidding. While saying nothing publicly, she was saying no privately. She had made her way to the top echelon, not as a woman but as a brain. Now she was saying no for the most womanly of reasons. She was saying no because she believed that her obligations as a wife, a mother, and a daughter would not permit her to go to Washington.

Although people are always reluctant to take a politician's stated reasons for any course of action at face value, many observers agreed that Mrs. Grasso truly had overriding family obligations. In the fall of 1967 her husband had two severe heart attacks. Although he was much better by February and back at his job as principal of the Center School in East Hartford, the doctors had advised him to lead a quiet, normal life. Clearly this would be impossible if his wife were to become engaged in a vigorous political campaign in which he would want to become involved because he is deeply interested in and concerned with her career.

Two years earlier the Grassos' daughter, Susane, almost lost her life in a serious automobile accident. Though she too was fully recovered by February, 1968, and a freshman at Hartford College, her mother still worried about her and kept an anxious eye on her needs. Jimmy Grasso, who was just sixteen, also demanded considerable attention from his mother, who is inclined at best to pamper her children.

During her most active years in politics, Ella Grasso's mother, who lives just across the street, was always on hand and happy to take up the slack at the Grasso home. But Mr. and Mrs. Tambussi were in their eighties and could no longer fill in for their daughter; on the contrary both required more attention from her, their only child. To Italians the family is always paramount, and Ella Grasso is a good Italian, reared in a tradition which would not easily permit her to leave her aged parents, her husband, and her children to their own devices while she spent five days out of every week in Washington.

At the Parma Restaurant, the unofficial Democratic headquarters of Hartford, a favorite lunch-time occupation during the early spring of 1968 was second-guessing Ella Grasso. Some of the regulars insisted that no matter what she was saying then, she would announce as a candidate before the June state party convention.

Another faction, convinced that Mrs. Grasso could somehow make the necessary family arrangements if she wanted to, was persuaded that her reluctance to run was based on other considerations: she had the long-time winner's dread of defeat; she was afraid of a Rockefeller sweep; she would only run if, by June, the signs pointed very strongly to Nixon. Another cogent argument ran that since Ella Grasso differs with the administration's Vietnam policies, she was unwilling to go through the ritual expected of a Bailey-endorsed candidate and promise total obeisance to the President.

There was also some concern expressed by the Parma-chair strategists that if Ella did not go to Washington she might wither on the vine in Hartford.

Such a thought is utterly foreign to Mrs. Grasso. As long as she holds the office of Secretary of the State — and certainly no Democrat is likely to challenge her for that position — her vine will be the state Capitol. She could never wither there, for her belief in the vitality of state government is fundamental. "It is here," she says, "in a great ferment of activity and concern that policies and decisions are shaped that will deeply affect the lives of the people."

On a morning in late February Ann Uccello and Ella Grasso appeared on the same platform as commentators at a symposium sponsored by Hartford College. The subject: Opportunities for Mature, Educated Women in the Greater Hartford Community.

INDEX

Index